"Simply written, thoroughly researched, resoundingly practical, gripping, sensitive, truthful and inspiring. Dr. Kojoglanian's book should be your go-to resource for understanding and conquering one of the greatest challenges facing society—weight gain and its relevance to cardiovascular disease and stroke. "

—Elizabeth M. Cooper, Research Scientist
 Staff Member, American Heart Association-American Stroke Association

"In his hope-filled and winsome style, Dr. Sam not only gives you the reasoning and motivation to sign up for your personal challenge, but he also gives you the recipe for achieving your success while attaining a healthier, more confident, and longer life. Get set to take the BIG step, sign up and embrace your new future!"

—Ken Wiseman, world record holder for both the Double and Triple Ironman
 CEO, AMS Fulfillment

"Remarkably enlightening, highly motivating, but most importantly, life changing, life enhancing and life saving. Dr. Sam, a fellow national speaker to top NCAA athletes, delivers a knockout!"

—Victor Marx, 7th degree black belt—Keichu-Do, trains Navy Seals, Marine Rangers, NFL players
 Founder and President, All Things Possible

"A captivating book conveyed with honesty, humor, medical expertise and spiritual insight. Dr. Sam gives no-nonsense solutions to an epidemic of obesity in a compassionate way. He provides fresh hope for those struggling with their weight, and points the way to those desperately searching for a relationship with their Creator."

—Jeff Lippencott, Emmy Award nominee and ASCAP Film & Television Music Award winner
 Composer, The Apprentice, The Biggest Loser, Who do You Think You are?, Shark Tank

To Kimberly

"Dr. Kojoglanian's insightful, creative and wholehearted book on claiming your life back is spellbinding. His distinct approach is mind-blowing, dispensed with great passion, invaluable perspective, and a life-changing purpose that will spare you from hardships. He is truly the Mender of Hearts—no "BUT(T)s" about it!"

—Susan Urbanski, Registered Nurse, Masters in Nursing
Chief Nursing Officer, Los Angeles County Health Services

Wishing you
GREAT
JOY, PEACE & LOVE!

2/20/13

DR. SAM'S SUREFIRE WAY TO LOSE WEIGHT,
KEEP HEALTHY AND FIND ABUNDANT LIFE

I GOT A
BIG
BUT(T)

SAMUEL A. KOJOGLANIAN, MD, FACC
Mender of Hearts

Library of Congress Cataloging-in-Publication Data
Kojoglanian, Samuel A., MD
I Got a Big But(t):Dr Sam's Surefire Way to Lose Weight,
Keep Healthy and Find Abundant Life
pp. cm.
Summary: Lose weight and cut your risk of cardiovascular disease.
1. Weight loss — Behavior modification
2. Weight loss — religious aspects — Christianity   3. Health
I. Title
RM222.2 2012
613.25
ISBN 0-9706625-5-6

The New International Version was used for all quotes,
stories, and paraphrases from the Bible.

Published by Rock Your Planet, Inc.

Layout and design by Jana Rade

Printed in the United States of America

Acknowledgements

I am thankful and humbled that my God gave me the strength and insight to write this book.

My heartfelt thanks to my friends and family who encouraged me through many drafts: Dr. John Akers and Russ Busby from the Billy Graham Ministries, Ashley Barton, Arpy Kojoglanian, Timmy Loan, Darren Paul and Dr. John Stead.

Many thanks to Houry Khechoumian, Raffi Khechoumian and Susie Parker for sharing your recipes; Armen Khechoumian for your keen artistic advice; Mike Wunsch and Craig Rasmussen from Team Results Fitness, and Ken Wiseman, Triple Ironman record holder, for sharing your exercise techniques.

Barney Klinger, entrepreneur, thank you for believing in the dream.

Paul Greasley, engineer, thank you for your invaluable input.

Creston Mapes, author, thank you for your exceptional advice.

Scott Keating, attorney, thank you for your loyalty.

Suzanne Wolfe, Registered Dietitian, who diligently facilitated making the dietary content comprehensive and practical; thank you for your nutritional adeptness throughout the book.

Jack Patterson, cardiologist, thank you for your heartfelt advice.

Russ Busby, photographer, thank you for your skills.

Tom Zaczyk, filmmaker, for walking alongside.

Lynn Lanning, editor, thank you for your matchless zeal and expertise, delivered with great care in editing multiple drafts of this book.

Jana Rade, graphic artist, thank you for your creative knack.

My patients, thank you for giving me the honor to serve you.

My parents, thank you for your unconditional love.

I am truly blessed! Dr. Sam

I Got a Big But(t)

Important message to the reader...

Although this book offers to share the wisdom of clinical experience and the gift of spiritual empowerment to sustain you on your path to healthier living, it is nevertheless only a book. A book must never be used as a substitute for professional medical attention. This book is intended only to complement the program by which you, your own physician and your other health care providers work to optimize your health.

No physician can address the particular health concerns of every person through the medium of a book. The recommendations made in this book are generic. All references, messages, graphics, charts and tables within this book are for exemplary and general informational purposes only. The author's discussion, anecdotes and opinions are not, and must not be taken as, a prescription for your personal care. Therefore, it is imperative that you first consult with your own physician about the appropriateness of any plan to lose weight or exercise so that appropriate modifications can be made relevant to your particular circumstances and condition. Never disregard medical advice or delay in seeking it because of something you read in this or any other book.

Nothing in this book constitutes an express or implied warranty or representation regarding the author's quality of care or skills as a medical practitioner. The results obtained by persons whose testimonials appear in the book may be unique to those individuals. You should be prepared that your own results may differ, depending upon your personal health profile and the course of treatment recommended by your own physician.

This book is not intended to be a complete treatise on the topics discussed. Rather, it is an overview of ways that certain lifestyle choices can be implemented for healthier living. No representation or warranty is made that all discoveries and advances in science, medicine and nutrition, whether existing prior to or arising after the date of publication, are necessarily included in this book.

The information and statements in this book have not been evaluated by the FDA and are not intended to diagnose, cure, treat or prevent disease. The mention of any product, food, brand or nutritional supplement in this book is for example purposes only, and does not constitute a medical prescription.

Foreword

On a scale of 1 to 10 (1 being small, 5 average, 10 extra large), how big is your butt? I'm not trying to be crude, so set aside the image and face the stark truth. Largeness in this category is not a good thing because the choices that lead to a large butt will ultimately cause havoc to your health. A Big Butt comes with a hefty price, and that price will not only impair the quality of your life, but it will claim your life prematurely.

June is a 43 year old who showed up at the emergency room with chest pains. She is the mother of two teenage sons, and the owner of a bakery shop. As a single mother, she does not get much sleep, caring for her kids and trying to keep up with the unending overhead of operating her own business. She was told to sit down and wait her turn because the front desk triage personnel dismissed her as simply "anxious." June had never experienced such chest pressure in the past.

She got up from her chair in the ER waiting room and told the front desk personnel that her pain was worse and that she was starting to sweat. Once more June was directed to have a seat as there was a trauma case that took precedence.

On her way to the chair, June's breathing became labored. She got to her seat, but by then her world of colors grew black and she could no longer see. Her 230-pound frame slammed to the floor and blood started pouring from her forehead where she sustained a deep laceration.

An EKG revealed that one of her heart arteries was shut down and she needed an emergency intervention. Given that there was no cardiac catheterization laboratory in the facility, June arrived at my hospital via helicopter within one hour.

I remember seeing her for the first time. She could not speak because she was on a ventilator. I checked her birth date twice, finding it disturbing that a 43-year-old female was on my cardiac lab table at such a young age. I checked her left artery first making sure it was intact, knowing that her culprit artery was the right. And there it was: a 100% shut down right coronary artery. As I opened her artery, I saw her heart rhythm slow down to the 30s and gave her a drug to increase her rate. But when her heart rate failed to increase, we placed a temporary pacemaker in her to secure a healthy rate.

The ventilator and the temporary pacemaker were discontinued the next day. She wanted to know about her kids, she wanted to know about her store, and she wanted to know what in the world she was doing in our hospital. All things were squared away, and upon discharge, she was diagnosed with coronary artery disease, myocardial infarction (heart attack), diabetes, hypertension (high blood pressure), hypercholesterolemia (high cholesterol), and obesity.

What June, you and millions of others must grasp this minute is that your weight is the very 'epicenter' of your physical being. In most cases, one's *weight* is the very cause of high blood pressure, high cholesterol and high sugar levels, which in turn can cause heart attacks, strokes, disability and premature death. It's a cascade or domino effect, and the weight—or in our case, the *Big Butt*—erodes the strong foundation of your physical being.

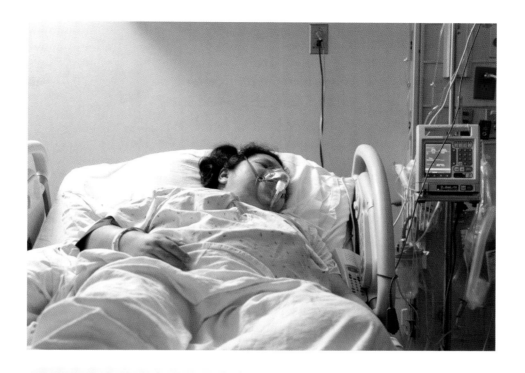

Dr. Sam's Insight
Your weight is the very 'epicenter' of your physical being.

June announced that the solution to her weight problem was going to be "a lap band" or gastric band—an adjustable silicone belt placed surgically around the upper part of the stomach to diminish its capacity—and that she was set to research the benefits when she got home. A lap band is not the solution for all, but being responsible for your own weight solves the problem for everyone. Doctors can change your anatomy, but if we can't change your mind and your heart, then no amount of gastric bypass or lap band or magic diet "cures" will enable you to achieve your goal.

Dr. Sam's Insight

Changing your anatomy will give you temporary results. Changing your mind and heart will give you lasting results.

Losing weight is difficult, *but it is simple*. Which brings us to the "but" component of this book. The ***Big But*** says, "I've called myself an emotional eater all this time…to tell you the truth, I crave fatty, fried and sugary foods. I'm a glutton, I can't stop myself, and I'm so ashamed…I'm so discouraged, having failed countless times…I've tried everything and I've never gotten it right…"

"***But*** I will forgive the past, forget my old ways, learn a new way to live with Dr. Sam's guidance, wear my mantle of discipline, and turn my life around!" This is an intervention that I call "*reframing*," or changing your perception. As you bite into this book, you'll experience a transformation of your heart that will proclaim, "I may have a ***big butt*** now, ***but*** that's going to change! I've always thought I couldn't do this, ***but*** after reading *I Got a Big But(t)*, I will not only wear my jeans, but I'll own my jeans, and I'll rock my jeans!"

This book will not only show you the consequences of a big butt, but it will give you the tools to overcome the addiction of overeating. It addresses the physical (Section I), psychological (Section II), and spiritual (Section III) aspects of losing weight. The testimonials of some of my patients who have lost weight are placed not as a scientific "prospective double-blind randomized study," which is the cornerstone in the world of cardiology, but as true, hope-filled stories that show how practical it is when one wears the mantle of self-discipline, cuts down on portions, and follows the guidelines set forth in this book.

The truth is that we don't measure the butt in cardiology, but we do measure the gut. The larger the gut, the more likely you are to have heart disease in the future. Obesity distributes itself differently: arms, thighs, guts and butts. The "big" problem is that we have grown accustomed to seeing men with medicine ball bellies and women with bulging thighs. In the meantime, we unfasten the top button of our blue jeans, buy a new wardrobe, create a bunch of excuses, rationalize our gluttony as "emotional eating," blame diabetes instead of our overeating that causes the diabetes, deny the truth, and make ourselves feel better by pointing fingers at yet even fatter people.

If the foundation of your being is glazed with sugar and salt, your body's structure will not be able to withstand the daily blows of life, and you will be plagued with illnesses that could have been avoided. But no matter whom we blame, we will have to face the dire consequences ourselves, in our own flesh, as we continue in our tragic and frenzied march of indulgence and self-gratification.

Dr. Sam's Insight
No matter whom we blame, we'll wear the consequences in our own flesh.

There is one more *but* in this book that you'll encounter in Section III, where more than your weight is weighed and where you'll find the true purpose of your life. If your weight is the epicenter of your physical and temporary being, then your soul is the epicenter of your spiritual and eternal being. If the body is saturated with excess sugar, salt and fat, then its solid foundation breaks and it is exposed to unnecessary illnesses that could have be prevented. On the other hand, if the body is nurtured with nutrient dense foods, it will weather through storms, and the risk of illnesses and cardiovascular disease will decrease while your quality of life will abound!

Similarly, if your soul is coated with the "sugar, salt and fat" of pride, past hardships, loss, bitterness, hopelessness, fear and regret—its foundation will be swept and tossed about like a building in an earthquake. In this section, you will not only set aside the bread for life, the worries of life, and the reality of the frailty of your life, **but** you will meet the Bread of Life, the gracious God who longs to heal you and set you on a solid, secure, sure and eternally blessed foundation.

No matter what the past, no matter what the shortcomings, no matter what the shame, you *can* change, lose the pounds, keep them off, look better, feel stronger, have more energy, decrease your risk for cardiovascular disease, and secure a healthy tomorrow—*today*. And no matter what the pain of your heart or the emptiness of your soul, you *can* change, be renewed, be revived, and be restored—*today*. You will find how to build this solid foundation and for the first time in your life, stand firm and stand with confidence, knowing you have done everything in your power to secure a healthier, happier future with an improved quality of life.

Simply put, the plan in this book is progress, and not perfection. This book ain't no mind game. I don't fix the brain with a scalpel or a gamma knife. By God's grace, I mend the hearts and heal the souls!

Place the gear of self-discipline on you.

Get your gaze fixed on your new journey.

And let's press on!

Dr. Sam
Mender of Hearts

CONTENTS

I. BIG BUTT: The Physical, The Portions

1. What's My Weight Got to Do With It? 3
2. Claim Your Big Butt 11
3. Dr. Sam's HAT Trick: 3 Steps to Healthy Living 15
    Testimonial #1 23
4. Do the Math 25
5. The Big Butt: Defined 29
6. The Building Blocks of a Big Butt 37
7. Alcohol: The Good, The Bad, The Inebriated 45
    Testimonial #2 52
8. But…It Tastes So Good! 55
9. One Fine Day 67
10. Big Butt's Pay Day 71
11. Dr. Sam's "Simple 2-Step Health Plan" 81
12. Tips on Healthy Living 87
    Testimonial #3 96
13. Effortlessly Effortless 99
14. From Supersize to Slim Size 107
15. Will that be Fresh Fish or Fatty Fries? 113
16. I Said, "Move that Big Butt!" 119
    Testimonial #4 124
17. Bitter Sweet 127
18. Sugar Cubes and Belly Aches 135

19. Kicking Sugar's Sweet Butt 143
    Testimonial #5 147
20. Smitten by Salt 149
21. Big Fat Disappointment 161
22. Busted 169
23. Big-Ol' Ugly Ashtray Butts 173
    Testimonial #6 178
24. Bad Break, Heart Ache 181
25. Empty Syringes and Broken Hearts 185
26. Potato Chips and New Hips 189
    Testimonial #7 192
27. Wrap it up with Dr. Sam's Top Ten Foods 195

II. UGLY IMAGE: The Psychological, The Problem

28. Portion Bias vs. Portion Control 203
29. The "Clean Plate" Syndrome 213
    Testimonial #8 218
30. Culture Bias 221
31. Mirror, Mirror on the Wall 227
32. So Far from Being a Track Star 231
    Testimonial #9 235
33. Doughnuts and Pies through Childhood Eyes 239
34. It's to Die For 241
35. I Got a Big Butt, *but…* 245
    Testimonial #10 249
36. A Bitter Root 251
37. What Golden Years? 253

III. TRANSFORMING TRUTH: The Spiritual, The Promise

38. Feed Me the Truth, the Whole Truth,
    and Nothing But the Truth   261
39. Irrefutable Truth   265
    Part I: Finding Pleasure   265
    Part II: Finding Perspective   270
    Part III: Finding Purpose   279
40. Benefits of the Big BUT   289
    Testimonial #11   296
41. Building to Code   299
42. The Bread of Life   303

IV. TOMORROW'S TALE: The Reality, The Future

43. Heart Portfolio   313
    Testimonial #12   315
44. Risk Portfolio   319
45. Living Portfolio   325
46. Sign Up for Tomorrow's Portfolio, Today   329
    Testimonial #13   331
47. Dr. Sam's 7-DAY COOK OUT   335
48. Lunch and Dinner Recipes   355
49. Dr Sam's 7-DAY WORK OUT   373
50. My Journal and Fun Facts   385
    Testimonial #14: It's Not Too Late   389
    References   391

I.

BIG BUTT

The Physical, The Portions

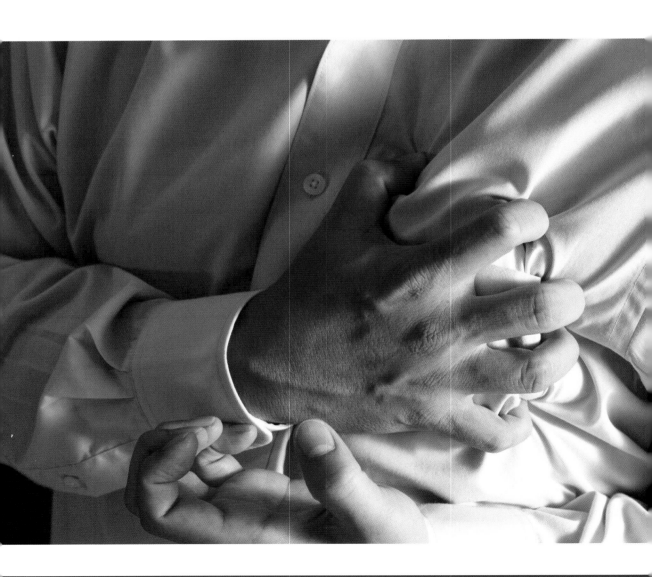

1 WHAT'S MY WEIGHT GOT TO DO WITH IT?

Suppose you are like Ted, who stuffed himself beyond the natural limits of his stomach's lining, then faced an emotional uproar in the family. His wife and he exchanged words they now wish were never spoken.

"You are a worthless piece of junk!" He jabbed a finger at his bride of 15 years. "I hate you!"

Anger has a funny way of distorting truth and love.

"Why don't you just die!" Nicole struck back.

Furious, Ted screamed even louder: "Die? So you can collect? I'll kill you first!"

Words are more powerful than we can imagine. With a word one can heal. And with a word one can kill. But once spoken, a word can never be retrieved. No little fairy can appear out of nowhere and say, "Please strike that, Your Honor. Jurors, be advised, you are to disregard those words when reaching a verdict."

Life doesn't work that way. Instead, Ted and Nicole's three teenagers unwillingly witnessed a horrible fight, which only got uglier as more words were spoken. Ted came within inches of striking Nicole, but hurled a stack of dishes onto the kitchen floor instead, and then stormed out.

Ted was a 45-year-old obese diabetic, mostly because of poor eating habits. He popped pills for high cholesterol and high blood pressure and injected himself with insulin daily to calm the sugar levels.

As he steamed out of the kitchen that day, shaking his head in disgust, an unwelcome and unfamiliar pressure built up in the center of his chest. The gnawing pain seemed to lodge there and radiated down his left arm, all the way to his fingers.

Way too stubborn to stop, Ted kept walking toward the porch.

Then, the profuse sweating, the shortness of breath, and the voice of fear.

He could not take another step.

Indigestion? A muscle strain?

Or just his imagination?

His hands automatically grasped his chest.

His family froze in shock.

He dropped to the floor.

Unconscious.

After a frantic 911 call and minutes of sheer terror, paramedics raced in, ripped Ted's shirt open, and began compressing his chest, his children bawling as they looked on.

"Dad, come back. Dad!"

His wife sobbed uncontrollably, recalling with horror and crystal clarity the venomous words exchanged minutes earlier.

After his heart rhythm was visible on the monitor, patches were placed on Ted's chest and he was shocked over and over, but normal rhythm was nowhere in sight and a pulse could not be found. Thirty minutes of resuscitation and suddenly, life returned. The strangers in blue, with Medic patches on their sleeves, were breathing for Ted via what's known as an ambu bag.

The 10-minute ride to the hospital must have further crushed Nicole's already shattered heart. When I introduced myself to her, she grasped my hand and would not let go. "Please, doctor, whatever you do, please I'm begging you, whatever you do, bring him back!" She stopped her sobbing for one second, and looked at me with a desperate plea, and said, "I have to tell him I'm sorry. Oh, God, I have to tell him I'm sorry. Please bring him back!"

"I'm going to do everything possible for Ted and for you," I said while holding on to her hands. What else could I say? "No sweat, I got this!" Or, "I'll bring him back!" Or, "Don't worry, it'll be all right." Or, "We do this all the time. Why are you so nervous? Just sit and relax." No, none of the above, but I pray and hope that my love for my patients speaks louder than any words.

Ted was rushed into our cardiac catheterization lab, and the first picture said it all: a 100% blockage of the "widowmaker," an artery so essential that a blockage can lead to death and leave a spouse a widow. Within minutes, catheters, wires and balloons were all set and lined up for the task. The wire crossed the 100% blockage. Then I sent a balloon down to the site of the blockage, inflated it, and the blockage was opened—but debris and a clot went downstream, adding to the insult. We aspirated the clot out of the vessel with a special catheter and then placed a stent within the blockage. Oh, how I wish you could have seen the next picture, simply beautiful! From 100% blocked to 100% open…no traffic jams in this widowmaker…a sweet sight to behold!

Our patient's heart was back in full gear, but only time would tell whether Ted's brain would come back to life. His whole body was in shock, and an "incidental" heart attack had wreaked havoc to his whole body, causing multi-organ failure including his kidneys, lungs, liver and brain.

Why was *I Got a Big But(t)* written? So that I could help bring healing to your body, your house, and your soul—and prevent the

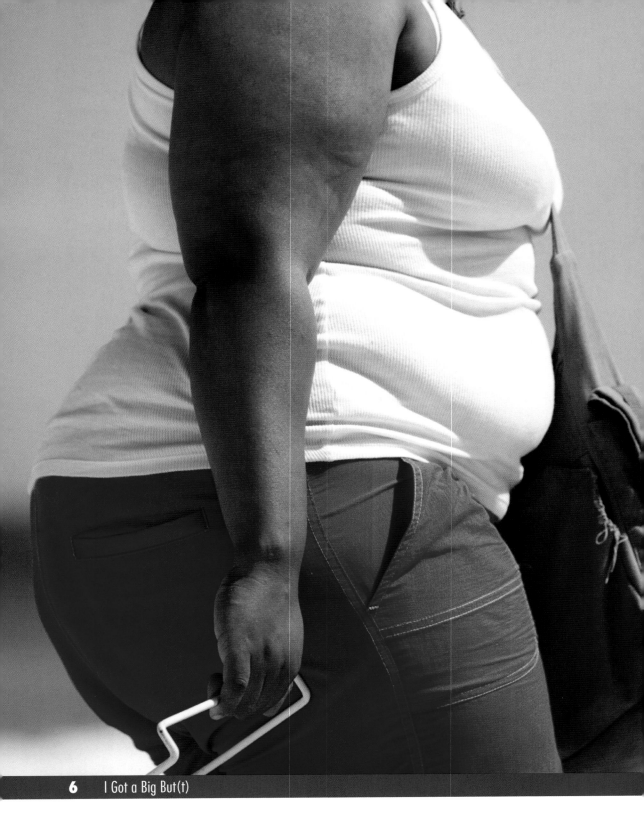

cruel hardship and uncertainty that Ted's family was facing. No matter what you think, ignoring your health while catering to your belly will lead to a dead-end road of hardship, pain, a poor quality of life and premature death.

"What's my weight got to do with it?" you ask. How about the quality of your life, your lifespan, increased self-respect and improved agility. It all starts with what foods enter your mouth, which translates into your weight—*but* there is a way out.

You might ask, "What's all the fuss about? Isn't Ted's story rare? And, what's it got to do with me, anyway?"

Here are the facts. According to the 2012 Heart Disease and Stroke Statistics Update, the American Heart Association notes that cardiovascular disease (CVD) accounts for one out of every three deaths in the United States; 33% of all deaths are attributed to CVD, which includes heart attacks, strokes and heart failure. Every single year since 1900, except 1918, CVD accounted for more deaths than any other major cause of death in the U.S. Each day, nearly 2,200 Americans die of CVD; that's an average of one death every 39 seconds. One out of 6 deaths is due to coronary heart disease, one out of 9 deaths is due to heart failure, and one out of 18 deaths is due to a stroke. CVD claims more lives each year than accidents, cancer, and chronic lower respiratory disease—combined.[1]

So, the answer to your question about Ted's story being remote, uncommon, and "Oh, that's not gonna happen to me," is an emphatic *"No!"*

Dr. Sam's Insight

**Every 39 seconds, someone in America dies
of Cardiovascular Disease (CVD).
The top two ways to decrease CVD and death:
1) If you smoke, stop.
2) If you are overweight or obese, lose weight.**

The hard truth is that one in three adults is *obese*. According to the 2012 Heart Disease and Stroke Statistics Update, the prevalence of obesity is 33.3% among adult men (20-74 years of age) and 36.2% percent among adult women,[2] translating into 75 million obese adults in the U.S. alone.

In the year 2000, there were *no* states with the prevalence of obesity greater than 30 percent of the population. By 2009, there were nine states with the prevalence of obesity greater than 30%: Alabama, Arkansas, Kentucky, Louisiana, Mississippi, Missouri, Oklahoma, Tennessee, and West Virginia.[3]

Dr. Sam's Insight

**Though obesity seems to be the new "normal,"
it is the very soul of health hazards,
contributing to illnesses, heart disease,
stroke, disability, and early death.**

Why is a big butt or big gut such an issue? Because eating too much food high in salt, fats, and added sugars causes weight gain. Weight gain causes high blood pressure, diabetes, and high cholesterol, which, in turn, cause CVD, disability, and death.

Dr. Sam's Insight

Excess food is a major cause of Cardiovascular Disease, causing weight gain, promoting high blood pressure, high blood sugar, high cholesterol and leading to premature illness and death.

Why should you change your ways?

Because, tragically, Ted was pronounced brain dead and lost his battle to survive.

It's my desire to help you have a different and healthier course in life. I don't want to talk to your family about donating organs. I don't want your life to smolder away. Aren't you tired of the guilt and old habits, anyway? You are going to find new hope, reach your goals and celebrate your success, and I'm going to lead you through it.

If you are overweight or obese, you do not have to follow in Ted's footsteps. You can overcome with a victorious shout and a light-hearted dance. You can have a solid foundation of health that will fuel the hope of a joyful life.

I truly hope you consider yourself precious enough—because you are—to make the changes and reap the benefits!

2 CLAIM YOUR BIG BUTT

Think of it—in the past 30 years, the number of fast-food restaurants has increased by 147 percent, as golden arches and flame-broiled burger joints have strategically popped up on virtually every corner. If you grocery-shopped 30 years ago, you would have found approximately 10,000 food products; today you can march in and gorge yourself on as many as 46,000 items, strolling aisle-to-aisle in the "supersized" grocery stores.

The problem of weight gain and obesity is readily blamed on our surroundings, our circumstances, and our environment—isn't that what modern society has engrained in us to think? There's got to be a good reason for our out-of-control eating habits, so we blame genetics, society, parents, our tragic past, TV commercials, failed relationships, and fast food chains.

In theory, all of these contribute to one's big butt.

But in truth, these factors deny personal responsibility and help us justify our daily poor choices.

The trouble is that we are careless out-of-control creatures, addicted to finding comfort for an hour or two by filling our growing bellies, regretting it, then mindlessly rising and searching for more comfort in foods that tear at the very foundation of good health.

We are the ones who salivate over the menu and end up ordering the fried chicken, the mammoth steak burrito, the brownie-and-vanilla-ice-cream dessert. We are the ones who pick up the doughnuts, dump the sugar in the coffee, hit the drive-thru for that afternoon shake, secretly snack on the "small sized" candy, and gorge away on the energy-dense cheesecake that lacks nutrients.

It's time to stop calling yourself an emotional eater. It's time to stop saying, "Yes, well, I might be a bit overweight…" After all, it's not all your genes; it's your choice. If it were your genes you would be forced to ask the question, 'Have my genes been on steroids the past two decades?' Because that's how long obesity has been on the rise, yet, all of a sudden genes are to blame? Genetics certainly influence body types and shapes, but daily choices are up to you. It's *not* your local fast-food chain, and for the most part, it's *not* that your mom or dad had diabetes—it's your sodas, it's your portions, it's your will. Quite simply, it's *you*.

Deep down, you already know the truth. It's just easier and helps you justify the matter by blaming someone else regarding your circumstances. But you're not getting anywhere without speaking the truth. Let's just call it like it is. It's time to say, "I'm obese. I'm responsible. I've got a big butt. I'm out of control. I love eating and I eat too much. It's my choice. I've made myself disgustingly unhealthy. I'm ashamed and embarrassed. I desperately want to change. And I need help!" Take responsibility for your actions. The desire to lose weight isn't enough. As you "reframe" your past mindset, you'll be happily astonished by the results as you bring self-discipline to the table.

Dr. Sam's Insight

Speak the truth and claim the blame. Good health starts with the truth and is cultivated with self-discipline.

I am excited for you! Why? Because, when the reality of a big butt casts an unsightly shadow of gloom in your heart, it's not too late—it's time for a new start! Do you remember the pills that were recalled, the ones that caused heart valve leaks? Do you recall the shots you've endured? Do I have to remind you of colon cleansing kits, laxatives, the boxes of prepared and expensive foods that you ordered, and the little "magic" granules or mystic droplets you put in your food? It's not too late when you have failed every single diet known to mankind. It's not too late if guilt is beating you down and shame is putting you in shambles. And it's not too late if you've already been branded with diabetes, hypertension, a heart attack,[4] a stroke,[5] or an illness.

If you are breathing and amongst the land of the living, then you have hope!

It is your time to change. It is your time to look better. It is your time to honor yourself. And it is your time to regain your self-worth.

Getting a smaller butt and a smaller gut will take tremendous effort and self-control, and I am here to encourage you to choose this path, the path that leads to a healthy life. I urge you to see yourself as worthy of a new beginning, and to picture yourself with a bigger smile and a lighter step. I encourage you to accept the temporary pain of discipline today—as it is so miniscule compared to tomorrow's regretful pain of a stroke or heart attack. And I beseech you to let the past failures fade away as you embark on a fresh hope filled journey with Dr. Sam.

3 DR. SAM'S HAT TRICK: 3 STEPS TO HEALTHY LIVING

Losing weight is difficult, and we continue to fuel this notion by repeatedly stating that it is. When we change our mindset, and reframe our circumstances, we will begin to understand that while losing weight may be difficult, it is *simple*. In three clear steps, you will grasp the essential tools that will help you lose the big butt and maintain a comfortable, healthy weight.

We can all learn from Carl. Ten years ago, Carl underwent bypass surgery for coronary artery disease (CAD). Now, at age 59, he is again plagued with chest pains. Overeating caused his obesity. Obesity caused his diabetes. And diabetes caused his clogged heart arteries.

I didn't know Carl back when he had his bypass, but met him five years later. At that time, he had a hefty gut and I warned him of the dangers that could lie ahead.

"Doc, I'm all right," he assured me. "I'm doing good. I don't feel a thing!"

His weight was out of control. His gut was like a medicine ball that hung over his belt. And his attitude—which is so prevalent today—was one that ignored self-control, while embracing the belief that his medications gave him the right to splurge on his diet and indulge without discretion.

Dr. Sam's Insight

Medications are not intended as a crutch for overindulgence.

Some time later, Carl developed more chest pains. He was having a hard time walking half a block. When he couldn't ignore it any longer, he was rushed to the hospital where he sustained another heart attack, weakening his heart muscle even further.

After the angiogram, Carl was disappointed that three of his five bypass grafts were completely shut down. And, of the two grafts remaining open, one was 99 percent blocked! I opened that graft by placing a stent. His pain went away and he was discharged in stable condition.

"Carl, the medications will only help so much; you need to work with me here, bud! Hello, it's time to pay attention," I said sternly.

To my disbelief, he looked at me in denial, as if he hadn't done anything wrong. So I decided to get a little graphic.

"I feel like I'm standing in front of a bridge whose foundations are faltering, and you're just cruising carelessly," I said. "I'm trying to flag you down, because the bridge is collapsing and you need to slow down so repairs can be made, but you just keep going, ignoring the deadly abyss ahead, as if you don't care or don't believe me. You're living in a lie and deceiving yourself, acting as if you don't know trouble is dead ahead. I mean, are you gonna just soar off the bridge and die? Is that what you want?"

I'm usually not that blunt, but I was obligated to intervene for the sake of my patient's life. As I spoke of the shattered bridge, I saw regret in his eyes. I saw a broken soul. And I saw someone who desperately needed compassion. I stopped talking and held his hand as I sat by his bedside. He knew this was it. He knew he had cheated death. He knew he'd been given multiple chances. And he knew it was time to make some extremely difficult decisions.

Because of the reality of Carl's situation, having lost three grafts, and fearing what might happen tomorrow, he looked into my eyes humbly and said, "Okay, Dr. Sam, I messed up—I really messed up, didn't I? Now what? Can you help me?"

"Child, I thought you'd never ask!" I exclaimed as my Southern accent slipped out. Can I help him? *Sweet!* That's what I was waiting for! I love my patients and don't like seeing them ill, but many times, it's at that low point when they finally allow me to step in and make the greatest impact. "You've come to the right person, bud," I said. "Got your note pad? Start taking notes!"

That day, Carl got a clear view of hope as he drank in every word of Dr. Sam's 3 Step Plan for Healthy Living: ***H**ydrate, **A**mbulate, and **T**abulate—the **HAT** trick!*

Step 1: HYDRATE

Drink at least eight glasses (each eight ounces) of pure water daily. We get water from our food sources, and there is nothing set in stone about "eight"; quite simply, it is reasonable, doable, and healthy. In fact, an adequate intake for men is roughly 3 liters (13 cups) daily and for women 2.2 liters (9 cups) daily; more is required depending on exercise, environment, pregnancy or breast-feeding.[6] I have stuck to the "8 by 8" rule (1.9 liters) because food provides about 20% of the total water intake, making up for the rest of the daily requirement. Get rid of the sodas (regular or diet), energy drinks, "athlete" drinks, coffee drinks, and cut down on fruit drinks. Drink an extra glass of water when you are feeling hungry as it curbs the appetite.

Our bodies are approximately 70 percent water and our brain is approximately 90 percent water by weight, yet most of us run around dehydrated, depleted of water. Though it's impossible to nail down the exact amount of water one should drink daily, I have found the 8-by-8 rule to be the simplest: drink eight cups of water daily, each cup having eight ounces. If you drink the 16.9 ounce water bottle, that's four bottles daily. Please consult with your doctor as excess water can place some folks into congestive heart failure. When your urine color is clearing and lips are not chapped, you are becoming well hydrated.

If you are still stuck on diet sodas, consider this: Aspartame, an artificial sweetener prevalent in sodas, is partially composed of Methanol, also known as wood alcohol. When exposed to the heat in our digestive tract, Aspartame releases Methanol. Methanol is converted to formaldehyde (embalming fluid for preserving the dead) and formic acid.[7] Unless you have a bizarre desire to be embalmed in the land of the living, I suggest that pure water is the better choice. Most of us are dehydrated and are flooding our veins with glorified coffee and lattes, which are pregnant with calories that we neglect to count. You'll also find out that all the "sugar free" drinks come with a "bitter price" on your health. If you want to spike your water, then try a squirt of natural lime or lemon.

Dr. Sam's Insight
Bottom line—Water detoxifies.
Sodas will cause your demise.

Step 2: AMBULATE

Walk as if your life depended on it—because it does. Walk six days a week. Start by walking slowly for 10 minutes daily, and gradually increase up to 30–60 minutes daily, if possible. Walking is gentle on the joints, there is no gym fee, and you can work it around your busy schedule. Instead of the 10 minute coffee and doughnut break at work, walk around the block. If you want to decrease heart disease, headaches, arthritis, and constipation, stop watching TV and walk. Too tired to walk? Get someone who will hold you accountable and who is willing to walk with you. No "buts" about it: get up off your butt, stop with your excuses, and walk. You will reap great benefits by walking, one being that a daily brisk walk for 10 minutes will reduce your heart-attack risk by approximately 50%, and the more you walk, the greater the benefit. More on the benefits in Chapter 49!

> **10 minutes of brisk walking daily will reduce your heart-attack risk by 50%.**[8]

Step 3: TABULATE

Watch your portions, tabulate the amount you eat, and count your calories—because most of us are eating for two people instead of one!

Decrease total calories, solid fats, added sugars, and breads.

Increase vegetables, such as celery, carrots, cauliflower, asparagus, artichokes, lettuce, spinach, and broccoli. Also, increase fish intake to at least once a week, such as salmon and trout, and snack on raw, unsalted almonds. If, by chance, you are concerned about the mercury levels in some fish, consider the embalming fluid I mentioned earlier, as you cuddle up with your bubbly diet soda.

Decrease your overall salt intake. I understand you might not use the salt shaker, but that is only five percent of your total salt intake. Approximately 80 percent of salt intake comes from processed foods (*canned* foods such as soups, *boxed* foods such as TV dinners, and *bagged* foods such as chips). The new American Heart Association guidelines limit daily sodium intake to less than 1500 milligrams daily for adults with or without high blood pressure. If we were to eat 28 small pretzel sticks, we would accumulate 500 milligrams within 30 seconds.

Dr. Sam's Insight
Determine your portion size BEFORE you start eating, not while eating—and no seconds!

And that, in a nutshell, is the Dr. Sam's "HAT Trick:" **H** for Hydrate, **A** for Ambulate, and **T** for Tabulate.

Carl and I went on to discuss the Health Care Reform and its incomprehensible 2,300 plus pages.

"Don't think for a second that it's gonna save your fanny," I said. "We can save trillions of dollars by preventing disease before it starts and circumventing it after it has begun, by simply hydrating, ambulating and tabulating!"

"It's not that simple, is it, Dr. Sam?" Carl said. "I mean, what about my family history of diabetes?"

"When did you get your diabetes, Carl, at birth or when you got your big belly?" I said. "And who gave you your big belly, your genes or your habits?"

He didn't answer. "Hey bud, you mad at me or you mad at yourself?" I asked Carl.

"No," he said, "I'm mad at myself!"

"This is your time, pal," I said. "This is your life, and we're turning you around. I hear you. You've struggled in the past, but that was then. This is now! You've got this. Work with me here…and you're gonna be living proof that with a smaller gut, you're going to feel better, truly *be* better, and live healthier! We got a deal?"

"Deal," he exclaimed!

So what's the deal with you? Think about your health and future. Your path to a more fulfilled, enriching life does not require rocket science, I assure you. What seems impossible is within your reach. Read this book, taste the hope on these pages, dig into it as if your life depended on it (because it does), build a solid foundation of healthy living, and be set free! And if you've been searching for a foundation of hope, joy and contentment, you're going to find it in Section III!

Impossible? Yes, in the past, but not now, not anymore!

As you make this journey, keep in mind, each patient is different and requires individual care. Therefore, be sure to spend time with your physician to formulate a plan specifically designed to address your condition, your needs, and your hopes and dreams for the future. In so doing, you can prevent the cutting, the bypasses, and the lap bands. You can avoid getting the stents that I place in unhealthy heart arteries. You can avoid an unnecessary hospitalization. And you can avoid a medical tragedy.

Get ready! You are heading out of the doom and guilt camp, soaring above your past lies and limitations, and entering into a reality of a slimmer, happier, healthier you.

Testimonial #1

JIMMIE BEFORE

Sometimes in your life, if you are fortunate, you come across someone who truly changes your whole dynamic in life and teaches you what you have inside that you never knew was there, and points you towards a brighter future. Dr. Sam is that someone in my life.

Because of his hands, and God's grace, I am alive today!!

I came to him overweight and sedentary, with a blockage of four arteries. The Mender of Hearts not only mended my physical being, but instilled in me a will to improve and correct my lifestyle.

JIMMIE AFTER

Dr. Sam's ability to show such sincere concern for the family, not just the patient, puts him far and above all other doctors. During my crisis he stood beside me and my wife, and he encouraged her to help me get fit. Now I've lost over 30 pounds and I eat healthy. Exercise is not such a dirty word after all. I look darn good!

What do you call a man who is half your age and is like a father, son, friend, spiritual adviser and confidant…well that's easy… Dr. Sam!

His true passion for his profession transfers to his patients in a way that makes you believe in yourself and helps you become secure in knowing that you are a child of God, and in good hands with the Mender of Hearts. Thank you, Dr. Sam, for giving me my life back!

Oh, by the way, did I say, "I LOOK GOOD!"

—Jimmie Robinson

4 | DO THE MATH

Here's the truth. The number one killer in the U.S. today is Cardio-vascular Disease (CVD), such as heart attacks, strokes and congestive heart failure. Why do I make such a big deal of this? Because one out of three people die of CVD, and I don't want to see you fall to such a fate.

Cancer is associated with fear and dread. According to the American Heart Association, approximately 1 in 31 women dies of breast cancer, *but 1 in 3 dies of cardiovascular disease.*[9] Furthermore, approximately 1 in 34 men dies of prostate cancer, *but 1 in 3 dies of cardiovascular disease.*[10] There is no reason to downplay cancer, but there is no excuse to ignore your heart!

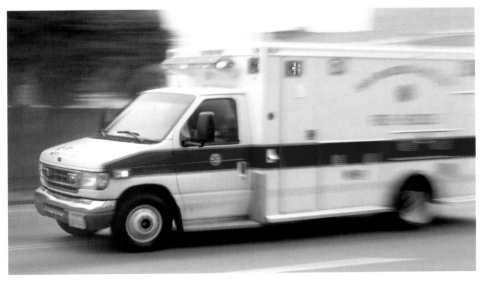

Dr. Sam's Insight

If heart disease is the number one cause of death, why are you ignoring your heart?

One in every three visits to emergency rooms can be attributed to cardiovascular events. While it is difficult, if not impossible, to prevent other causes of death or disability—such as cancer, Alzheimer's, or accidents—cardiovascular disease *can* be prevented or, at least, reduced significantly, simply by doing some math.

Bill was having a stress test in my office and was venting about the administration at the high school where he teaches. The kids must love Bill, because he's genuinely kind, pleasant, and has a great sense of humor. He told me that his school district is desperately trying to prevent absenteeism, so they are rewarding schools if they have good student attendance and punishing them when students miss school. For each student who is absent, the school gets charged $40 per day of school missed.

To make up for the days students missed, school teachers contemplated allowing students to receive lessons on Saturdays, but the administration was hesitant, because they didn't budget to pay teachers like Bill for holding Saturday school, and declared it would "mess up the system."

Bill was beside himself. "Do the math!" he insisted. "If 60 students are absent in one week at $40 per student, that's $2,400 dollars the school loses. If I teach those 60 students on Saturday, the school makes up most of that $2,400 loss; all they have to pay me is a small reimbursement, and the students will catch up. In the end, everyone wins. Just *do the math!*"

We talked about his administration, but I really wanted to talk about his heart.

"Bill," I said, "your heart is showing signs of disease."

"Whoa!" he said. "What do we do?"

"Well, pal, what do you think about your weight?"

"I guess I'm overweight. I know and I have to start working on things."

"Overweight?" I said. "Your Body Mass Index (BMI) is 35. The normal range is from 18.5 to 25; overweight is 25 to 30; above 30 is obese. Bill, your BMI is 35—*do the math!*"

He was shocked when I said, "*Do the math!*" I didn't say it in an ugly way, but I *wanted* to startle him. We'd talked about his weight for the past three years, and he was not only getting heavier, but his heart was paying the price.

Days later I told a friend in North Carolina, John, about "*doing the math.*" John drinks too much, smokes excessively, and eats like there's no tomorrow.

"John," I said, "I'm asking you to please cut your calories[11] to 2,200 a day. Reduce your wine intake to four to eight ounces daily. Drink 64 ounces of water each day and, goodness sakes John, stop smoking, see your doctor, and start walking. *Do the math*, bud!"

"Yeah, I got this algebra down," he laughed.

Two weeks later I received a tragic call from John's wife. While sitting on a commode, John had fallen face-first onto the hard tile floor. He wasn't able to move his entire right side, and doctors believed the stroke would not resolve. In essence, John could well live in a wheelchair the rest of his life.

Since then, John has lost all hope, shut himself out, and will not respond—except with bitter tears. Time will tell how things will play out for John, but it is not too late for Bill and his school district. It's not too late for my patients. And it's not too late for you. You still have time. You still have breath. You still have hope. And you still can change.

Please, I beseech you, listen to a voice that cares for you. Class is now in session...do the math!

5 THE BIG BUTT: DEFINED

Most of my patients tell me, "I know I'm overweight, Dr. Sam, but I really eat healthy. You should be proud of me. All I had for lunch was yogurt." Sometimes I am tempted to ask what was buried beneath the yogurt, perhaps an entire double-layer box of See's Candies®? But my compassion for them makes me hold my tongue.

Truly, I wish my patients just ranked in the "overweight" category. But we would all be fooling ourselves if we believed that, because most are actually "obese" and quite literally bursting at the seams. Obesity is an embarrassing term that has a destructive effect on people's health and psyche. People who are obese are, quite simply, setting themselves up for disaster. Snacking is quite deceptive as we all have done it mindlessly, but a little here and a little there adds up. And folks could very well be eating healthy foods, but the amount and the second portions all add up, become excessive, and lead to obesity.

Ever watch the kids play with Legos® as they create airplanes, dinosaurs, and houses on those large, solid foundations? It's the foundation that holds up their wild imaginary creatures. Without a solid base, their creations wouldn't get half completed before they toppled.

In your grown up world of Legos®, how firm is your foundation?

Don't ignore the question. This is the basis of my message and the secret to your healthy living. The building blocks for many people include excess salt, sugar, and fat, supersized portions, and a complete lack of activity. Building blocks like these form a foundation called obesity. Obesity nurtures conditions such as high blood pressure, high cholesterol, and diabetes. These risks, in turn, cause cardiovascular disease, heart attacks, strokes, heart failure,[12] disability, and death.

Take a minute and honestly examine your foundation. On a scale of 1 to 10—1 being rotten and 10 being excellent condition—how solid is your foundation? Of what does it consist? Is it woven flimsily with starch, sugar, and energy-dense foods, or is it constructed on a sturdy rock, with fiber, green vegetables, fruits, almonds, and nutrient dense foods? Are the building blocks made of unyielding love, or cracked with regrets and resentment? Is it held together with the fiber of forgiveness or falling apart from the wounds and deception of bitterness?

Obesity is a measure of excess weight associated with unfavorable health outcomes. Using the body mass index (BMI)—the ratio of weight in kilograms, divided by the height in meters squared—you can define normal weight, overweight, and obesity. So let's do some math. In adults, normal weight is defined as a BMI of 18.5 to 24.9 kg/m^2; overweight is defined as a BMI of 25.0 to 29.9; obesity is defined as a BMI higher than 30.0. Morbid obesity is defined as BMI greater than 39.

Be aware that a general BMI cannot be applied to everyone in the same way such as for children, the elderly, and athletes; it still faces scrutiny as to its accuracy. Please discuss your BMI with your doctor.

Please see the adjacent BMI table, or go to http://www.nhlbisupport.com/bmi to quickly and automatically calculate your BMI level.

	Body Mass Index	What is your BMI? http://www.nhlbisup-port.com/bmi/
Normal Weight	18.5– 24.9 kg/m²	
Over Weight	25.0–29.9 kg/m²	
Obesity	30.0–38.9 kg/m²	
Morbid Obesity	Higher than 39 kg/m²	

Did you calculate your BMI? Many of my patients are shocked to find that, like one out of every three people, their BMI is greater than 30 and, yes, they are "obese." Waistlines are also critical as we'll see in Chapter 10. Men with waistlines greater than 40 inches and women greater than 35 inches are at an increased risk for cardiovascular disease. Get a tape measure and go at it, but understand that your waist starts at your navel (belly button) and not your lower abdomen or hips. It's sad to see people misinformed or in denial, such as the man who has a 48-inch waist around the navel, wears 36-inch waist pants simply because he keeps his belt fastened below his big gut, and thinks he has a 36-inch waist. It's actually tragic as this behavior leads to disease.

We mask our behavior by labeling it "emotional eating" and insisting it's only "comfort food." But there must be a defining moment in our lives when we, very frankly, call it what it is. That liberating moment is the first step to the road to recovery.

It's not "emotional eating" or "comfort eating."

It is gluttony.

It is indulgence.

It is unrestrained behavior.

It is negligence.

It is uncontrolled self-gratification.

It is selfish.

It is a lack of self-control fueled by a desire that is *never* satisfied, and leads to tragedy.

Despite the delicious taste and temporary satisfaction of various foods and beverages, there is an important truth we must face. The "big butt" is only an exterior manifestation. Meanwhile and more importantly, the inner body takes a beating as it is overwhelmed with illness and crying out for relief.

If you are short-sighted, this book is not for you, because it will not satisfy your fanny or your fancy. If that's the case, reading and implementing Chapter 3 might be enough for you. But if you are truly concerned for your future health and well being, and are eager to reap great rewards, please, set aside the chips and dip and concentrate on the pages ahead. You will be happily overwhelmed by the goodness that awaits you.

Tony is a hard-working 45-year-old contractor who loves cheesecake. He is six feet tall, weighs 223, and is obese, with a BMI of 30.2; he also has high blood pressure. After a stress test last year, I recommended that he decrease his portions, lose weight, and undergo an angiogram. Instead, he gained weight and refused the angiogram. But denial has its payback.

One year later, I visited him in the emergency room. He had stopped taking his blood pressure pills, and was celebrating his wife's birthday at their favorite restaurant. His wife thought he looked a bit ashy, but he denied it. When his heart started to flutter and his head began to spin, he conceded that he was sick and needed help.

Tony's heart raced at 180 beats per minute. To complicate matters, he was so dehydrated upon admission that his kidneys were not functioning properly. He was a hard worker who had completely neglected his health. Medications were given him to slow his heart rate. On the second day of his hospitalization, because he continued to have an abnormal and potentially dangerous heart rhythm, I placed an ultrasound camera probe through his mouth and down his esophagus, taking pictures of his heart to make sure he had no clots in his heart chambers. Then I placed pads on his chest and back, sedated him, and shocked his heart back into a normal rhythm.

"Ouch!" Tony jumped up and shouted. "That hurt like a truck ran over me!" Once he was completely awake, he didn't remember anything, including our 18-wheeler drive-by special. His wife was at his bedside every hour of every day, suffering with him. After successfully shocking his heart into a normal rhythm, I wanted to shock his brain into submission, and so I asked him, "Tony, if you want to kill yourself, that's your business, but what about your family? Do you want to hurt them? Do you want to leave them behind?" Sheepishly, he said, "No."

After his discharge, Tony's heart jumped back into an abnormal rhythm, which forced him to take multiple medications. His uncontrolled blood pressure caused one of his heart chambers, the left atrium, to enlarge irreversibly, which "stretched the electrical unit" and caused what we call atrial fibrillation. He will soon get an angiogram. It's safe to say, Tony has learned that being uncooperative comes with loss—loss of time with loved ones at home, loss of time at work, and loss of life's goodness.

Excess weight will cause much harm to the person carrying it. Granted, there are medications such as steroids and antidepressants that can cause weight gain, and there are some illnesses such as autoimmune disease and cancer that wreak havoc on the body's foundation, but overall, weight gain and its subsequent destructive consequences are most often caused by making improper choices.

Dr. Sam's Insight

Being obese is most often a selfish act. It does not consider others. It is self-serving. It is self-seeking. And it is self-destructive. It fails at all counts, and it causes unnecessary pain for the patient and the whole family.

Are you up for an 18-wheeler drive-by special? Just in case you're on the verge of saying yes, or trading your health for that second piece of cheesecake, I want you to be fully informed. When obesity causes the shot knees and hips that need replacement, when it causes the diabetes that require the belly injections, when it causes the stroke that gives you a lame arm and leg, when it causes the bad heart rhythm and heart attack, when it causes your quality of life to shatter—you will walk in the land of dismay, depression, and regret.

Dr. Sam's Insight

Your health is the foundation of your breath, your hope, and your dreams. Cherish your health now—honor it today. In so doing, you will honor yourself, honor those who love you, and honor your future.

I'm not talking about the grave, because then it won't matter. I'm concerned about your life *today* and what you will face tomorrow if you ignore my plea. When you choose to abandon the path of the "big butt," your agility, awareness, and activity will increase exponentially. The risk of cancer and heart disease will plummet. Your quality of life will soar, as the years ahead of you multiply. You will relish the freedom of a lighter step, accented by a smaller butt.

Even a 5% total weight loss will capture the attention of your family and co-workers and begin to restore your health. You are only one decision away from being set free, and walking away from what binds you.

Dr. Sam's Insight

If you decide to wait, tomorrow may be too late. Why? Because, illnesses have their own rights and agendas. Soon, they will begin to dictate their own plan of attack, without asking for your permission.

You may think it's too late. You may feel too depressed to change. You may say, "Dr. Sam, you just don't understand my situation. I see no way out."

To you, I say, "That was yesterday. Today is a new day. I'm your advocate; walk with me. I'll be your counselor; listen to me. I will do my best to guide you and walk on this journey with you. Allow me to step in and make a positive impact in your life. It's your time, and maybe for the first time, you will open the doors of your heart to let courage walk in. Now is the time to forgive the past, stand in confidence, walk in strength, and live in hope. Now, let's press on!"

6 THE BUILDING BLOCKS OF A BIG BUTT

It's late at night, you've had a rough day, and you're exhausted. The TV remote is at your service and you stretch on the couch to get a moment's rest. But something is missing. So you grab the 20-ounce potato chip bag and the 1.5-quart container of low-fat ice cream. Your intention is to eat just a few chips and scoop a couple of bites of ice cream. The shows aren't what you wished for, but you're too tired to get up. You're surprised when you wake up, the TV is still on, the bag of chips is half gone, and the ice cream container is half empty, and your couch has also shared in the ice cream fest. You get up to toss the bag on the counter, the container in the trash, and head to bed. Here is the tragedy: the products eaten, the amount consumed, and the time it was ingested are all hazardous to your good health.

That's where obesity resides—on the couch.

That's when obesity thrives—after hours.

That's how obesity wins—when you are beat and down and make poor choices.

We can argue all day and all night that eating late is not the problem. I concur, because it's the amount we eat that sets us back—but most have their biggest portioned meals during the evening, indulging and eating in excess, without any inhibition, casting off all limitations, and disregarding moderation. And that's when nighttime becomes a big blunder in the big butt blueprint!

Things that seem harmless can become the most notorious causes of obesity. It's not the food itself that's the problem, but we, the consumers, who have no frame of reference as to what portions and calories are acceptable. If we are sitting in front of the TV, eating out of the 20-ounce potato chip bag or the 1.5-quart ice cream container, we're killing ourselves, because we have no sense of how much we are consuming.

The three major sources of calories are carbohydrates, fats, and proteins. These are the main ingredients that support our foundation. What my patients don't realize is that alcohol, sodas, fruit drinks and energy drinks play a major role in caloric intake. Make no mistake about it. The more fat, sugar, and starch in your blended Lego® world, the bigger the belly, the bigger the butt, and the higher the risk of heart attack and stroke. That's what happens when we build our lives on a wobbly foundation consisting of diabetic walls and hardened, caramelized pipes.

So, how do we define a healthy foundation? How many calories should we consume each day? The answer depends on how active we are. Most females require 1,600 to 2,200 calories per day. Most males require 2,000 to 3,000 calories per day. More active people require additional calories.

How do we calculate our caloric intake? From carbohydrates, proteins, and fats. And since alcohol is so prevalent, I'll be including it as the "fourth" food group.

Carbohydrates (CHO) offer 4 calories for every gram. If a food contains 10 grams of carbohydrates, we will ingest 40 calories (4 calories x 10 grams). Approximately 50% of our total calories usually come from CHO. For example, given an 1,800 calorie diet, 50% or 900 calories (50% of 1,800) are from CHO, which equals 225 grams daily (900 divided by 4 = 225).

CHO consist of:

1) Complex CHO such as starch: pasta, bread, potatoes, white rice, brown rice.
2) Simple CHO such as sugars: white, brown, corn syrup, honey, fruits (fructose).
3) Soluble and insoluble CHO such as fiber:
   a. Soluble: oats, peas, beans, apples, citrus fruits, carrots, barley, psyllium
   b. Insoluble: whole wheat flour, wheat bran, nuts, many vegetables

Dr. Sam's Insight

You may have been advised to cut down on your carbohydrate intake. That's partially good advice. Cut down on the sugars and starches, but increase the fiber!

Dietary fiber normalizes bowel movements, helps prevent hemorrhoids and colon related disease, can lower cholesterol levels and control blood sugar levels.

Fats offer 9 calories for every gram. If a food contains 10 grams of fat, we will ingest 90 calories (9 calories x 10 grams). Approximately 30% of our total calories usually come from fats. For example, given an 1,800-calorie diet, 30% or 540 calories (30% of 1,800) are from fats, which equals 60 grams daily (540 divided by 9 = 60).

Fats are the source from which we get our cholesterol, and our cholesterol intake should be less than 300 milligrams daily. Our liver already makes cholesterol on a daily basis, and by eating more, we add to the total intake. Cholesterol is only found in animal products such as meat and eggs. Fats from non-animal sources, such as nuts, do not contain cholesterol.

"Fat free" diets are not the answer to your problems. Your choices and your portions are.

The "Eat-Less" Fats

When you hear or read the words *saturated, trans-fats, and hydrogenated*, run for your life. When you see these words, link their excessive intake with heart disease. As we'll later see, this new outlook or perception is called "reframing," and helps us see food in a different way. These fats are found in pizza, sausage, bacon, ribs, burgers, food fried in hydrogenated oils (such as fried white potatoes and fried chicken), candy, butter, dairy desserts, and ice cream. Our daily saturated fat intake should be less than 7% of our total calories. So an 1,800-calorie diet mentioned above would have 126 calories (7% x 1,800); and 126 divided by 9 = 14 grams of saturated fat per day.

The "Eat-More" Fats

These fats include *mono-unsaturated and poly-unsaturated* fats. These are found in a variety of foods and oils, such as olive oil, peanut oil, canola oil, avocados, poultry, nuts, and seeds.

Proteins offer 4 calories for every gram. If a food contains 10 grams of protein, we will ingest 40 calories (4 calories x 10 grams). Approximately 20% of our total calories usually come from proteins. For example, given an 1,800 calorie diet, 20% or 360 calories (20% of 1,800) are from proteins, which equals 90 grams daily (360 divided by 4 = 90).

We should ingest at least a minimum of 50 grams of protein daily, or at least 1 gram of protein per kilogram of your ideal weight. Three ounces of poultry has 25 grams of protein. One cup of 1% milk or yogurt has 10 grams of protein. Grains, cereals and vegetables have approximately 2 grams of protein per serving. Nuts have 7 grams per serving.

Dr. Sam's Insight

Excluding healthy carbohydrates and clinging to an extreme protein diet is not the answer for losing weight.

The other day, I was on call and craving ice cream. The hospital cafeteria had Dove® ice cream bars with almonds and milk chocolate nicely packaged. One ice cream bar weighs 2.89 fluid ounces. I was impressed with the label, because it displayed what was inside each bar.

As a side note, food labels can be extremely deceiving. Many labels state that the "amount per serving" in the package is two or more. If a label states there are two servings in the package, you need to multiply all the numbers including calories and salt by two. This is where many people go astray! "The label said 200 calories," they insist. Yes, but did they read that the package had 10 servings and they ate the whole thing? That would be 200 x 10 = 2,000 calories! You need a translator? All right, it's called a "Big Butt."

Back to our delicious Dove® ice cream bar, which should be a treat and not a habit for us. The label says one bar contains 250 calories; total fat 17 grams (saturated fat 9 grams, trans fat 0 grams); cholesterol

25 milligrams; total carbohydrates 21 grams (dietary fiber 1 gram, sugars 18 grams); protein 4 grams; sodium 100 milligrams.

So let's break this down. How did they calculate 250 total calories?

1. Total fat 17 grams. We know that each gram of fat is equal to 9 calories. So 9 x 17 = 153 calories.

2. Total Carbohydrates (CHO) 21 grams. We know that each gram of CHO is equal to 4 calories. So 4 x 21 = 84 calories.

3. Total Proteins 4 grams. We know that each gram of protein is equal to 4 calories. So 4 x 4 = 16 calories.

4. We'll take 153 + 84 + 16 and get 253 calories (approximately 250 calories).

5. What's vitally important is that, of the total 17 grams of fat, the saturated fat ("eat-less" fat) was 9 grams.

6. What you also want to know is that, of the total 21 CHO grams, sugars comprised 18 grams. Note that the ice cream bar only contained 1 gram of fiber.

7. Also of importance is the fact that the bar included 100 milligrams of sodium (salt). People always tell me, "I don't use any salt," and "I rarely salt my food." The salt shaking part of their story may be true, but they are consuming gobs of salt in many of the foods they eat. Salt is everywhere and we should only be consuming up to 1,500 milligrams each day.

8. Many get the word "cholesterol" mixed up with "calories." But, as mentioned above, cholesterol comes from fats. We are supposed to consume less than 300 milligrams of cholesterol daily. So, if we eat the whole ice cream bar—and who doesn't—we've just ingested 25 milligrams, leaving room for just 275 milligrams the rest of the day.

Reading labels helps us identify what we eat and how much we eat.

Alcohol offers seven calories for every gram. Many alcoholic beverages contain 150 calories per serving. Suppose you drink a six-pack of beer daily, which would likely make you an alcoholic. You have just ingested 900 calories, which likely exceeds 50% of your total calories for the day! More on alcohol consumption and restriction in the next chapter.

Dr. Sam's Insight

If we don't read what's on the labels as we eat indiscriminately, our foundation will be cracked with diabetes, weakened by disease, and ruined by death. Morbid? Yes, but only if we ignore the instructions.

7 ALCOHOL: THE GOOD, THE BAD, THE INEBRIATED

The "healthiest" dose of alcohol has not been definitively determined by the experts. If you do drink, the ideal dose of alcohol is likely around 6 grams per day. One portion of alcohol (10–15 grams of ethanol) can be found in one glass of table wine (5 ounces), one glass of fortified wine such as sherry or port (3–4 ounces), one can or bottle of beer (12 ounces), one glass of malt liquor (8–9 ounces), or one small glass of brandy or spirits such as 80-proof gin, vodka, or whiskey (1.5 ounces).[13] In the largest study of alcohol associated with mortality, the maximum benefit occurred at a consumption of *one drink* daily for both men and women.[14]

In my opinion, no level of alcohol consumption can reliably be regarded as "safe" for some people. Conditions that make alcohol ingestion absolutely inadvisable include pregnancy, personal or strong family history of alcoholism, previous hemorrhagic stroke, hepatic or pancreatic disease, and operation of potentially dangerous equipment or machinery. People with active gastritis, esophagitis, premalignant GI lesions such as Barrett's esophagus, or a strong family history of breast cancer should also abstain from all alcohol.[15]

Ironically, many of my patients drink to feel happy, but alcohol is actually a depressant, altering a person's perception, emotions, movements, vision, and hearing. I often ask my patients what they consider to be "one glass of wine." Going by the books, a "glass" of wine is three to five ounces, but many people drink wine out of a 12 to 16 ounce goblets, designating it their daily "one glass of wine," which usually escalates to at least two glasses. I don't believe alcohol is intrinsically bad, but I do know that many people don't understand moderation, limitation, and alcohol's addictive dispensation. They believe that "whatever I'm drinking is fine." Don't let the burgundy color fool you, as it sparkles in its shiny glass and goes down so smoothly; in the end it bites like a snake and poisons like a viper.[16]

Dr. Sam's Insight
Many don't understand moderation, limitation and alcohol's addictive dispensation.

Not everyone who drinks will become an alcoholic, but I don't believe anyone who starts drinking alcohol ever states, "I'm proud to say that I'm going to become an alcoholic one day, hang out with a bunch of other alcoholics, waste my resources, lose my job, set a bad example, bring my family shame, and regret it forever." Neither do they think they will ever be caught driving drunk, hurt someone in an accident, or commit domestic violence. They don't plan on vomiting up blood, ruining their liver, or dying from pancreatitis. The spitting up blood picture may not be very pretty, but it's the truth both for the educated as well as for the uneducated.

The younger a person starts drinking, the worse the damage, and the tragedy. In fact, more than 4 out of 10 people who begin drinking before the age of 15 eventually become alcoholics. The overwhelming majority of youth—74 percent of 8- to 17-year-olds—cite their parents as the primary influence in their decision to drink or not to drink alcohol.[17]

Many of my patients minimize or underestimate their alcohol intake when reporting to me. It's very difficult to say, "I am drinking too much."

I had been struggling to control Ben's blood pressure when I asked him about his food and alcohol intake. He told me he drank two, 12-ounce beers per day, at most. Ben is 66 years old, five foot seven and weighs 180 pounds; his BMI is 28.2 (overweight). After he passed a cardiac test and underwent an extensive neck spine fusion, he was admitted to the ICU, where he began hallucinating, shouting, shaking, sweating, crying, and shivering uncontrollably. His heart rate increased, his blood pressure climbed, and he started experiencing seizures. Ben went into cardiac arrest and died in ICU. Amazingly, he came back to life after 10 minutes of CPR. But the road ahead in the hospital was extremely difficult.

With an expert staff and the right medications, Ben began to improve, and his alcohol withdrawals ultimately resolved. His rehab went well and he was eventually able to rest comfortably at home. Ben later told me that the two 12-ounce cans of beer he'd reported previously were in reality at least one 6-pack per day, and sometimes much more.

"We lost you pal," I said, "and now that you're back in the land of the living, you've got new hope!" Even then, Ben told me he might have one or two drinks in several weeks when he got better. "Not one, not two, not nothing—not ever!" I urged him.

I don't think Ben particularly liked hallucinating, when he insisted bugs were slowly creeping onto every square inch of his body, ravaging his skin as he was hallucinating. I don't think he liked shaking uncontrollably and foaming at the mouth. I don't think he liked the "spiders" that hung from the ceiling tiles of the ICU and swam in his soup as he rode the ugly wave of alcohol withdrawal.

Ben has stopped drinking. His blood pressure is normal. He functions better. His family can converse with him sensibly. He is a new person. And we're all grateful. Even if we did need the help of the ugly crawling bugs and nasty tasting spiders.

Dr. Sam's Insight

When drinking, don't exaggerate and don't underestimate. Alcohol has no consideration for your well-being. It is notorious for tearing the very foundation out from under you and stripping away the breath of hope within you.

I've never seen alcohol help anyone. It is associated with uncontrolled high blood pressure, high sugar and cholesterol levels, excess calories (up to 150 calories per drink), large guts, accidents, domestic violence, and death. I have comforted many people and their families who trusted alcohol as a close confidant, and were betrayed, even unto death.

Take Jay's case for example. Jay is gentle, yet bold; he can be calm, yet stern; he's a great leader, yet he's always approachable. He is the most sought-after manager at his work place, and employees wait months after placing their requests to work with him.

Jay showed up at my office one day complaining of chest pains. A previous chest CT showed that his aorta, the largest artery in the human body, was enlarged. His sugar counts had threatened to climb above the diabetes fence for years, but recently strutted their way across shamelessly. His alcohol intake exceeded the daily allotment.

Given Jay's aortic problem, we chose a gentle protocol on the stress test, yet within four minutes of starting the exercise, his heart began to beat erratically. I immediately stopped the test and watched

for deterioration of the rhythm. His color was pale and he was sweating profusely. The ultrasound pictures showed a portion of his heart muscle missing oxygen, consistent with a blocked artery.

The abnormal stress test results led us urgently to the angiogram suite. The diagnostic pictures in the cardiac cath lab showed an artery that was at least 95 percent blocked, in the middle of the most important artery on the left side. The balloon sailed easily to the spot while I opened up the blockage. The stent, which keeps the blockage open, was deployed, and the celebration was cut short when I witnessed his frail artery dissect, tearing in a way that looked like a candy cane swirl.

The second stent fixed the dissection just past the first stent, and once again, I thought we were finished. But another dissection began just before the first stent and my patient began having severe chest pains. We were seconds away from disaster, so I asked for the third stent. I got it up quickly and attempted to push it forward to cover this new dissection, but the stent got stuck. I thought, "You've got to be kidding me!" And I prayed, "Oh, Lord, help me now!"

My patient's vitals were changing for the worse and the calcium build-up in his vessels was waging war against me. With a tenacious attitude and God's grace, I wiggled the stent down to its spot, deployed it, held my breath, took the next picture, and there it was: a perfectly beautiful opened artery with no more blockages. "Why did you give me such a hard time, Jay? Can't you keep it simple for me?" I later asked my patient. "Got to keep you on your toes, Dr. K!" he responded. "Thanks bud, thanks for the challenge!" I said. "My pleasure, doc!" Jay replied.

We spoke about his alcohol intake, it was too much; his weight, it was too high; his activity level, it was too little; and his encounter with death; it was too close. Jay was sick of it all. His hospital stay was unremarkable, just the way my patients and I like it, but what was remarkable was Jay's response: decreased portions and increased walks. Visit after visit to the office and here is the new Jay: 25 pounds lighter. He is slimmer, faster, and healthier. No more alcohol because according to Jay, "It's not worth it!"

Dr. Sam's Challenge

See if you can stop drinking alcohol for 30 days. If even the pure suggestion bothers you, seek your doctor's help!

A drink of alcohol here and another drink there—it can start out so innocent, yet it can attack like a rattlesnake and sting like a scorpion. Get your sugar, cholesterol, and blood pressure tested. Know your limitations. If you don't dare pick up a snake by its tail, then listen to the blood-curdling rattle when you reach for your goblet.

Dr. Sam's Insight

If you don't dare pick up a snake by its tail, then listen to the blood-curdling rattle when you reach for your wine goblet.

"Well, don't experts say that alcohol is good for you?" you may ask, being a little irked after reading this chapter. Because many alcohol consumers don't understand limitations, or "moderation," and think they are somehow exempt from drinking in excess or causing harm to themselves or others, they end up tagging on the calories and tearing down their lives.

Well, you've now heard Ben's story.

And you've heard Jay's story.

What's your story?

Testimonial #2

EUGENE BEFORE

Meet Eugene Padakowski, a 59-year-old husband, father, brother, and friend. He used to weigh 200 pounds, and now weighs 175 pounds, having decreased his BMI from 30.67 to 27.40.

When I first met Dr. Sam, he told me that I had a heart problem. I really didn't want to hear it, and never thought that this could happen to me because I've been strong and healthy all my life. When I was in Dr. Sam's office, he told me I would need an angiogram. It was only when we got to the hospital that it hit me that I was a patient. It amazes me how our minds work, not wanting to deal with our own truth because we're so busy with family and work. Dr. Sam thought he was only going to put in one stent, but had to put in three…in one of the most important arteries. Hard to believe that my heart artery was 95% blocked.

I always thought of myself as being overweight, but I guess on Dr. Sam's scale, I was obese. It didn't take me long to figure out that I was going in the wrong direction—being diagnosed with obesity, high blood pressure, high cholesterol, and diabetes. With Dr. Sam's help, I've stopped eating junk, stopped alcohol all together, and started to walk. Man, I feel better and have more energy.

EUGENE AFTER

I really want to live, especially because I almost died. Imagine living in denial? I did it, and know how it feels. But I now know that denial can kill. 'Why would you want to hurt yourself?' Dr. Sam asked me. I don't. I don't want to hurt myself. I want to grow old with my family and love them. I want to be responsible. It's on me. It's my choice. I pick up the food. I put it in my mouth. I'm the one who chooses to drink. Instead of drinking alcohol, I drink water. Boring? Nothing is boring when I have the privilege of living! Instead of sitting, I'm now walking. Like Dr. Sam says, 'Celebrate life, walk, you're amongst the land of the living!' Well, the course of my life, my health, and well-being has changed, and I'm never going back!

— Eugene Padakowski

8 BUT... IT TASTES SO GOOD

Gloria sat on a chair, looked me straight in the eye with her 285-pound frame and said, "Really doctor, I'm hardly eating anything! For breakfast I had an apple, and for lunch just some lettuce, I swear! And at times, I only eat once a day!"

Since Gloria's weight had been going up, I asked, "Seriously Gloria, how big was the apple?" And Gloria knew I was not buying her story of "the little world of apple and lettuce fairy tale."

Dr. Sam's Insight
You may lie, but your weight will testify!

Stop messing with me! When you eat once a day, what in the world are you eating? How *much* are you eating? When you eat the apple, do you soak it in caramel? Stop lying to yourself. Here's Dr. Sam's prescription: Shut your mouth, stop watching TV, get off your big butt, and start walking. This is your new life. This is your way to healthy living. This is your new journey of hope. No talking back. No looking back. And no going back. This is how we press on!

Dr. Sam's Insight

It's not the food: it's the amount.
It's not the circumstance: it's the person.
It's you. It's me. Take responsibility.

I'm going to list the top ten foods that, when eaten in excess, are killing my patients. The top three alone are the biggest culprits of weight gain amongst my patients. Nothing is inherently wrong with any one; however, because we lack self-discipline and just can't stop at one serving, we're chipping away at our firm foundation and choking out our future well-being.

1) Ice Cream. Oh, how my patients devour this sweet treat—not from a small cup, mind you, but right out of the container, until the whole thing is gone! And then follows the justification: "But it's a good source of calcium!" One scoop of ice cream is enough. Place the scoop in a bowl and put the container in the freezer. You say, "That's not enough!" Two words: big butt!

Dr. Sam's Insight

Big scoops come with big butts—and big heart attacks.
It's your move, your choice, your life, and your health.

2) Cheese. Seriously, don't mess with my cheese! Oh my, your cholesterol is about to explode out of your arteries, so please, put the cheese down and walk away. I don't mind if you eat cheese daily, as long as you can control your portions. Cut your portions in half and reap the benefits!

Dr. Sam's Insight
**If you have a big butt and a bulging gut,
your portions are out of control.**

3) Breads, breads, and more breads! Oh, how people love bread. First, unless you enjoy the thought of sucking on bleach, stop eating white bread. How else do you imagine they turn that gray slice of dough, that looks like a cadaver, into a white-washed beauty?

Bread is what you get when you first sit down at the restaurant. It's free, it's hot, it tantalizes, you're starved, and the pretty little basket it comes in makes it so appealing. If the restaurant had a syringe and you could see what ingredients went into making the bread, that syringe would be filled with salt. 100 calories per slice can add up quickly! People complain about being bloated. They swear up and down that they don't eat much and can't figure out why they are gaining weight. Many times the culprit is *too much* bread. Calories add up, whether from bread, crackers, croissants, or bagels. What you eat is important, but how much of it you eat is critical to your good health.

Dr. Sam's Insight

Choose whole wheat bread over white bread, any day and every day. Instead of a whole bagel, eat half.

Eating too much ice cream, cheese, and bread is a sure way to get a big butt. Recently, Becky visited my office and I could tell at first glance that she had gained weight; I didn't even have to look in the computer to check the recorded vitals to know she was heavier. She trembled as she got on the treadmill, her husband watching.

"I'm here with you Becky," I said, "you'll be all right."

"I'm scared Dr. Sam."

"What are you so scared of?"

"That I'll fail this test and you'll find something wrong."

Her stamina had decreased and her heart walls had thickened and one chamber had enlarged. One of the problems was that her hip joint didn't allow her to walk far and her big gut pushed up on her diaphragm and limited her breathing. After the test, we reviewed the results and went over the above three major foods that, when eaten in excess, promote weight gain.

"Nope, I don't eat those foods, Dr. Sam," she said. "Today for lunch I had some lettuce and a yogurt. I've been watching my weight."

"Wait up, Becky," I said. "You've gained 10 pounds in four months. You're five foot five inches tall and you weigh 230 pounds—that's five pounds away from the category of morbid obesity; not just obesity, but *morbid* obesity."

I didn't want to be cruel, I didn't want to hurt her feelings, and I didn't want her to feel helpless. But I also realized Becky needed a wake-up call. If I didn't deliver the message, who would? "Becky, hon, your BMI is near 39 and you don't eat much? You may not be eating bread, cheese, or ice cream, but you're eating something other than lettuce and yogurt—and you're *overeating*. You're limping. It's affected your walking. Are we going to get a cane next? Are we going to get a hip replacement?"

Her husband chimed in. "Tell him, Becky. Tell the doctor what you had at the banquet last night." Becky looked at him in shock, as if he had betrayed her. She dropped her head in embarrassment, and her husband continued. "Okay, I'll tell him. She had a huge dessert last night. And she's been making that a habit. Late night desserts, helping herself to one, two, three servings."

That was that. I restricted Becky from eating after 6 p.m., except for salads, fruits, and vegetables. She could eat one small portion of dessert after a meal, but that was all. Becky would return to my office nine pounds lighter in three months. How do I know? She faced the fact that she was limping, and it affected her soul. She got a glimpse of her future, and it lacked a sure foundation. She caught a vision of a longer life span, and it restored her hope. She gave me her word, and I believed it because it was written in her tears.

What we desperately need are two things: 1) accountability, to help us face denial as in Becky's case, and 2) simplicity, to help us decipher between healthy choices and unhealthy choices. Our diet often lacks nutrient-dense foods such as fruits, vegetables, greens, beans, fish, and almonds. It's not the healthy, nutrient-dense foods that are killing us and causing the big butt to get bigger, but the unhealthy energy-dense foods and drinks. Here are some other energy-dense foods, which, when eaten in excess, are destroying good health.

4) Chips, salty foods (such as canned soups). These will, quite simply, blow the cap off your head as they increase your blood pressure due to the increased salt content that extends the food's shelf-life. How else are the manufacturers going to bypass refrigeration? Be warned and flee from these sodium-soaked troublemakers. Don't know how? I'll help you. Stick to the perimeters (except the bakery) of the grocery store. The central aisles are where the processed foods, sugars and salt reside.

Dr. Sam's Insight

**If you simply watch your salt intake,
you'll invariably decrease the fats and starches.**

5) Wine, beer, hard liquor, "glorified" coffee (with sugar and cream, and lattes and cappuccinos), whole milk, soft drinks, sport drinks, fruit drinks, and energy drinks. Drinks are deceptive; many don't consider counting them as a food product, ignoring the sugar or empty calorie content. The serving size for juices is 4 ounces. Just because it's liquid does not mean it is free of calories! Many do not consider that liquid items have calories and can cause weight gain because they do not view drinks as "food." But even "innocent and healthy" drinks such as fruit juices have sugar contents that will blow your mind and your waistline.

6) Any ranch dressing (made out of buttermilk, sour cream and mayonnaise), blue cheese dressing (also made out of sour cream and mayonnaise), and dips. Why smother natural foods in fat and salt? Why not use olive oil and vinegar? The heavy dressings and dips will clog your arteries and make your heart work overtime. Instead of pouring the dressing on your salad, have it on the side, and use only a small portion. Dip your fork in ever so lightly, then fork the lettuce. You'll save yourself a ton of excess calories and salt intake. The "light" version can also cut 50% of the fat. Exclude croutons and bacon from your salads.

7) Fried foods, French fries, chicken skin, oiled and salted nuts. Stay clear of oils that are solid at room temperature, such as butter and margarine. Which is better for you, butter or margarine? Neither! Reach for the olive oil. Otherwise, it will be a big butt outside and clogged arteries inside. Enough said.

Dr. Sam's Insight

Fried foods cause a big butt outside and clogged arteries inside.

8) White rice, white flour products, such as white bread and flour tortillas. Now that you know that white bread is bleached, stick to whole wheat. White rice has less nutrients and fiber than brown rice. Choose whole wheat tortillas over flour tortillas. Delicious Ezekiel bread is flourless and made from live, sprouted grains. Other fiber-rich products that get thumbs-up include brown rice, whole-grain pastas, and whole-grain cereals. If you are allergic to wheat, millet bread is a healthy alternative.

Dr. Sam's Insight

White bread is dead. Whole-grain is gain.

9) Cookies, pies, cakes, chocolates, doughnuts, candy, brownies, pastries, and sugar—cleverly disguised on labels as 'sucrose,' 'dextrose,' 'maltose,' and 'fructose.' When it comes to these sweets, people usually say, "Okay, just this one time, I'll indulge." But everywhere you go, it's "just this one time." There's always a birthday, anniversary, wedding, or baby shower, and there will always be office goodies, graduation parties, picnics, and random celebrations, and before you blink, Thanksgiving and Christmas.

My patients, like Becky, either "forget" the fact that they eat these foods, or simply ignore or downplay their hazardous effects. Then

I hear, "Oh, Dr. Sam, I had lost so much weight, but the holidays messed me up!" Listen, Thanksgiving and Christmas didn't mess you up, you messed yourself up! Call it like it is and stop sitting, eating, bloating, belching, bulging, and complaining.

Dr. Sam's Insight
What's the major cause of the weight gain?
Hands down: portions...sweets, snacks or sandwiches...
it's portions!

10) Low calorie, fat-free foods, packaged foods and meals. Because many foods are "low in calories," people overlook the salt content and tend to eat in excess. Because it is "fat free" or "sugar free," people snack more and drink from extra-large, gulp-sized cups.

A word of caution: if the food glitters, beware. Don't underestimate the packaging and marketing! It may look good on the outside, but once it hits your esophagus, it turns into illness, sickness, and ruthless death. However, if the food is natural, once it hits the esophagus, rejoice, because it turns into health and life.

Dr. Sam's Insight
If God made it and it grows naturally, eat it. If it's
processed, put on your running shoes and run away!

Want some comfort foods, like pizza or chocolate? Set aside a "free day" every now and then when you "reward" yourself with these foods—but *don't* overindulge. You can even have some of these things *daily*, *if* you exercise portion control!

How will you know when you've had too many comfort foods? The life of my patient Hank will enlighten you about that in the next chapter. The one thing you don't want to do is eat so many comfort foods that you're comforting yourself all the way to my angiogram table with a massive heart attack, because you insisted on having too many hot dogs, fast food burgers, cold cuts, and pizzas.

Let me ask you, point blank, are you eating too many comfort foods? Ask your big gut and your big butt—they will speak louder than any words. Words lie, but the butt and the gut speak the truth, loud and clear. Keep in mind, if a little is good, more is *not* better. For instance, when you enjoy pizza, that's fine, but stop after your second slice. Beyond that is just wrong. Moderation will save you! One slice of cheese pizza has approximately 300 calories. Two slices, 600 calories, and a salad with low fat dressing to boot…you've got yourself a reasonable meal.

We may kid about the big butt and the big gut, but these are serious warning signs of likely health hazards on your horizon. Once you learn how the butt grows, your newly found hope will instruct you to run away from the wicked grasp of eating too much of the above foods.

This is your time to choose life over death. It's your time to choose freedom over captivity. It's your time to experience contentment and not guilt. And it's your time to enjoy God's green earth with health that accompanies your every step!

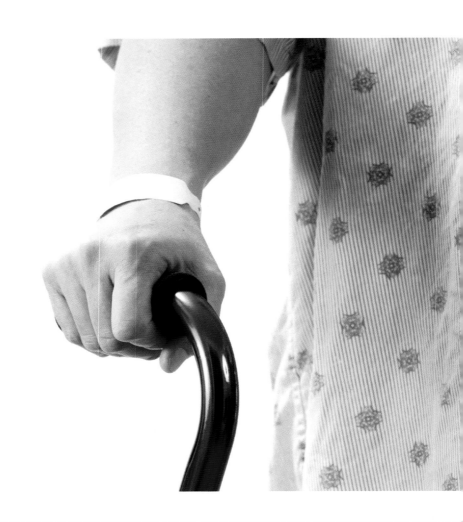

9 | ONE FINE DAY

"What's all the excitement about?" you ask. "So I've got a slight gut and a rather large butt. Look around! I'm not the only one. And I'm not that bad, compared to a lot of people. What's up? Why can't I eat, drink, and be merry?"

You can live that way if you wish, but I will let my patient, Hank, tell you all about the cost.

Hank served our country as a Marine in his early twenties. Back in those days, he was slim and cut at 170 pounds. Thirty years later, however, in his fifties, Hank got up to 320 pounds. I remember seeing him eight years ago and advising him to lose weight.

How did things get so out of control?

For years, Hank's routine was the same. He would arrive home from work after 7 p.m. and plant himself in front of the TV, eating potato chips and ice cream, and drinking his favorite diet soda. His favorite move was walking to the fridge. And his favorite saying was, "I'm not that bad. Have you seen my neighbor? I'll stop this one day."

Well, that one fine day has arrived.

Hank is on a dozen medications, including insulin injections, which he needs twice daily. The other medications include three different prescriptions for high blood pressure, two for high cholesterol, two for gastro-esophageal reflux, one thyroid medication, two for joint pain (following surgery for total hip replacement), and one to reduce the swelling in his legs. At night he uses a machine to help him sleep because he suffers from severe sleep apnea, when he stops breathing momentarily due to excessive neck weight.

When he walked into my office recently, my heart cringed. He wheeled an oxygen tank with him, with tubing connected to his nostrils to provide continuous oxygen to the lungs. His blond hair was white. He did not make eye contact, but looked at the floor. His once strong, proud back was now bent in humility.

My eyes filled with tears when he said, "Have you seen the new me?" And my spirit sank when he said, "I thought it wasn't so bad, until I had to carry this tank; I guess what hurts the most is that all this is self-inflicted."

There was no room in my heart to say, "I told you! You should have listened. Look at you now. Some fine mess you're in!"

While on a recent vacation, Hank had been hospitalized for congestive heart failure, a condition where fluid backs up from a weakened heart and fills the lungs. He'd aged dramatically in just two months. Although his weight had dropped from 320 to 290, I had to wonder if it was too late.

We are all human, we all err at times, and we all have our downfalls. But can you give me just a few seconds to shed some light and hope in your life? Take it from someone who knows about hearts and arteries, the human body and long life. *You don't have to be on all those medications. You don't have to suffer. You don't have to struggle with guilt day in and day out. And you don't have to live in failure.*

Dr. Sam's Insight
Sufficient food sustains you.
Excess food kills you.

You can start changing your life right now. Please, listen to me, before that "one day" comes, and it is too late to turn back the hands of time.

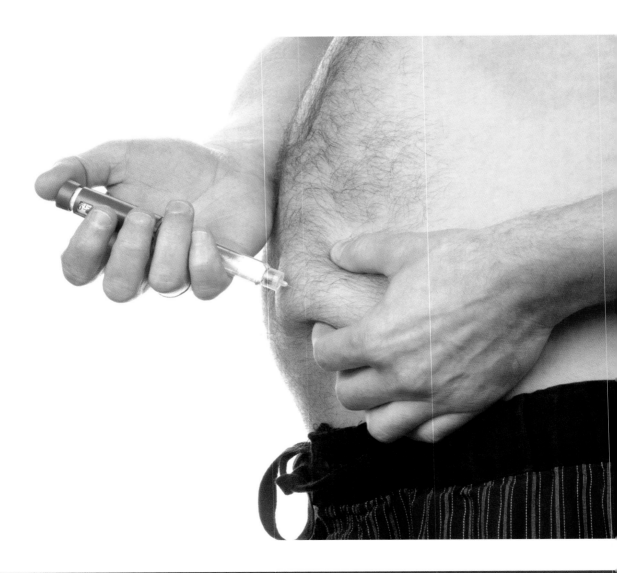

10 BIG BUTT'S PAY DAY

Parties, fun, family, laughter, games, comfort, joy—and food. Doesn't it all go together? And there is nothing wrong with it unless we consider the dire consequences of over-eating. Seriously, is there really a cost for making poor decisions or being in denial or mere ignorance? Are cardiovascular events that grave? Since you won't know until it hits you, I'll spare you the pain and help lead you in the path of health. But you must make the choice—to follow or stray.

 **Warning: hazard ahead!** Please get your payments ready. The toll booth is fast approaching, and your payment for a big butt is your health. "No way!" you say. Say what you wanna say, I see what you have not yet seen, and I, as your advocate, want to change your world into a healthier place.

The following are what I consider to be the consequences of a big butt, the dirty dozen:

1) Diabetes (high blood sugar). Let me testify on the record that when it comes to ruining your body's sound foundation, this is one of the nastiest risks for trouble, havoc, destruction, and utter devastation. High blood sugar is not just a condition that suggests you prick your finger, adjust your insulin injection, eat another dessert, and smile for the family picture. But that's exactly the way Julie, a 53-year-old, 250-pound obese patient of mine, chooses to live.

Julie has an insulin pump, which was implanted into her body by doctors to control her diabetes. Every time she is faced with a decision to eat or not eat the delicious desserts set before her, she simply injects herself with a little more insulin than usual, and proceeds to gorge herself on chocolate. When she pricks her finger later, she is quite happy with her glucose numbers, and all is justified because she conscientiously drinks only "healthy" *diet* sodas.

What a tragedy! If Julie were to drop 25 pounds, she would decrease her insulin intake. And by losing more weight, she could possibly get rid of the pump. Imagine the freedom!

"Julie, you need to bump up your veggie and fruit intake," I said.

"Dr. Sam, you know I can't eat apples and oranges and most fruits, right?"

"No, please tell me why."

"Those things will raise my blood sugar."

Sometimes I really want to stand up and yell and scream and shout!

"Hello, people—are you working for yourselves or against yourselves? Are you ready and willing to be disabled, and to die at a young age and leave your family and friends behind? Are you really that numb to the truth that you are going to continue lying to yourselves and destroy the bodies and minds God has given you?"

If you can adjust your insulin injection for a banana split with five scoops of ice cream, can't you adjust it for an apple? If you can judge how much more insulin you will need for a third chocolate chip cookie, can't you do the same for an orange or a peach?

Did I miss something here? Are my patients trying to tell me that their 250-pound frames are okay, as long as they continue to manipulate their insulin and smile like they can get away with it? For a limited time the answer may be, yes, but for tomorrow, it's an emphatic, "NO!"

Julie has been gaining five pounds per year, but she doesn't feel any different because her pump is her best friend, and her best friend is doing her just fine. Not really! Soon, she will be on dialysis three times a week, each session requiring four hours, so that a machine can clean her blood because her kidneys are unable to do so. Did anyone bother to let her know, "Julie, diabetes will eat you alive?" Yes, I did!

The fact is, Julie has been warned multiple times, but she will not listen. Her appetite is enslaving her. And it is extremely sad, because we know she does not want to live this way. Perhaps when she gets her right leg amputated below the knee, she will realize that it is time to stop the madness. Julie has an infection in her right foot. Although the infected tissue has been surgically removed and she is on antibiotics, her foot is not healing. She has very poor circulation due to destroyed vessels from diabetes, her foot is changing colors, and amputation is imminent.

Why am I relaying such a sad story? I am telling you the truth, so the truth can lead you to hope and healthy living. Are you feeling this? Your appetite is not your advocate—I am.

Dr. Sam's Insight

If you insist on listening to your appetite rather than your advocate, you will soon realize that your appetite is your worst adversary.

2) Hypertension (high blood pressure). High blood pressure increases the tension of the walls of our arteries, damaging the inner lining or layers and causing:

- Strokes
- Heart attacks
- Blindness

- Kidney failure
- Heart failure
- Aortic disease (aorta is the largest pipe or artery in the body, originating from the heart)
- Aneurysms (weakening, bulging, and ultimately bursting of the artery)
- Heart muscle thickening and stiffness
- Heart muscle weakening
- Heart chamber enlargement
- Shortness of breath

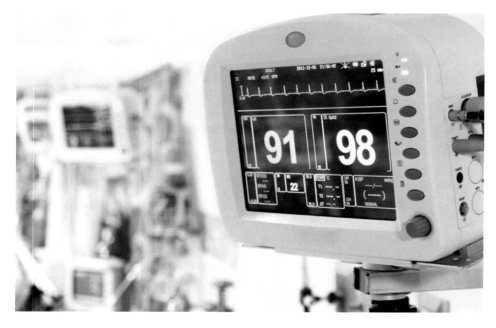

Julie already suffers from heart muscle thickening, shortness of breath, and eye problems. She is losing her vision and receives laser eye treatments each year, but can still see for now. She is on a high-powered blood pressure medication and a second one was recently added in an attempt to get control of her skyrocketing blood pressure.

3) Hypercholesterolemia (high blood cholesterol). This build-up in the lining of the arteries weakens them and opens the door for cardiovascular disease, including heart attacks and strokes. Julie has not had a stroke or a heart attack—yet. The problem is, she is content with her cholesterol numbers, which require three medications to increase her good cholesterol (HDL) and decrease her bad cholesterol (LDL).

4) Central Obesity (fat gut). Women, your waist size should be below 35 inches. Men, your waist size should be below 40 inches. Don't cheat! As we discussed in Chapter 5, we correctly measure the waistline at the navel, or belly button, and not below the bulging belly! The fatter the gut, the more susceptible one is to cardiovascular disease.

5) Metabolic Syndrome. This is a condition that incorporates all four of the above problems (diabetes, hypertension, high cholesterol, and obesity) in one nasty package. It will lead to medical hardship upon hardship, causing devastation to the body, mind, heart, and soul.

6) Bone disorders. Bone disorders include conditions like arthritis and hip and knee degeneration, which lead to a vicious cycle of reduced activity, depression, continued excessive eating, and an even bigger butt. Did I mention that Julie's left knee is scraping bone-on-bone, because she places more pressure on her left side, due to her right leg infection? Her 250-pound frame is too much for the knees to negotiate.

7) Cancers. Various cancers, such as colorectal cancers, may be significantly reduced by consuming more fiber.[18]

8) Endocrine problems. These disorders involve diseases related to the endocrine glands of the body. The endocrine system produces hormones acting as chemical signals secreted through the bloodstream. Hormones help the body regulate different processes, like breathing, fluid balance, and weight control. Endocrine problems can result in diabetes (high blood sugar), which can lead to strokes, blindness, heart attacks, kidney failure (leading to hemodialysis), and neuropathy. Because Julie cannot feel her feet due to neuropathy, she might accidentally bump a toe, get a cut, not notice it, and fail to treat it. It will become infected, ultimately resist antibiotics, burrow itself to the bone, wreak havoc, and lead to an amputation. Never happens? Ask Julie.

9) Peripheral Vascular Disease. The valves in the leg veins can only take so much weight. The bigger the butt, the more inept the valves in the leg veins become, and the more swollen the legs appear. We've got Julie on a diuretic so she can decrease her leg swelling, but a 25-pound weight loss could improve and even reverse the swelling altogether. When cardiovascular illnesses are left unchecked, they can lead to varicose veins; heart failure; incompetent valves in leg veins leading to leg swelling; narrowed kidney arteries, further exacerbating high blood pressure; and narrowed neck arteries (carotid artery disease) causing strokes.

10) Gastrointestinal ailments. These cover the gamut, from acid reflux disease to hiatal hernias, gallbladder problems, diverticulitis, diverticulosis, constipation and hemorrhoids. Hemorrhoids? Serious? Yeah, I'm serious. Decrease your portions, increase your fiber intake, and give your bellyache a break! How about bloating? Start drinking water instead of sodas and sugar drinks. Start eating more apples and less chocolate chip cookies. Start eating more fish rather than red meat. And start eating more vegetables rather than breads.

11) Musculoskeletal issues. These painful troubles can include fibromyalgia, which leads to severe pain from the slightest touch; bursitis, caused by tissue inflammation; and arthritis, that causes joint degeneration due to excessive weight bearing.

12) Neurological mysteries and sleep disorders.
Neuropathy—the loss of sensation in the extremities, associated with pain—often visits overweight diabetic patients. Attention deficit disorder—short attention span—is another consequence that can be greatly reduced, I believe, if we taper down on sodas, sugars, video games, and computer time. Sleep disorders—which are often overlooked when it comes to over-eating and eating late—plague millions of Americans. Sleep apnea (snoring, followed by a span of not breathing) can be controlled by eating less, eating earlier, and losing weight.

Julie sleeps using what we call a CPAP (pronounced C-PAP) machine, which includes a mask that is placed on the face to provide oxygen and open the breathing airway. Sleep apnea causes harm to the heart and can ultimately result in bad heart rhythms, which dent the quality of life and even shorten one's life span. Believe it or not, it is usually not the 70-year-old who comes to me with sleep apnea problems; instead, it is the 30- to 50-year-olds.

"I'll just take pills and treat the illness," people often say.

But how long can you continue like that? How long can your body take the hits? When will what I'm saying begin to sink in—before or after your hospital stay? That is, if you make it to the hospital! Fifty percent of people who have heart attacks die within minutes at their own homes, work places, or en route to the hospital, and fail to even make it through the hospital's emergency doors alive.

Dr. Sam's Insight

Regardless of what you believe, your pills are not your savior. Daily wise decisions pave your road of strength, your way of hope, and your path to healthy living.

We must all make the choice today. It is a simple choice: do I choose to live, or do I choose to die? Do I choose to be healthy, or do I choose to have a cabinet full of pharmaceutical wonders that will blow a hole in my finances and trample my joy? Do I keep suffering in pain and guilt, or am I willing to make adjustments in my game plan? Do I dare destroy my body, or will I live a disciplined life that builds a strong foundation of healthy living, driven with an unmistakable and undaunted spirit of hope?

Discipline hurts. That's true, but a broken foundation is far worse. It will plague you every day with unbearable and hopeless pain. One choice leads to another choice, just like one habit leads to another. Will you choose to be enslaved to food and pain and doctors and hospitals—or will you slay your demons and take the road to recovery and restoration?

Dr. Sam's Insight

Quite simply, it's one choice, leading to the next choice. But make no mistake, it is your choice.

Are you still with me? If you drop just 10 pounds, your blood pressure and cholesterol will noticeably improve. Losing excess weight will help you get rid of the pills, rid yourself of the guilt, silence your critics, and lift your spirits. How fast? A two- to three-pound weight loss each month will help you develop life-changing habits and, by the end of the year, you will have shed 25–35 pounds! Read the next chapter and find out how.

"Hey, wait up," you say. "You don't know how hard it is."

No, you don't know how awful it is to be sick like Julie.

"I won't get that bad," you say. "I've got plenty of time to change."

Oh how Ted, our 45-year-old brain-dead diabetic, whom you met in the beginning of the book, would beg to differ.

You have no idea what it's going to be like to grasp your chest, fall on the ground, and slobber all over yourself while people around you panic and call 911. You can't even fathom what it feels like when you lose the ability to talk and move your left side. So stop making excuses and get off your big butt, because the danger is coming your way, and kicking back and justifying your actions, or the lack thereof, won't help you one ounce.

Dr. Sam's Insight

Many say they will "one day" start exercising. But as diabetes, arthritis, and life's heartaches beat them up, and joints fall apart, reality rudely reminds them that "one day" should have started yesterday!

What in the world are you waiting for? This is your time. This is your life. This is your victory shout! Get up and march to health. Your "one day" has patiently been waiting for you. Your "one day" has arrived. Your "one day" is here. And your "one day" is now. Embrace your "one day" today, get your game face on, and let's press on!

11 DR. SAM'S "SIMPLE 2-STEP HEALTH PLAN"

Why am I concerned about your big butt? For two reasons. First, because I have seen too many precious people fall into depression, become enslaved to their appetites, and fall victim to heart disease, disability, and early death. Second, because in my years of work as an interventional cardiologist—performing angioplasties and stenting of the heart, kidney, and leg arteries—I have learned the keys to healthy and happy living. In a nutshell, I have been blessed to serve my patients, acquire wisdom to help people, and by God's grace, am able to heal, teach, and inspire people to take better care of their hearts, minds and souls.

Ten years after most medical books and "facts" are written, half of the information will invariably change. But I will share with you the two things that will not change. To get rid of the big butt, we must first, decrease our portions and second, increase our activity. There is no magic trick involved. There are no "secrets." There is no food, drink, supplement, granule or droplet, appetite suppressant, fad diet, snack, pill, or energy bar that will lead us to the Promised Land. None of these things will save us.

Dr. Sam's Insight

There are two simple steps to lose weight after we admit that we have a problem. First, decrease those portions. Second, start walking. No secrets—just steps—one step at a time!

We are faced with many decisions in life and perhaps for you it is time to believe the truth, accept my challenge, set the big butt aside, and live with passion. I'm pleading with you: please don't order miracle "sprinkles" or "droplets" to place in your food. Hold fast to our plan of lesser portions and more walking, and you will have started the transformation to a new and healthier you!

My "Simple 2-Step Health Plan" will not only improve the quality of your life, it can lengthen the span of your life.

Let's start with portions. Our society as a whole is in overdrive when it comes to consumption. I'll let you crunch the numbers in your own diet, but the bottom line is this: the less we eat, the healthier we'll be; the more we eat, the sicker we'll be.

You can go ahead and get the lap band or gastric bypass, you can drown yourself in Phentermine and appetite suppressants, you can place yourself on the latest fad diet or extreme protein or shake diet, but I don't suggest any of it. You will end up ill and looking unnaturally gaunt. Wait, did anyone tell you about the side effects or complications? Did you read the fine print? Plus, with these "secrets," you will likely fall back into regaining every ounce of your weight. Why? Because you never changed your *heart*, just your big butt—and that, only temporarily.

Let me take a second to share one more truth with you that I've found over the years in working on people's hearts: the answer to healthy living is not found in a high-fat regimen or high-protein diet.

Nor is it found in boxed meals, shots, injections, pills, elixirs, colon cleansing, or laxatives, or by assigning point values to certain foods, doing a gastric bypass, or strapping on a lap band.

Some weight-loss clinics do not assign points to fruits and vegetables, meaning their clients are encouraged to eat as much of these foods as they want throughout the day. What does that tell us? It confirms that the solution does not reside in gastric bypasses and lap bands, but in nutrient dense foods. The solution lies in our hearts and in our choices. If we change our hearts, we can change our lives. That's why *I Got a Big But(t)* was written—to change your heart, mind and soul.

Almost 100 percent of my patients who spend hundreds and thousands of dollars joining weight-loss programs end up losing weight, gaining it all back, and adding a few pounds for good measure.

Dr. Sam's Insight
You can change your stomach size, but if you don't change your heart, you have only temporarily changed your weight!

I would be thrilled—and I think you would be too—if we were to start with a five percent loss of your current body weight. If you weigh 190 pounds, a 9- or 10-pound drop in weight will start reinforcing your heart's foundation with strength, joy, freedom, lightness, hope, and long-lasting health. Not everyone may be able to achieve a BMI of 25 or less, and that may not be practical for all my patients. Your ultimate goal should be to become a healthier, happier person with an improved quality of life, sporting a foundation less saturated with fats, sugars, and salt, and better sustained with more nutrients. *(See Dr. Sam's 7-Day Cookout and 7-Day Workout in Chapters 47 and 49, respectively.)*

The answer to good health is found in eating more nutrient dense products, and eating less energy dense foods. It is to walk more around the block, and less around our excuses. It is eating less refined sugars (doughnuts) and more natural sugars (fruits). It is eating less processed foods, fast foods, canned foods, packaged foods, fried foods, and fatty foods, and eating more fibers (vegetables).

Dr. Sam's Insight

**The answer to good health is found in eating more nutrient dense products, and eating less energy dense foods.
It's to walk more around the block, and less around our excuses.**

The first steps you take will be the most difficult.

Let's say Fred and Shelly are indulging themselves with hot chocolate chip cookies and sweet vanilla ice cream, and there you are. What are you going to have? Raw almonds! Are you kidding me? This is the tough part, but remember, we are working to set you free from guilt today so you can soar into an enormously healthy new you tomorrow. Just the hope of this new identity, which will allow you to be slimmer and lighter, and to wear the clothes and styles you so desperately long to wear, will help you take the first step.

Just think, turning down those cookies and ice cream, or eating half the portion as a treat once in a while, will lead to a brand new independence; no more condemning yourself. Your success lies in lesser portions. You'll benefit from the freedom of moving faster, the pleasure of feeling better, the joy of looking younger, the contentment of breathing easier, and the satisfaction of silencing your critics—all this will help you stay on the high road of self-discipline.

Remain on the course of healthy living and your blood pressure, cholesterol, and blood sugar levels will drop, while you experience a psychological lift that is filled to the brim with contagious hope.

12 TIPS ON HEALTHY LIVING

The other day, one of my friends handed me a package of dried blueberries. The package read "Naturally Fat Free," and "Source of Antioxidants." Inherently, we go along with it, automatically thinking, "Blueberries are good for me, there is no fat here, and I get antioxidants. Let me eat the whole thing!"

Then I read the bag label on the bag. The nutrition facts showed that there was indeed no fat, no cholesterol, no sodium, and no protein. How about our carbohydrates? Total carbohydrates: 35 grams, with 3 grams of fiber, and 32 grams of sugars. The whole bag was packed with sugar. One can easily argue that 4 x 35 grams = 140 calories, and that's a good snack. Because the food glittered with sugar, I doubt that all the sugars came from the fruit. Blueberries have high antioxidant content and low glycemic index,[19] and are a good source of phytonutrients.[20] And when feasible, purchase fresh organic blueberries over glittery dried blueberries any day! If you were to eat half of the blueberries with a small handful of nuts, the sugar content would decrease and you would introduce more balance. Simply, read the nutrition labels, examine your food and count the calories.

Dr. Sam's Insight
"Low fat" and "no fat" can mean high salt and high sugar! Fresh foods trump packaged foods any day!

The fact that we have become anti-sugar is not necessarily a good thing. Why? Because, we have made "sugar free" products our savior. In reality, these items are laced with our friend Aspartame, the artificial sweetener we discussed in Chapter 3, and partially composed of Methanol, which is converted to Formaldehyde when exposed to the heat in the digestive tract. Smile and say hello to formaldehyde, the embalming fluid, as you embrace diet drinks and foods.

Dr. Sam's Insight
"Sugar free" can be more dangerous than sugar!

People who are conscientious about maintaining the right body weight face a twofold problem today: we treat fat like the plague, and we have become anti-sugar everything.

Does the problem with our weight gain stem from carbohydrates? Remember, carbohydrates can contain sugars, starches, and fiber. Carbohydrates with fiber are shunned by most, while carbohydrates with sugars and starches now dominate our daily food intake. I believe carbohydrates have taken a lead role on center stage in our society's ongoing battle with obesity, but one's portion size is the factor that wins the war over obesity!

In order to maintain an ideal body weight, adults require approximately 30 calories per kilogram of body weight each day. The calculated energy expenditure for an obese man weighing 250 pounds

(113 kilograms), for example, is approximately 3,390 calories per day (113 kilograms x 30 calories = 3,390 calories). With a variability of 20 percent, based on how much energy he expends, that number could go as high as 4,068 calories per day (active), or as low as 2,712 (not very active). The critical point is that an average deficit of 500 calories per day can result in weight loss of approximately 0.5 kilograms per week, or one pound per week.[21]

Dr. Sam's Insight
An average deficit of 500 calories per day can result in a weight loss of one pound per week.

So, how do you reach that deficit of 500 calories per day?

It is challenging to count calorie by calorie, but the Internet has made it easier to help us calculate the amount we eat. Sites such as www.myfitnesspal.com post popular restaurants and calculate the amount of calories per serving. Other sites such as www.choosemyplate.gov or www.caloriecount.about.com can help educate us. Many apps such as "Lose It" are also available on smart phones.

One rule of thumb is to "stop eating when you feel full." The tricky part there is defining "full." Some people may not hit "full" until they begin regurgitating! But be of good cheer—after your body adjusts to lesser amounts of food, you will start feeling full with smaller portions!

The past decade has seen a proliferation of "low fat" and "no fat" foods, and people have gorged themselves, but have you noticed? Obesity is increasing! The "low fat" diet is *not* the solution. On the other hand, people who swear by the "high fat" diet may be losing weight, but they will one day pay the price when their arteries shut down because they are so clogged with plaque.

What in the world *can* we eat then? That is exactly what Pat, my 60-year-old patient with psoriasis (a benign, yet troubling skin condition) asked me. One year ago while lifting boxes at work, he clutched his chest and sat down. He rested for five minutes and the chest pains resolved. Because he felt better, he dismissed it as indigestion, did not tell anyone and continued about his work.

Dr. Sam's Insight

Dismissing chest pains as indigestion temporarily can lead to a quick death…permanently.

Weeks later, Pat came to my office for a stress test. When he failed miserably, we sat down to talk.

"What are you going to do, Doc?" he said. "Don't tell me I have to have my chest cracked open."

"Let's do an angiogram first, Pat," I said. "Then we'll figure it out right then and there. You up for it? You set?"

We did the coronary angiogram (taking pictures of the heart arteries), and found a 99 percent blockage in his right coronary artery. With small wires, balloons and stents, and by God's grace, I opened up his artery and sent him home the next day.

"Are you serious, Doc? I had a 99 percent blockage?" Pat said. "I could have died. And now I'm going home? I can't believe this. Is this happening to me? Am I better now? Am I going to live? When can I go back to work? What am I supposed to eat? When do I eat?"

At that time, Pat was five feet seven and a-half inches tall and weighed 200 pounds, which gave him a BMI of 30.9, and categorized him as obese. "You really want to change, Pat? You really want to be a new man?"

"Look at me Doc. I love to eat, but I'm disgusted with myself!" he said. "I shouldn't weigh this much. I've made every excuse in the book. I choose to pig out every day."

Together, we walked through Dr. Sam's health tips, which I hope you will take to heart.

Dr. Sam's Health Tips

1. "Let's get the timing down. No eating after 6 p.m.," I said.

    "Can we make that 7, Doc? I get home at 6:30 p.m."

    "Okay, 7 p.m. it is. If you are going to eat after that, only salads, fruits, or vegetables."

2. "If it is 'low fat' or 'no fat,' it is likely high in sugar, nasty sugar," I said. "You ever count the creamer in your coffee as sugar? Lots of people don't even consider the little things. It's the little things that add up. Cut these little things in half."

3. "You drink soda?" I asked.

    "Yeah, it gives me energy at work."

    "Well, bud, it's time to stop. One drink has about 12 little white sugar cubes in it and we're only allowed up to nine cubes for the entire day."

4. "Doc, I drink diet soda with less calories. It doesn't have all that sugar," Pat said.

    "Yeah, but it's got Aspartame in it. Some researchers say that artificial sweeteners actually *increase* hunger.[22] No more diet junk!"

"You're kidding, right Doc?"

"Pat, we just opened up your heart artery. This is for real. No more diet drinks. Period."

5. "You like water? Let's get you on water! I know…it doesn't taste as good as the sodas. Want some flavor? Add lime or lemon to it."

6. "You like tea? Let's get you drinking hot tea—big time antioxidants."

7. "You like fruit juice? This is tricky, because although it may look and sound natural, it has *lots* of sugar. Most people drink too much, thinking it's good for them. Instead, it's killing them. A serving is 4 ounces, and that's a healthy portion for you. Even the so-called 'athletic drinks' and iced tea drinks that look so innocent can have tons of sugar."

8. "Hey Pat, what kind of dressing do you like for your salad?"

"Ranch, blue cheese, you know..."

"Yeah, I saw some of that ranch in your artery!"

"Are you serious Doc, you saw some ranch?"

"Nah, I'm just messing with you, but the ranch didn't help your artery. Let's go after things that will help you. Try vinaigrette, light Italian dressing, lemon, olive oil, and balsamic vinaigrette. Forget the bacon and croutons. And, instead of drowning the salad in dressing, dip your fork into the dressing, then take a bite of lettuce. You with me?"

9. "Always take the food you are about to eat out of its large container or package, and place it in a bowl or on a plate. That's your portion. No seconds."

10. "Bump up your veggies, fruits, almonds, beans, and greens, like spinach and asparagus, and eat 'em with gusto!"

11. "Indulge sometimes. Splurge everyday, if you want, as long as it is *small* pieces and *small* portions."

12. "Skip the restaurant appetizers. They may have as many calories as your main course."

13. "Watch out for foods high in salt (read the amount of 'sodium' on the label), like canned soups and other canned foods, frozen entrees, condiments, pickles, olives, and pay attention to the boxed foods."

    "You see this plastic bag?" I asked Pat as I pulled out of my doctor's coat the bag containing 28 small pretzels. This has about 500 mg of salt in it, Pat. I can finish this in 30 seconds flat…500 mg of salt! You are allowed 1,500 mg of salt a *day*. You see, bud, this is going to take some reading on your part."

14. "Hey Pat, you really want to lose weight? Want the real deal?"

    "You're not going to tell me to fast the whole day…are you Doc?"

    "Putting aside some meals with your physician's supervision can lead to good health, but what I was going to say is, decrease eating fast foods. Hey man, *that* will change everything!"

15. "Candy is dandy, but little by little, it leads to a cavity and an unsightly belly."

    "You can rhyme like that, Doc?"

    "That's how we make it fun!"

16. "Cakes and pastries are delicious, but they contain excess amounts of the simple sugars and mega fat. For the most part, walk away, or show restraint."

17. "Have fish at least twice a week and eat your chicken without the skin. Oh, by the way, watch out for the ready-made foods, like the whole chickens and turkeys where we get our sliced lunchmeat in the grocery stores—they are extremely high in salt. See Pat, that's why small portions will save you."

Dr. Sam's Insight

Eat like a king in the morning (minus the sausage, ham, cheese, and syrup), like a queen in the afternoon, and like a pauper in the evening.

18. "Many people only have coffee for breakfast, and that's all. Skipping this most important meal slows the metabolism into a coma state. Then they snack the whole day on foods like doughnuts and chips. Man, I pass the doughnuts all the time in the hospital cafeteria. You think I don't want them? But I know what they do to me…not to mention, people are watching what I eat…so I'm usually a good boy…but sometimes, I just go for it."

"In the past, I've tried not to eat much during the day," Pat said.

"That's not the answer, either, bud, because people who starve themselves all day set themselves up for catastrophe at night. That's when they have their biggest, heaviest meal, then go to bed. It's tragic. The butt just got bigger and the artery blockage just got tighter."

"You crack me up, Doc."

"Thanks Pat. Let's just get you healthy. This is the new you. I can see the banner now: 'Pat, new man, new hope, new life!'"

19. "I need you to decrease pizza and red meat in your diet."

"Come on, Doc."

"No one is telling you to stop eating these fatty foods, Pat, but when you buy the lean red meat, you decrease the fatty content. How about pizza? You should stop after you eat the second slice, because the next piece will slash a wicked crack in your health's foundation. Seriously, the third slice is just wrong!"

"But just one extra slice—what's the big deal?"

"The big deal is not one slice, the big deal is one slice, plus another, plus another. It's a 'big deal' because it leads to a big butt, a big gut, and big health problems!"

20. "Pat, do you exercise?"

"I'm on my feet a lot at work."

"Okay, I want you to stop watching TV at home, get away from the computer, and start walking regularly. Walking burns calories. Any walking you add to your day is going to help you get rid of your big gut."

"But won't that just make me even hungrier, Doc?"

"So, snack on walnuts and almonds and carrots and celery—and drink plenty of water when you feel hungry. Do this and I'm telling you, pal, you are going to start to know what it feels like to live again! You'll be a different person in one month!"

I saw Pat in my office one month later and he had dropped five pounds and felt like a new man. One year later Pat weighed in at 165 pounds for a total weight loss of 35 pounds and his BMI had fallen from 30.9 to 25.4. With another few pounds of weight loss, he would achieve the "perfect" 25, but he had successfully reached a reasonable and healthy weight, which I recommended he maintain.

"Hey Pat, I'm so proud of you," I said. "You could be the poster child for my practice, Mender of Hearts."

"Thanks, Doc," Pat said. "It's thanks to you, and all the walking and water!"

Pat went on to tell me that some of the other key secrets for him were cutting way down on fast foods and not eating after 7 p.m. He passed his next stress test, as predicted, and is now quicker, slimmer, and more agile than ever. Next time you drop by The Home Depot®, watch for the slim guy on aisle 9!

Testimonial #3

PAUL BEFORE

Paul Newman (no relation to the late actor), a 69-year-old gentleman is one of my patients who has decided to turn his life around.

I remember when I met Dr. Kojoglanian, he told me that I had 'classic chest pains,' meaning the chest pains I was having were caused by a heart artery blockage. I guess it doesn't hit you until it hits you. I mean I had a major heart artery that was almost closed off. I always thought I was a bit too big, and it didn't seem to bother me much, so I thought.

Anyway, I wanted to lose weight, but I didn't know how. It's not as hard as it seems. Dr. Kojoglanian told me, "It's simple, but at first it'll be hard!" Man, was he right! I cut out the fast foods, brought my own lunch to work, and stopped eating after 7 p.m. And 35 pounds later and lighter, I feel so much better!

Why I didn't start earlier, I don't know. That's when I started feeling bad about what I've done, but Doc says, 'Paul, it's always too soon to quit, but never too late to start!' He's right, it's never too late. I'm now enjoying my days like never before. I thought food brought me happiness. No, too much food actually made me more tired and less active. Too much food made me walk slower and breathe heavier. In reality, too much food made me feel guiltier. It's not food that makes me happy, it's my good health that brings me happiness!

— Paul Newman

PAUL AFTER

13 | EFFORTLESSLY EFFORTLESS

The other day, I wasn't watching TV, but it was on. There was a commercial that was off the wall, and it got my attention enough to get me to sit on the couch and gaze in disbelief. They were advertising a product you sprinkle on food, a plan that allows you to eat anything. Buy it monthly, sprinkle the granules on your food, don't exercise, splurge, and lose weight! In fact, the "scientific study" they conducted revealed that their subjects lost an average of 30 pounds by simply dashing granules on their foods without practicing any discretion or discipline.

"It was effortless," one lady boasted, and "look at me now!" "Effortless…you've got to be kidding me!" I said, as if she could hear me through the tube. This special invention is supposed to trick your taste buds, which in turn tricks the brain into thinking you're full; but the fact is, most of my overweight and obese patients eat whether they are hungry or not!

Effortless? You mean like the redwoods in Northern California that endure the storms, winds and fires and stand in majesty in the forest? Like the most beautiful china that is subjected to flames at least three times until their rich crimson colors emerge? Like the pianist who sits eight hours a day through intense practice sessions so she can play Sergei Rachmaninov's *Piano Concerto No. 2* effortlessly?

Effortless will not get us healthy. Effortless will not get us fit. Effortless will not get us strong. Are you with me? It is through effort and discipline that we stand tall, and shine with our crimson colors, and play our song with beauty.

Well, how in the world does someone get the big butt in the first place? There are ten key reasons why people fall into the big butt trap. We'll get a glimpse of each point in this chapter and then follow through with more details in the chapters to come.

Here are Dr. Sam's 10 bad "S" words:

1 — Supersizing

The larger the portion, the bigger the butt. The bigger the butt, the sicker the individual, due to risks like high blood pressure and high cholesterol, which we know by now can lead to disastrous cardiovascular events. On the contrary, the smaller the portions, the smaller the butt. The smaller the butt, the healthier the individual!

When asked, "Will that be a small, medium, or large?" without hesitating, say, "Make it a small, please." But then again, what are we doing in the fast food drive-thru? This is the simplest rule, yet one of the most difficult to follow. Perhaps that's because people don't think the difference between a large and a small will make any difference in their lives, but remember: big meals = big butt, and small meals = small butt. This is true whether you're in a restaurant or in your own house. Portions are portions and calories are calories wherever you go!

2 — Slippery Slurpy

I can't proclaim this enough: what we eat has a *direct* correlation with how we feel, what we look like, how we live, and what our future holds. I tell you the truth—slip-sliding our lives away on 64-ounce frozen slushy drinks, candy bars, cocoa and lattes, cakes and doughnuts, extra large burritos, second servings, and the enormous portions in restaurants will escort us to the corridors of the emergency room.

3 — Sedentary

Left, right, move your butt! This may sound strange, but the less you move, the more tired you become. Conversely, the more you move, the more energy you will have. Why? The more active you are, the more endorphins are released. Endorphins are the healing neurotransmitters that are secreted from your brain into your bloodstream; they make you healthier, happier, and more agile. Press on!

4 — Sugar

Saturated within almost everything we eat and drink is sugar—be it white, brown, sweet, natural, or artificial. You've got to hear me on this and understand: the higher our sugar intake, the higher the risk we face of becoming diabetic. Taking this lightly is simply deadly.

5 — Salt

It's usually the small, hidden, almost unnoticeable things that creep up on us and set us back, disable us, and yes, even kill us. Those tiny, seemingly harmless grains of salt you shake onto your eggs in the morning are one of those deadly culprits. Surprising to most, an excess of salt has a direct correlation to high blood pressure in many people, which leads to strokes. And remember, it's not just the salt from the shaker that's bad. Check the salt (labeled as sodium) content on the label!

6 — Saturated Fat

Warning: processed foods and pastries generally have high fat content and are *screaming* with trans-fats and saturated fats. So what's the big deal? Let me break it down—the higher the trans-fats and saturated fats, the higher the cholesterol in your blood; the higher the cholesterol, the filthier and more clogged become the body's arteries. Do you want to avoid hospital visits? Cut the trans-fats and saturated fats, or I'll just meet you in the cardiac catheterization lab.

7 — Smoking

Would you lick hot tar off a newly paved road, or sip on cyanide, or place your mouth over the car exhaust and inhale carbon monoxide? No? Then why are you smoking? Smoking is not correlated with being obese, but it's placed here as one of the "S" factors because it ruins your health. The nasty ingredients in tobacco jackhammer your arteries and lead to strokes, heart attacks, cancers, and the complete demolition of a solid foundation.

8 — Stress

When fear and stress strike, they often drive people to open their mouths wide and stuff their faces with excess food. Please, even when you are under pressure and feeling the need to eat, make a point to munch on healthy foods, such as fruits, raw almonds and raw veggies.

9 — Strain

Through stress, fear, and pressure, life has a way of beating up your mind, soul and spirit. Anger, bitterness, and depression can set in. You may now be experiencing such unbearable strain that you are about to crack! Keep reading—we will visit the way of escape on the pages ahead in Section 3.

10 — GAP'S'

GAP'S' is an acronym I've created that stands for 'Gender,' 'Age,' and 'Parents' (genetics). None of these three can be changed, so they are considered non-modifiable risks for cardiovascular disease. Each one has a sneaky way of working on our big butts. What places some people at a higher risk than others in these areas? Males who are greater than 50 years old, and those whose parents have experienced premature cardiovascular disease—such as a father who had a heart attack prior to age 65, or a mother who had a heart attack before age 55—are at greater risk.

But even if you are at higher risk, I've got good news for you. These factors can be greatly minimized when you implement Dr. Sam's HAT Trick: Hydrate, Ambulate, and Tabulate! *See Chapter 3 for details.*

So, will it be sprinkles of granules for you? Or will there be a droplet of a very expensive substance in your water that curbs your appetite? Are you going to stock the same foods in the pantry and fridge and hope to get slim? Are you going to sit on your butt, keep watching TV and expect to get fit? If so, you are living a lie.

Let me "sprinkle" the truth in your diet. The answer and the sure fire way to do this is to mix your desire with self-discipline and effort, and start living. It is never effortless. It actually takes great effort. But isn't the effort worth it? The new you will be able to walk better, feel better, breathe better and be better; it will allow you to spend quality time with your family and friends and enjoy life more fully; and it will prevent or even *reverse* the very disease that has you staggering.

Why should you adhere to the truth?

Because you are worth the investment!

14 FROM SUPERSIZE TO SLIM SIZE

My patient, Tom, 50, is five feet nine inches tall and weighs 328 pounds, giving him a Body Mass Index of 47.7, which classifies him as morbidly obese. His foundation has been shaken and badly cracked by his sheer heaviness.

The solid structural frame of bone and muscle that once stood erect has been soaked with sugar, and diabetes is making his "house" unsteady. His pipes are hardened, beaten up, and riddled by hypertension. The electricity of his heart has decided to beat irregularly. And the floorboards of his insides are waxed thickly with cholesterol.

I first saw Tom 10 months ago. "Hey bud, are you trying to kill yourself?" I asked.

He looked at me, then to the floor, with tears in eyes.

"Tom." I placed my right hand on his shoulder, which seemed to be carrying untold pains of years gone by. "Don't you want to live? I'm here to help you."

Tom began to weep. I'd said enough, so I just took his hand and let him cry. When he was finished, he said, "Sorry, Dr. Sam. I'm sorry. Yes, I'm ready to live. I'm just tired of all this. I'm tired of failing. I'm tired of looking this way. I'm tired of people staring at me. I'm tired of feeling guilty. I'm just tired of all this mess. It disgusts me. My weight is disgusting!"

After that day, Tom wanted to become accountable to me, with regular follow up visits. Since then he has lost 20 pounds. "Big deal," you say? Yeah, it is a big deal, because all of a sudden Tom is sleeping more soundly, breathing better, walking more easily, and looking different. His blood pressure has improved and the pain in his hip has decreased. I may never get Tom to a BMI of 25, nor do I think that's necessary in his case, but I have promised to walk the road of hope and healthy living with him. And that has made all the difference in his life!

How is Tom losing weight? By downsizing instead of supersizing, by refusing seconds, and by walking 30 minutes a day.

Does he indulge? Yes, at times.

Dr. Sam's Insight
Is breaking the rules of eating allowed? You bet!
Why? Because extremes on either end will discourage you.

I'm thrilled for Tom, because he is taking the initiative to change the foundation of his house! He now clearly understands that supersizing causes illnesses that he can avoid; Tom came face-to-face with the reality that supersizing would ultimately send him to an early grave.

I have heard experts say, "Eat whatever you want; all you have to do is stop eating when you become full." Hey Monsieur Expert, the problem is, many of my patients don't want to admit they are full.

What has Tom learned out there in the real world of hard knocks?

Don't supersize.

Don't go for seconds.

Downsize your plate size; eat from a smaller sized plate.

Dr. Sam's Insight
Eat small, walk big.

When given a large portion, eat half of it and take the rest home for another meal.

In fact, let's start with the small things. If you normally drink a venti, downsize to tall. If you put two portions of heavy cream in your coffee, cut it to one. Put half the sugar in that drink.

If you eat the Double-Double from In and Out®—and I will confess, in case you catch me at the drive-thru, I treat myself to my favorite burger by having it "animal style" (special fatty dressing) with fries and a vanilla milkshake to boot, once every six to eight weeks—eat a single-patty hamburger instead; even try it protein style—wrapped in lettuce instead of a bun; or skip out on the cheese.

The average American eats five pounds of food each day.[23] If a person lives to be 77, he or she will consume up to 70 tons of food, equivalent to 40 mid-size cars.

Dr. Sam's Insight
The average person gains two pounds in a year.
Doesn't sound bad, until you do the math...
that's 20 pounds in 10 years!

That probably doesn't mean a lot to most 20-year-olds, but ask a 40-something how he's doing with his bulging belly, or how she's doing with those massive thighs. Some gain the pounds even faster. How? If you eat 500 extra calories a day for 7 days, you'll accumulate 3,500 unused calories, or are you ready, you will have gained one pound!

Inversely, you can lose that pound by consuming 250 less calories daily and burning off an extra 250 calories daily for one week.

Dr. Sam's Insight

**500 extra calories in 1 day = 3,500 calories in 1 week,
3,500 extra calories = 1 extra pound gained!
You can also lose that pound in a week
by a daily 500–calorie deficit.**

Why shouldn't we supersize? Because, supersizing a meal at any fast food chain or at home will one day cost you much more than the change in your pocket; it will cost you your life.

Remember when I told you that people require approximately 30 calories per kilogram of body weight to maintain an ideal weight? A man who weighs 155 pounds (70 kilograms) should eat about 2,100 calories a day. But wait up: the average American consumes approximately 2,700–3,700 calories per day![24]

In general, men should consume approximately 2,000–2,500 calories per day and women should consume approximately 1,500–2,000. Your age, weight, height, and level of activity are what make these numbers different for different people. If you are trying to figure out how many calories you need, you can calculate your basal metabolic rate (BMR). This rate is simply the amount of calories you need to ensure that your body processes can function normally.

To calculate your BMR, take your current weight and multiply it by ten. So, if you weigh 155 pounds it's 155 x 10 = 1,550 calories per day is your basal metabolic rate. With a low activity factor of 1.2 (desk job), that works out as 1,550 x 1.2 = 1,860 calories per day. With a light activity factor of 1.375 (light exercise 1-3 days per week), that works out as 1,550 x 1.375 = 2,131 calories per day. With a moderate activity factor of 1.55 (moderate exercise 3–5 days per week), that works out as 1,550 x 1.55 = 2,403 calories per day. And with a heavy activity factor of 1.725 (heavy exercise 6–7 days per week), that works out as 1,550 x 1.725 = 2,674 calories per day. Each individual is different, and these numbers are only guidelines. To calculate your BMR, you can check www.caloriesperhour.com/index_burn.php and please seek the advice of your doctor and your dietitian to implement a plan that is right for you.

Dr. Sam's Insight
To lose weight, the amount of calories needs to be cut down. Don't supersize, downsize!

Females should have at least 1,200 calories daily, and males 1,500 calories daily. It's important to realize that BMR doesn't tabulate your physical activity. If you exercise regularly, your caloric intake needs may be higher.[25] Some use the "droplet diet" to curb their appetites and decrease their daily intake to 500–600 calories a day and successfully lose weight; that's plainly dangerous, unhealthy, and a set up for future weight gain! Please check with your doctor and registered nutritionist to determine the caloric intake that will enable you to lose weight, but will keep your body functioning properly.

15 WILL THAT BE FRESH FISH OR FATTY FRIES?

We are captivated by fried fatty treats and sweet sugary eats. But these foods are *dead*—lacking essential nutrients and proteins. That's the bad news. But wait up, don't despair. The good news is that there are *living* foods that can energize us, keep us trim, and saturate our lives with hope! What are the living foods?

1. *Fresh fruits* and *vegetables*. These should be a major part of our diet—at least 5 servings per day (one serving ranges from ½-cup to a full cup, or four to eight ounces). Most vegetables have a lower glycemic index—which measures how fast a carbohydrate triggers a rise in the blood sugar—than fruits. A low glycemic index is 50 or less. Fruits and veggies that have a glycemic index of less than 15, which is exceptional, include artichokes, asparagus, avocados, broccoli, cauliflower, celery, cucumbers, eggplant, green beans, lettuce, peppers, snow peas, spinach, young summer squash, and zucchini. The index for an apple is 36, banana 53, sweet potato 63, pineapple 66, watermelon 72, and dates 103. Food with a lower glycemic index is preferred, especially in a diabetic patient.

2. Foods high in *fiber*. The recommended goal is 25 to 30 grams daily, but most of us eat 12 grams or less! Foods with fiber help us combat constipation, hemorrhoids, diverticulosis, colorectal cancer, elevated cholesterol, and irritable bowel syndrome. Some tasty fibrous foods include: pinto beans, artichokes, kidney beans, navy beans, apples,

figs, oranges, green peas, raspberries, barley, blackberries, mangos, bananas, whole wheat noodles, whole wheat breads, and brown rice.[26]

3. Fish. When shopping for fish, keep in mind that "wild" caught fish are far superior to "farm" raised fish, given the high toxin content in farm-raised fish. Most grocery stores have a decent variety of wild fish, including wild salmon. For some, the taste and price are deterrents.

Omega-3 fatty acids are excellent for you and can be found in cold-water fish, like salmon, tuna, halibut and herring, and in flaxseed and walnuts. Two good acids—DHA (docosahexaenoic acid) and EPA (eicosapentanenic acid)—are found in fish and provide adequate Omega-3 balance. EPA has anti-inflammatory, cardio protective, anticancer, and antihypertensive properties, reducing the risk of strokes, heart arrhythmias, dementia, and heart attacks. DHA protects against Alzheimer's, dementia, and attention deficit hyperactivity disorder.

4. *Whole grains*. Sprouted grain breads, brown rice, whole-grain pastas, and whole-grain cereal have a high concentration of nutrients, vitamins, minerals, and fiber—with a great tangy taste to boot. These should become "regulars" in our diet—far better for us than regular pasta, white rice, and bleached breads.

Refined white flour is highly processed, eliminating the most important nutrients—bran and germ.[27]

5. "Eat More" Fats. There is a structural difference in saturated versus unsaturated fats. Saturated fats are *not healthy* for you, because they contain more hydrogen, which makes "clumping" easier, and promotes clogging of the arteries. mono-unsaturated fats, on the other hand, are associated with decreased risk for breast cancer, lower risk of heart attacks and strokes, weight loss, reduced belly fat, and reduced cholesterol levels. These mono-unsaturated fats can be found in organic or regular peanut butter, avocados, olives, almonds, and walnuts. I urge my patients to stay away from salted, roasted, and caramelized products.

You may be wondering, "What are the 'dead foods' that I should be steering clear of?"

'Dead foods' that should be avoided include processed foods, fast foods, foods high in sugar, white breads, soft drinks, and cereals drenched with sugar. If we stop buying processed foods, our cabinets and fridges will sport a new and healthy look over time. Except for the occasional treats, it's time to clean the cupboards. Out of sight, out of mind is a method that *will* work for you. Start replacing your processed foods with fresh produce and start living healthy!

We shouldn't cave impulsively and stop at the nearest drive-thru; we should refrain from eating fast foods as much as possible. The potatoes used to make French fries and the breaded fried chicken are not only processed, but often deep-fried. These foods are high in calories and contain loads of saturated fats. We should also avoid desserts like apple pie and chocolate chip cookies, cake, and ice cream sundaes—they are drenched with sugar and butter. Ingesting these products should be a "limited habit," and not part of our routine meals.

Limit your consumption of processed meats such as ham, bacon, hot dogs, bologna, and other packaged cold cuts, which are chemically treated. Processed meats contain high amounts of sodium and saturated fats. Over-consumption of red meat puts you at risk for colorectal cancer. The American Institute for Cancer Research suggests we should eat less than 18 ounces of red meat per week.

As part of caring for yourself, make it a habit to eat at home. Pack your lunch for work. You will save both your health and your money.

It's time to face reality and ask yourself some life-changing questions. To live or to die? The apple or the cake? The almonds or the fries? The sweet smell of hope, victory, ability, clarity, and stability—or the irrevocable regret of a bitter stroke, coupled with debilitating guilt? "Come on," you say, "strokes don't happen that often. What are the odds—one person in my town each day, at most?"

Not quite. According to the American Heart Association, someone has a stroke every 40 seconds, and in every four minutes, someone dies of one.

It's time to put your pretty little white bread down, lace up your comfy shoes, stop making excuses, eat smaller portions and start walking big for your good health and your future!

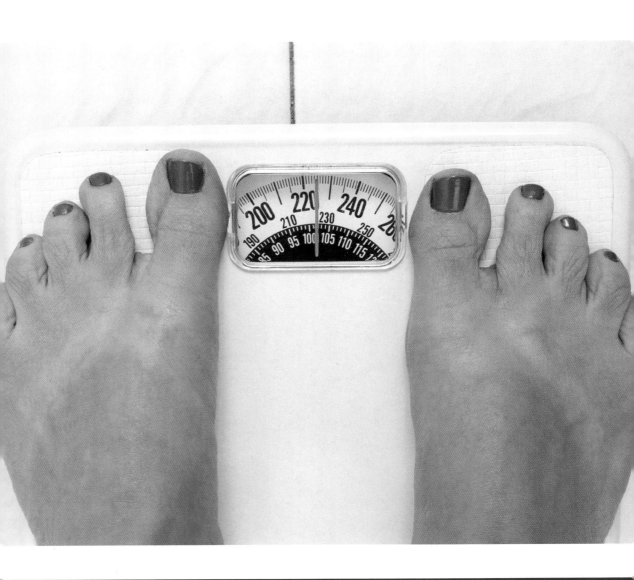

16 I SAID, "MOVE THAT BIG BUTT!"

I was looking at Jodi's driver's license picture that was scanned into my computer as she was sitting next to me, complaining about her recent increase in blood pressure. I thought to myself, "Is this the same person?" The picture on her license was taken maybe 10 years ago, and Jodi's smile took center stage; her countenance was bright and cheery; and her confidence was delightful. But the Jodi in my office did not smile. She had gained over 100 pounds, her hair was disheveled, and her heart was shattered.

She had met a wonderful man who didn't stay so wonderful. Soon after they were married, he began beating her, threatening her, and demeaning her. Jodi would hide her bruises, but her eyes could not hide the tears. After five years of physical and emotional abuse, she took her two little girls and left him. But one abuse usually leads to another, and Jodi found "rest" in narcotics and antidepressant medications.

She swore up and down that she did not eat much. I don't let my patients get away with that. "I swear doctor, I don't eat that much," she said. So I pressed her about it. She didn't budge. According to her, she ate hardly anything.

It's difficult to gain weight when you don't eat much…I'm just saying. But what I have found is that pain taints perception, heartache shuts out the truth, depression encourages the dejected soul to reject hope and embrace despair.

Dr. Sam's Insight
**Pain taints perception
and heartache shuts out the truth.**

When Jodi got on the treadmill, her heart rate rose quickly; and when she got off, her heart rate stayed high for over 10 minutes, a sign that she was not exercising and living a sedentary lifestyle. Sedentary, as in chair bound, deskbound, bedbound, self absorbed-bound.

I offered her advice, but she said she already exercised. I offered her guidance on what to eat, but she said she does that already. I offered to direct her to a local care ministry that nurtures the broken, but she declined. She didn't want to make another appointment for her heart despite two leaky valves and an enlarged heart chamber. That broke my heart. Indeed, at times, nothing I say or do can break through the pain to touch a person's life and heart. My prayer is that God will send kind souls into Jodi's chaotic life and that she will somehow begin the healing process.

Jodi's spiritual heart needs a touch of grace, while her physical heart needs a touch of cardiovascular activity. What do I mean by "cardiovascular activity," and how much exercise am I talking about? Not everyone is built the same and not everyone has the motivation to run marathons. I admire the people who run them, but this is not on my top 100 "to do" list; you can't even find it in my top 1,000!

I encourage my patients to walk daily. Why? Because it's free and you can do it any time, even on breaks during work. Doesn't fit your schedule? Remember, as we mentioned in Chapter 3, even a daily, brisk 10-minute walk could decrease your heart attack rate by 50%.[28]

Start by walking 10 to 15 minutes daily and increase up to 60 minutes, if able. It can even be done in short increments. Exercising such as walking secretes endorphins from your brain that restore your body. Let someone else have the parking spot by the front door at the mall. Instead of stressing about the parking spot, park further away and walk with a smile while others fight over a meaningless space. Take the stairs instead of the elevator. Please obtain a clearance from your physician before you begin moderate to heavy exercise.

People tell me all the time, "Walking? Just walking? That's not going to help me lose weight!" Well, sitting on your big butt isn't going to do it either. So get up off the cozy couch covered with chocolate chip cookie crumbs, declare a state of hope for your future, and start marching!

Try to touch your toes without bending your knees, at least 10 times. You can do this standing up or sitting on the floor. This is a good sign of your health and physical condition. If you can't do it, keep walking, keep drinking water, keep eating vegetables, and keep trying to touch your toes with your finger tips—you'll get closer every day as you follow Dr. Sam's advice!

People make up a lot of excuses about why they can't walk. For many it's the weather. They say it's too hot, too cold, too wet. Go to the mall and start walking. The wind doesn't blow and it doesn't rain in the mall! If you can't go to the mall, exercise at home, do gardening, dance, walk up and down the stairs, get a stationary bike. Not everyone will be able to do the same exercise. Biking and swimming are gentle on your joints. Start with being active a few minutes five to six days of the week. Make it a routine, and watch yourself change!

Once my patients start walking daily, I encourage them to have a good cardiovascular workout, achieving 85 percent of their predicated maximum heart rate, which is 220, minus your age, times 85 percent.

Let's do the math. If you are 50 years old, the equation would look like this: 220 − 50 = 170, and 170 x 85% = 145. So I would encourage my 50-year-old patient to reach 145 beats per minute for at least 10 minutes of a 30-minute workout. Many tell me they are unable to reach 85% or work out for 30 minutes. I, in turn, will gladly accept anyone's attempt to walk—no matter how far or how short the distance, no matter how high or how low the heart rate—because that person has decided to finally embark on the journey to better health!

Dr. Sam's Insight

If you want to decrease your anxiety, pain, depression, arthritis, blood pressure, cholesterol, and risk of heart disease, just start walking!

It is your time to embrace life by walking on this journey of health and hope; it is your time today to build a solid foundation for tomorrow—despite your yesterday!

Come on.

Get your shoes on.

Get your game face on.

It's time to press on!

Testimonial #4

ROY BEFORE

I was to retire by the end of December 2008, at the age of 64. In the next year, another cardiologist told me that I needed a pacemaker, but I refused. Because of chest pains, I ended up in the hospital. I asked for recommendations, and I got to see Dr. Kojoglanian. He came to see me and gave me hope. He told me how my weight was causing a great burden on my heart, body, joints and entire system. He didn't see the imminent need for a pacemaker at that point.

At the time I was released from the hospital, I weighed 330 lbs. I didn't drink or smoke. Dr. Kojoglanian encouraged me on this journey, warning me about the consequences of obesity and inspiring me about the benefits of losing weight. From 2009 to 2012, I've lost 50 pounds. I still haven't gotten a pacemaker, because my heart is doing so much better and it's not erratic. I can breathe now, I can move! My joints feel better, my sleep apnea is gone, and my diabetes and blood pressure are better controlled. My life has changed and I am so excited!

ROY AFTER

Thank you Dr. Kojoglanian for taking good care of my health and always encouraging me. You've brought out the spark, color, and joy in my life that were long buried. You have given me hope!
——Roy F. Morse

17 | BITTER SWEET

I got called in on a Sunday to see a patient with a fast heart rate due to pancreatitis, a condition where the pancreas is inflamed. The patient's wife was telling me how he was being watched for borderline diabetes. I asked her what his sugar levels usually ran at home when he was healthy. "About 200 to 220," she said. "220?" I asked. "That's not borderline, that's in the diabetic range," I continued, in hopes of educating the family. "Well he is watching it, and I'm proud of him!" she exclaimed.

Because my patient was very sick, I let it slide for the time. His BMI was 32 (obese), he had blood sugar in the 250s (diabetic), he had blood pressure of 170/95 (hypertension), and he had cholesterol of 270 (hyperlipidemia). What in the world was he "watching?"

I hate the term borderline diabetes, pre-diabetes, or insulin resistant, conditions where the glucose in the blood is elevated, yet the patient is not clinically diagnosed with diabetes. When you talk about pregnancy, you don't say, "Yes, we're so excited, she's borderline pregnant!" The toll on the microvasculature (small vessels) and macrovasculature (larger vessels) is alarming, yet many "pre-diabetic," "borderline diabetic" or "insulin resistant" patients are placed on "watching my numbers with diet" and many are given a medication to prevent the onslaught of full-blown diabetes.

We all are responsible, but I fear that labels like "pre-diabetes" give patients an option to opt out of their responsibilities. Whether or not you are diabetic, take charge and make the right choices. For instance, when eating pizza, put the third slice down and walk away. Enough is enough. The best way to treat diabetes is to avoid it.

Whether it is "pre-diabetes" or "real diabetes," the common problem still lingers: obesity. This relates to adults who have a choice, who have adult onset diabetes, not juvenile diabetes, which kids have. People have all kinds of euphemisms to make their big belly feel better, trading it in for a big butt and an unhealthy future. Too strong? No, too true. Let the truth set you free! Otherwise, you are skating on thin ice.

Dr. Sam's Insight
Terms like "pre-diabetic" or "borderline diabetic" are euphemisms. You're either diabetic or you're not. Best way to treat it? Avoid it.

Foods with high sugar content are the gateway to diabetes and a troubled future. Of all my patients, diabetics are the most depressed, because they not only have to deal with their sugar levels, but their disease usually comes with a tiresome regimen of injecting insulin into broken bodies that have brittle, fragile foundations.

Certainly, there are skinny people who have diabetes, usually young people with Type I Diabetes, linked with genetics. And adults likely have a predisposition, given their family history. But the truth is, most people with this disease have Type II Diabetes, which usually hits adults who are overweight and obese. Being diabetic is not a pretty picture. It will lead to eye, brain, heart, kidney, and vascular diseases, which ultimately can lead to blindness, strokes, heart attacks, and amputations.

Patients with Type II Diabetes have high levels of sugar built up in their blood, because their bodies are not making enough insulin or are insulin-resistant. Insulin helps the body's cells absorb sugars from our bloodstream. A marker called Hemoglobin A1C, a blood test, helps physicians track the severity of their patients' diabetes.

Symptoms of diabetes include: urinating frequently, feeling tired all the time, being more thirsty than usual, being very hungry, having blurry vision, and having numbness of hands and feet. Surprisingly, the first sign may be a sudden weight loss that is not associated with cutting back on calories or exercise. Reduced calorie intake, portion control and exercise are the antidotes for diabetes and its overwhelming consequences.

Dr. Sam's Insight
Diabetes places a person at four times the increased risk of having a heart attack or stroke.

How can you lose weight and avoid diabetes?
1. Exercise daily.
2. Eliminate soft drinks and sodas (regular or diet), and decrease processed and genetically modified foods.
3. Eat a limited amount of breads, grains, noodles, corn, potatoes, and other starchy foods.
4. Eat fruits and vegetables, especially the green, leafy kinds, like spinach and collard greens.
5. Read the labels and avoid foods with unnatural additives. Seriously, if you can't read or understand the names of the ingredients on the label, you should not eat it.
6. Drink purified water and herbal teas.
7. Sugar is sneaky and we eat way too much of it. Sugar is frequently found in sources we forget to consider, such as

juice, dried fruit, peanut butter, and spaghetti sauce. Get into a habit of reading the labels—it will pay high dividends for your healthy being.

• • •

The other day, I was called to testify as an expert witness in a Santa Ana courtroom some 60 miles away from my office. I arrived at 6:30 a.m., two hours early, in order to beat the morning traffic. Since I didn't want to sit in the car for two hours, I found my way into a fast food restaurant nearby. I had already eaten breakfast, so I asked if they had any milk. They had reduced-fat milk (2%) in eight fluid ounce bottles for $1.40. I grabbed one, sat down, and you guessed it—I couldn't help but read the nutrition facts. Here is what I found:

Serving size: one bottle (236 ml). Remember this number, because 8 fluid ounces is equal to one cup, or 240 milliliters (ml), and is the normal serving size for a glass of milk.

Servings per container: 1. This is critical, because the serving size can be 2 or 3, in which case you would have to multiply everything by 2 or 3, in order to calculate the fat, cholesterol, sodium, carbohydrate, and protein contents. However, in this case, we can simply multiply by a factor of 1.

Calories: 130 (this is the total amount of calories in one small bottle of milk).

Fat calories: 45 (this is the amount of calories from the fat content in the milk bottle)

Total Fat: 5 grams (since we receive 9 calories from 1 gram of fat, we multiply 5 x 9 and get 45 calories, just as the label stated).

Saturated Fat: 3 grams. Notice, 3 out of the 5 grams of fat were saturated (3 x 9 = 27 calories).

Trans–Fat: 0 grams; none of the 5 grams of fat was in the form of trans-fat.

Cholesterol: 25 mg. This content comes from the fat portion.

Sodium: 130 mg. What I started paying attention to was the "% DV," which is Percent Daily Value. According to the bottle, this was based on a 2,000 calorie daily diet. Some of my patients can have more than 2,000 calories and some need less. So I wouldn't take the "%DV" as the gospel. Another thing is that some of my patients are restricted to 1,500 mg of salt instead of 2,000 mg, due to heart failure. Anyway, look how easy it is to get 130 mg of salt from several gulps of milk.

Total Carbohydrates: 13 grams. Since we receive 4 calories from 1 gram of carbohydrates, we multiply 13 x 4 and get 52 calories. Once you hear the word Carbohydrates—first think sugar! *I believe of all foods, carbohydrates are most deceitful!* When you eat fat, you know it is fat, but carbohydrates are tricky. Excess starch, sugars and overall surplus of daily calories and portions are killing my patients. *The carbohydrate trap is addictive and sets many an unsuspecting consumer up for the snare of diabetes.*

Dietary fiber: 0 grams (no dietary fibers are found in milk). Dietary fiber is what we desperately need every day.

Sugars: 13 grams (all the carbohydrates in this bottle of milk are sugars). This is not terribly bad, because we need carbohydrates, but other foods with extreme sugar contents are wreaking havoc on us.

Protein: 10 grams. Since we receive four calories from one gram of proteins, we multiply 10 x 4 and get 40 calories.

Calcium: 35% of daily value.

Vitamin A: 10% of daily value.

Vitamin D: 25% of daily value.

So the label tells us we have 45 calories from fat, plus 52 calories from carbohydrates, plus 40 calories from proteins, to equal 137 calories in all (the discrepancy between 130 calories on the label and 137 calories calculated manually is likely due to approximations). I've broken this down to help us become aware of nutrition labels, and to encourage us to read and understand labels, because our health depends on it! It's all in the amount, the portion size. Reading the label is not only informative, but imperative!

Dr. Sam's Insight

**It's all in the amount, the portion size.
Reading the label is not only informative, but imperative!**

While we are on the topic of milk, I should mention that milk is an essential part of many people's diet. You are probably aware that there are alternative milk brands now available. Cow's milk is the cheapest and, yes, still the gold standard for dunking cookies! Rice milk is the most expensive. Almond milk has the least calories and is reasonably priced. Soymilk is also reasonably priced, but can leave a bitter or 'beanie' aftertaste. And, in case you're worried about the calcium content of the alternative milks, it appears they supply adequate amounts of calcium; just make sure you shake the carton, because the calcium tends to settle at the bottom. These milk substitutes have added sugars, not natural lactose, but some are unsweetened.

Okay, so it had been a long day in court. I was a little hungry and didn't have access to any healthy snacks, so I decided to splurge and have a Kit Kat® bar. I have a hunch you know how this tastes—simply delicious! There are four crisp wafers in one wrap, and I ate them all. The net weight was 1.5 ounces, which was 42 grams. Here's a run-down of the "Nutrition Facts" on the label:

Serving Size: 1 package.

Calories: 210 calories.

Fat Calories: 90 calories (90 out of 210 calories are due to the fat content).

Total Fat: 11 grams (11 x 9 = 99).

Saturated Fat: 7 grams (7 x 9 = 63).

Trans–Fat: 0 grams.

Total Carbohydrates: 27 grams (27 x 4 = 108 calories. Note, more calories from carbohydrates than fat, which makes sense, as approximately 50% of our calories are from carbohydrates)

Dietary fiber: < 1 grams (meaning less than one gram).

Sugars: 21 grams. (21 x 4 = 84 calories).

Welcome to the world of sugar!

Protein: 3 grams. (3 x 4 = 12 calories)

Calcium: 6%.

So, we have 99 calories from fat, 108 calories from carbohydrates, plus 12 calories from proteins, which equals 219 (the discrepancy between 210 calories on the label and 219 calories calculated manually is likely due to approximations). I consider the Kit Kat® treat as "empty" or "easy" calories, which can give us quick energy: they're all right…once in a while.

The day in court went well and I headed back to work, stuck on the Southern California freeways with a 220-calorie Kit Kat® smile on my face.

Anyone got toothpaste?

18 | SUGAR CUBES AND BELLY ACHES

My office staff tell our patients to bring a water bottle with them when they come for their stress test at the office. One slim young lady brought her sports drink bottle. She passed her test and we were looking at her blood work which showed she was a diabetic. We checked for the glucose (blood sugar levels) in the blood, and many labs vary, but if one's fasting glucose level is above 100, they are considered to be in the diabetic range; my patient had a glucose level of 150. I really didn't expect this for someone who had a BMI of 23 (normal) at the age of 45. I asked how many bottles of the sports drink she has daily. At least two. How about coffee with creamer. "Oh, I love my creamer, and I can't give it up!" Wow, these "innocent" drinks and condiments had elevated her sugar levels to an all time high. She was stunned, and said, "Maybe I can cut back." "That would be a good move!" I said, encouragingly, anticipating that we will see healthier numbers backing the future.

Dr. Sam's Insight
How do you win this fight? Cut down, cut back, back off, stand up and walk on!

How much sugar are we allowed to consume? According to the American Heart Association, 6 to 9 teaspoons per day. Remember, carbohydrates are broken down into sugars, starches, and fiber. So, we are speaking about the sugar component of carbohydrates.

For most women, this would be no more than 100 calories per day (about 6 teaspoons), and for most men, no more than 150 calories per day (about 9 teaspoons) for added sugars. Hold up! The average American consumes up to 22 teaspoons of sugar every day, and much of that is in the form of canned drinks![29] Is there a conspiracy in labeling? The labels usually depict sugars in grams and not in teaspoons, especially in soft drinks. For clarification: 1 teaspoon = 4 grams = 16 calories (4 grams x 4 calories/gram) = 1 white sugar cube.

Can you see how "innocent" foods and beverages can contain so much sugar? With one can of a soda, you have already exceeded your daily recommended allowance of sugars, the maximum being 9 teaspoons. For example, in a 12 fluid ounce can of soda (335 ml), there can be 43 grams of sugars. If 4 grams equals 1 teaspoon, then 43 grams is equal to approximately 11 teaspoons of sugar, or 11 white sugar cubes—in *one can* of pop!

Dr. Sam's Insight

1 teaspoon of sugar = 4 grams = 16 calories = 1 white sugar cube. We are allowed 6-9 sugar cubes a day. One can of soda usually contains 11-12 sugar cubes!

To educate ourselves, the following illustrates the nutrition facts in one can of clear soda:

Serving Size: 12 fl oz / 335 ml
Amount per Serving: 1
Calories: 170, from fat 0

Total Fat: 0 grams, 0%

Saturated Fat: 0 grams, 0%

Mono-unsaturated Fat: 0 grams

Poly-unsaturated Fat: 0 grams

Cholesterol: 0 mg, 0%

Sodium: 65 mg, 3%

Potassium: 0 mg, 0%

Thus far, good, right? Okay, are you ready for this?

Total Carbohydrates: 46 grams, 15% (note: the 15% designation is placed here, but is deceptive)

Sugars: 46 grams (note: the 15% designation is not placed here, because 46 grams exceeds the daily sugar intake)!

Dietary Fiber: 0 grams, 0%

Protein: 0 grams, 0%

Notice the sugar content: 46 grams, approximately 11.5 teaspoons, or 11.5 white sugar cubes! Notice something else: when the company uses the % Daily Value, they place 15 percent beside carbohydrates, meaning that this is 15 percent of the total carbohydrate allowed in a day. But do they place the % Daily Value beside the sugar content of the carbohydrate? No! This is deceptive because we are not allowed 11.5 teaspoons of sugar daily; if it were marked on the label correctly, the % sign would be beside the word "sugars" and it would read over 100% Daily Value in the sugar category. Sweet nibbling, I think I've got a bellyache!

Dr. Sam's Insight

Soda cans contain 12 fluid ounces (335 ml), over the limit of the "normal" serving size. Check your serving sizes when reading labels, as many drinks will have 2 or more servings in 1 bottle or can.

Natural Fruit Drinks

Aren't the natural fruit drinks better for me? Yes, they are. A 15.2 fluid ounce (450 ml) container of 100 percent orange juice (from concentrate with Vitamin C) has 24 grams of sugar, according to the label. But beware. Because our serving size is 4 fluid ounces (120 ml) for fruit juices, there are almost 4 servings in this container. Therefore the bottle has 24 x 2 = 48 grams of sugar. This is equal to 12 teaspoons of sugar, and this is where many of my patients are making mistakes—drinking healthy fluids, yet in excess. If you were to drink half the bottle, then you would be consuming 24 grams of sugar, or six teaspoons, within the allowed limits.

Fruits

Do natural fruits have sugars? The natural sugars found in fruits are healthier than processed sugars, because they have antioxidants, vitamin C, and a rich source of soluble fiber. But remember, eating too much sugar of any kind can raise blood sugar levels and cause weight gain if it's more calories than we need in a given day. There are fruits low in sugar content, which will help you avoid the insulin spikes.[30]

Strawberries have 7 grams of sugar per cup. They are a good source of anthocyanins,[31] which may help protect the body and brain against free radical damage.[32] They also have antioxidants and anti-inflammatory properties related to their high phenol content. Blackberries and raspberries also have lower sugar content.

Fresh cantaloupe is the lowest sugar-containing melon with 3 grams in one cup.

Lemons contain 2 grams of sugar per cup as compared to 14 grams for a medium orange and 11 grams for a grapefruit. Then again, how many of us eat lemons the way we do oranges and grapefruit? Other fruits that are low in sugar content include kiwi and plums.

Artificial Sweeteners

How about the artificial sweeteners—are they good for us? Marketed as "sugar-free" or "zero" or "diet," these fake sweeteners are found in sodas, chewing gum, baked goods, candy, fruit juices, pudding, canned foods, jellies and jams, dairy products, and ice cream. They have trumped regular table sugar, sucrose. But be warned, sugar substitutes are not "natural," they are processed and refined, and they are *not* the answer to losing weight. The reason they are attractive is because they add virtually no calories to your diet. Manufacturers argue that these sweeteners have no calories and therefore help in weight control.

But some research suggests that these sweeteners may be associated with *increased* weight.[33] The weight-conscious public often considers artificial sweeteners "health food." But the San Antonio Heart Study examined 3,682 adults over an eight-year period, and noted that drinkers of artificially sweetened beverages consistently had higher BMI numbers during their follow-up.[34] Precisely because they are sweet, artificial sweeteners encourage sugar craving and sugar dependence, and the repeated exposure trains flavor preference.[35]

Many sodas that use artificial sweeteners claim they have zero calories, zero fat, zero sugars, zero protein, and only 40 mg of sodium. Some even claim they are "good for you," complete with the "heart" logo stamped on the can! So, drink all you want, right? Slam dunk? Wait up. *Check the label.* I cannot stress this point enough! Look at the list of ingredients. It usually starts out with things like carbonated water, caramel color, phosphoric acid, and you guessed it, aspartame. If this didn't hit you the first time, let me break it down for you: 1) substituting a natural sweetener for an artificial sweetener is not going to help you lose weight, and it is likely contributing to your weight gain, and 2) preservatives may enhance flavor, but they don't "preserve" you and they don't contribute to your good health.

Then why don't we just drink regular soda instead? One product states that it has "100% natural flavors," and natural is good, right? In a 20 fl oz (591 ml) plastic bottle, there are 240 calories and 110 mg of sodium. Total fat: 0 grams. Total protein: 0 grams. Total carbohydrates: 64 grams (21% of DV). But then, that 64 grams equals 64 grams of pure sugar! How did they get 240 calories? 64 grams x 4 (4 calories per gram) = 252 calories (close to 240 calories). Do you realize that 64 grams of sugar is equal to 16 white sugar cubes? Oh my goodness, my belly is killing me!

According to some experts, the risk of becoming overweight or obese by drinking one to two cans of *regular* soda per day is 32.8%. It rises to 54.4% if you drink one to two can of *diet* soda instead![36] Diet sodas may be the choice of overweight and obese people in the first place, but sugar substitutes may be causing increased hunger, "tricking" the body that it's not yet full.

Dr. Sam's Insight
Though both diet and regular sodas are associated with obesity, diet sodas pose a higher risk than regular sodas.

The major ingredient in some sweeteners is Sucralose, which is not natural, but is derived from sugar. This sweetener can have multiple side effects: bloating, abdominal pain, gas, diarrhea, headaches, migraines, heart palpitations, increased urination at night, depression, anxiety, joint pain, dizziness, and blurred vision.

Think about how many times people get refills on their drinks. These are far from free! Your health will pay the price. Your foundation will be soaked with sugar, and your world will crumble. "Come on, be real, from a simple soda drink?" you object. No, not from one drink. But one drink followed by another and another.

Dr. Sam's Insight
"Free" refills are far from free! Your health will pay the price.

Stevia®, another sweetener, is considered safe by many experts. Other natural products are recommended over artificial sweeteners, such as chicory root, lo han, and xylitol. Instead of sugar in hot tea, try natural honey; it will taste just as sweet.

The last decade saw an explosive increase in the number of food products containing the non-caloric artificial sweeteners. More than 6,000 new products were launched in the United States between 1999 and 2004.[37] During this same period, obesity was dramatically on the rise. Coincidence? I think not. It seems that the non-caloric sweeteners are not as benign as we consumers are led to believe.[38]

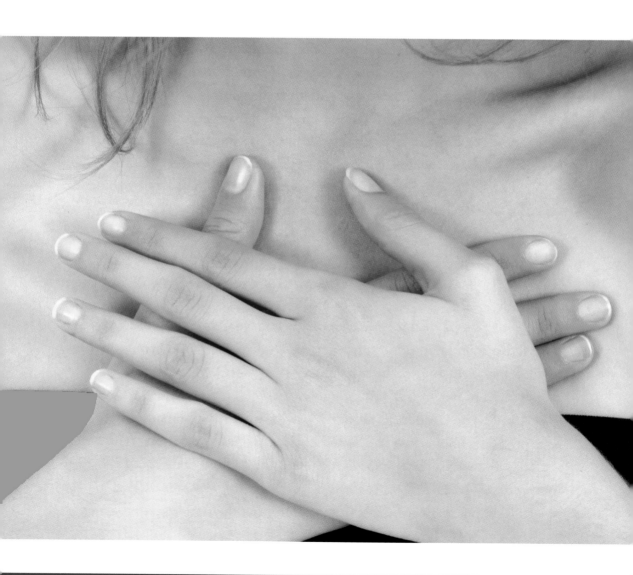

19 KICKING SUGAR'S SWEET BUTT

Kate was walking uphill when she felt a gnawing pain in her throat. (Beware, not all "chest pains" from heart disease occur in the chest!)[39] She tried to march through it, but the pain stopped her will to walk. After a five minute rest, her symptoms resolved and Kate returned back home. During a wellness check with her primary doctor, she stated that she had one episode of throat pain while walking. Her doctor sent her to me for a heart check up.

Not all "chest pains" occur in the chest! Angina (chest pain from heart disease) can occur in the shoulders, throat, elbows and wrists. It can manifest as shortness of breath, fatigue, and even back pain. Please don't ignore your symptoms—seek medical attention.

Dr. Sam's Insight
Not all "chest pains" occur in the chest!
Please, don't ignore your symptoms—seek medical attention.

Kate underwent her stress test and a specific area of the heart muscle weakened during physical stress.

"Kate, we're going to need an angiogram."

"You sure I need this doc, I mean, I don't want this if I don't have to have it, you know."

"You need this, Kate. Look at the ultrasound with me; you can see it for yourself. The muscle just gave up the ghost, it's not moving, and that means you have a tight blockage."

So we went in, and there it was: a 99% blockage smack in the middle of her most important coronary artery. One day in, one stent later, next day home. A 99% blocked area turned into a 100% wide open artery.

"I guess you were right, doc, I did need it, huh?"

"Good choice Kate, glad you joined me!"

"Yeah, good going doc!"

Whatever happened in the past, happened.

But what has happened since, is a new beginning.

Kate has turned her life around and now celebrates life instead of food. Her favorite sweets are not so important any more. But her life is!

As was true for Kate, most of the desserts she ate seemed harmless. But we should be aware of the amount of sugars per serving. Cookies, for instance, can contain 8 to 18 grams of sugar per serving. A cookie with 8 grams of sugar means the cookie contains 2 teaspoons of sugar, or 2 white sugar cubes (1 teaspoon = 4 grams = 1 white sugar cube). A chocolate chip cookie with 18 grams of sugar contains 4.5 teaspoons of sugar, or 4.5 white sugar cubes.

Why should we avoid sweets? So we can avoid the deadly D's: Dental decay, Diabetes, and Deterioration of our health's rock solid foundation.

Dr. Sam's Insight

Why avoid sweets? To avoid the three deadly D's: Dental Decay, Diabetes, and Deterioration of our health's rock solid foundation.

The big question is, how do we avoid consuming all this excess sugar?

1. Have fresh fruit for that sweet dessert instead of cakes, cookies, pies, and sweets.

2. Choose veggies over candy, fruit over pastries, and yogurt over cookies.

3. Have a bowl or bag of chopped raw veggies in the fridge to munch on at all times: carrots, celery, green peppers, cauliflower, broccoli, etc.

4. Cut out the sodas—drink green tea or water instead.

5. Limit the candy.

6. Skip the sugary and frosted cereals.

7. If you choose canned fruit, make sure it's packed in water or juice, not syrup.

8. Drink more milk and water, and less fruit juice and fruit drinks. Remember, even the 100 percent fruit juice has a high concentration of sugar. Even alcohol contains sugar—lots of it.

9. Cut down on blended coffee drinks.

10. Eat fewer added-sugar processed foods, such as sweetened grains, like honey-nut waffles.

11. Beware—there is a lot of sugar in some salad dressings, salsas, and condiments; check your labels!

12. Choose the reduced-sugar syrups, jams, and jellies.

13. Ice cream and sweetened yogurt contain considerable amounts of added sugar. Cut your serving size in half or find a healthier substitute.

14. Beware of low fat desserts, as they are usually high in their sugar content.

If we translate grams of sugar into teaspoons and cubes, we will not be deemed ignorant. If we understand that we are limited to 6 to 9 cubes of sugar over a 24-hour period, we will be considered well-informed. And if we cut our portions by 50 percent, we will be known as wise stewards of our health who stand firmly on the grounds of hope, and who display a foundation built on wisdom, joy, and healthy living.

Testimonial #5

ANN BEFORE

Ann Socher is 53 years old. In one year, she has lost 40 pounds, and has dropped her BMI from 34 to 27.9.

Thank goodness I was referred to Dr. Kojoglanian (Dr. K), the Mender of Hearts, by my primary care physician. I knew nothing about Dr. K, but felt comfortable with him immediately. I came for what I thought may have been a chest cold, and I didn't like his suggestion of an angiogram ASAP, and begged him for an alternative.

To top it off, we were talking about my weight, and I told him that I was overweight. "No, you are obese," Dr. Kojoglanian said to me without judgment in his voice as we talked about the angiogram. The way he uttered that statement shook me up along with his very strong recommendation to have the cardiac catheterization.

I'm so thankful that I listened to Dr. K's advice because he performed an angioplasty on my 99% blocked LAD (Left Anterior Descending artery), and I'm only 53! After Dr. K inserted a stent in my heart one year ago, I grabbed onto

ANN AFTER

my second chance at life with gusto. I am worth it. I want to be here for my kids as they navigate life. So far I have lost 40 pounds. Becoming normal sized seemed an impossible feat one year ago as did walking up an incline. However, healthy food choices and exercising regularly (cardio and weights) resulted in normal cholesterol, blood pressure and sugar levels.

Taking my blood thinner medication each morning reminds me that I am lucky to be alive, but I should not take my life and health for granted. I still want to lose 10 more pounds but am confident it will come off as I continue to care for my body and my being which includes visiting the good doctor for checkups and tending to other medical issues immediately.

Without Dr. K's gentle prodding, I probably wouldn't be alive to write this testimonial! I can't say enough about his bedside manner. During our visits, I feel like I'm his only patient because he always gives me as much time as I need answering my list of questions. I actually look forward to my office visits with him as he is my biggest cheerleader, acknowledging my efforts in losing lots of weight and improving my heart's condition with exercise and diet. I appreciate that he took me off blood pressure medications saying that he doesn't believe in medicating where unnecessary. And just to let you know, Dr. K's office personnel are great, compassionate and caring just like him. Dr. Kojoglanian is truly the 'Mender of Hearts!' He saved my life!

— Ann Socher

20 SMITTEN BY SALT

Howard has been dealing with high blood pressure for 10 years. Recently he's been working long hours and getting paid less, a sign of shaky economic times. His blood pressure is climbing with his stress levels. For lunch he's been ordering Mandarin food because it has vegetables. "I don't put any salt in it, Doctor Sam, and I watch my salt intake."

"You know how much salt is in your food, Howard?"

"No, not really," he admitted.

"How often do you eat out?"

"Almost every day."

"Serious?"

"Yeah, serious."

"Since when?"

"Three months."

"When did your blood pressure get out of control?" I asked.

"Oh, about two to three months."

"Bam! We got it, bud, we figured it out!" I exclaimed.

"What, what is it?" He asked.

"The type of food you're eating is high in salt. Cut it out, and watch your pressures improve, unless…"

"Unless what?" he asked nervously.

"Unless you want me to add one more pill to your regimen."

"No thanks, doc, I think I'll stop eating at the restaurant."

"Good choice, Howie! Good choice!"

Salt preserves and enriches the flavor of foods, but it's safe to say, we are often unaware of just how much salt we consume. Although salt is essential to help us maintain our normal body functions, most people's salt intake well-exceeds the daily required amount.

Dr. Sam's Insight

High salt intake can lead to hypertension or high blood pressure, also known as the "silent killer."

Nearly one-third of adult Americans have hypertension, and roughly another one-third are pre-hypertensive, according to the most recent national survey data.[40]

How much salt are we allowed? According to the *old*, 2005 Dietary guidelines for Americans: 1) Healthy adults should not exceed 2,300 mg of sodium per day. 2) Those with high blood pressure, kidney disease or diabetes, or who are greater than 51 years old, should not exceed 1,500 mg of sodium per day.

Dr. Sam's Insight

1 teaspoon of salt = 2,300 mg of salt.
Little things in life can cause BIG problems!

The *newer* 2010 dietary guidelines recommend sodium intake to be less or equal to 1,500 mg per day for adults—this does not apply to individuals who lose large volumes of sodium in sweat, such as competitive athletes and workers exposed to extreme heat stress (foundry workers and firefighters).[41] The American Heart Association recommends 1,500 mg of sodium daily whether or not one has hypertension.

Even with those solid guidelines in place, the average American consumes about double the daily goal, approximately 3,500 mg of sodium per day. In 2005–2006, the estimated average intake of sodium for all people in the U.S., ages two and older, was 3,436 mg per day![42]

The main sources of sodium in the average U.S. diet come from:

- **5 percent added while cooking**
- **6 percent added while eating (salt shaker)**
- **12 percent from natural sources**
- **77 percent from processed and prepared foods.**

According to the Mayo Clinic,[43] a dash of salt here and a pinch of salt there can quickly add up to unhealthy levels. One teaspoon of table salt has approximately 2,300 mg of sodium, which exceeds the day's limit (1,500 mg) for many healthy adults! Most everything we eat and drink contains salt. Just because we don't shake the saltshaker, doesn't mean we don't eat salt! Celery, cheese, milk, canned foods like soup, processed meat, and shellfish all contain salt.

Dr. Sam's Insight

Most everything we eat and drink contains salt. Just because we don't shake the saltshaker, doesn't mean we don't eat salt!

My take on it is that we should stick to 1,500 mg of sodium a day, and I have noticed that if we watch our salt intake, we usually watch our weight! The 1,500 mg daily decreases your water retention, reduces leg swelling, and decreases blood pressure. How easy is it to hit the 1,500 mg limit? Simple. If we were to eat 28 slender pretzels, we would add approximately 500 mg of sodium (depending on the brand) to our diet in 30 seconds flat!

Why is your blood pressure so important? Blood pressure is the force of blood against your artery walls. Although the pressure varies throughout the whole day, if it stays up over time, it's called high blood pressure. This in turn can lead to heart attacks, heart failure, strokes, and kidney disease.

Blood pressure is made up of two numbers: the top number, systolic blood pressure, which is the force of blood when the heart beats; and the bottom number, diastolic blood pressure, which is the force of blood when the heart relaxes. A blood pressure of 120/80 is normal. A blood pressure of 140/90 is elevated.

Losing just 10 pounds can help lower your blood pressure and make a significant difference in how you feel. It's okay to lose weight slowly, aiming for a half-pound to one pound per week. If you weigh 250 pounds and you drop two pounds per month (about a half-pound per week), you will lose 24 pounds in one year! Why so slow? So you can form a lifetime habit, and avoid losing water weight and muscle mass!

Dr. Sam's Insight

Losing just ten pounds can help lower your blood pressure and make a significant difference in how you feel.

How do you eat healthy, stay happy, and avoid high blood pressure? That's what I asked Yvonne, a 78-year-old patient who was admitted to the hospital after being diagnosed with pneumonia. I was asked to see her as a consultant because her troponin (heart enzyme measured in the blood) levels were high, and she was said to have had a heart attack. Yvonne is five feet two inches tall, weighs 125, and has a BMI of 23. She teaches piano, walks 60 minutes a day, plays golf twice a week, socializes with friends, and volunteers in her community.

After speaking with her, finding she had no symptoms, and looking at her EKGs that were all normal and an ultrasound that showed a strong heart, I determined that her troponins were falsely elevated and that she had not had a heart attack.

"How in the world do you keep yourself so healthy, Yvonne?" I asked.

"Oh, it's really nothing," she said. "I just walk every day and eat only what I need."

Bam!

How simple is that?

Walk much, eat less. You think she read my book?

We laughed about how this was her first visit to the hospital since she had her babies. She was discharged to go home, and was soon back on the golf course.

Unlike Yvonne, the main problem with the majority of my patients is, they *love* to eat. Food is a delight, a treat, a joy, and feeding the appetite is done with enormous pleasure! It then becomes difficult to eat healthier foods and to stop at smaller portions. Then they ask for diet pills, blood pressure pills, cholesterol pills, and diabetic pills…so long as they can continue to indulge.

Dr. Sam's Insight

You have to decide what you love more: your fattening, salty foods, your big butt, and your imminent downfall, or your health, your hope, and your sure foundation.

Ironically, overeating should be "labeled" as selfish, because if you could only see what I see—shortening of your life span, decreasing the quality of your life, and putting a strain on your family members—you'd agree. One of the best pieces of advice I can give you is, avoid salt—and *please*, do not shake the salt shaker, especially if you haven't even tasted the food yet (how do you know it even needs salt?)! Throw out your salt shaker. Use pepper and salt-free spice blends, flavored vinegars, lemon or lime juice, garlic, and fresh or dried herbs and spices to embellish your foods. Be aware that ketchup, mustard, relish, dips, sauces, salad dressings, and soy sauce contain truckloads of sodium. One tablespoon (15 ml) of soy sauce has 1,000 mg of sodium. Again, I've observed that those who watch their salt, also watch their calories, curb their portions, and lose weight.

Many salt substitutes contain potassium chloride.

Too much potassium can be harmful if you have kidney problems. On the other hand, a moderate body of evidence has demonstrated that a higher intake of potassium (in people with normal kidney function) is associated with lower blood pressure in adults, and a daily intake of 4,700 mg of potassium is recommended.[44]

Dr. Sam's Insight
A higher intake of potassium is associated with a lower blood pressure in adults.

The lifestyle changes I'm talking about will give you more energy, a sharper mind, and you will feel so much better about yourself. If you're concerned about your future:

- Ask your doctor about the low-in-salt DASH® diet.[45]
- Eat more fiber, such as fresh fruits, vegetables, and whole grains.
- To reduce your high blood pressure stop smoking and drinking.
- Increase your magnesium, potassium and calcium (ask your doctor first).
    - Some foods that have one or more of these minerals are:
        - Fruits like bananas, dates, grapes, oranges, melons, peaches, prunes, raisins, strawberries and tangerines.
        - Vegetables like carrots, green peas, squash, broccoli, spinach, green beans, lima beans, and sweet potatoes.
        - Nuts, seeds, and dried beans, like almonds,

hazelnuts, peanuts, walnuts, sunflower seeds, kidney beans, and lentils.

- ♦ Lean, cooked meats, like chicken and fish.
- ♦ Yogurt and cheese (watch your portions on the cheese, please)!

- Avoid processed foods. Foods that have a "healthy" sign may not be so healthy. If you buy processed foods, at least choose ones that read "low sodium," and still be diligent in checking that they are not high in fat and sugar. Be aware of the high salt content in boxed and canned foods.
- Read food labels to see how much sodium is in each serving.
- Be active.

Dr. Sam's Insight

Increased salt intake can increase your blood pressure. Increased fruit and vegetable intake—coupled with regular exercise—will decrease your blood pressure, boost your energy, and help you sleep better!

Before you finish reading this short paragraph, another American will have suffered a stroke. Don't let it be you. Honoring simple truths will bring benefits that reward you with a hope-filled future and a solid foundation of healthy living. Ignoring these facts will bring hypertension, obesity, regret, despair, depression, and, ultimately, the most unwelcome of guests, strokes and heart attacks, masquerading themselves as "to die for" foods.

Dr. Sam's Insight

Change your mind
Change your heart
Change your choices
Change your portions
Change your habits
And change your life!

This is your life and it is your time for good health. You may have failed over and over again in the past, **BUT** you are now being educated and finding out "to die for" is not worth it. Turn the page in your life. Start to walk briskly, hike, jog, swim, climb stairs, or bike. This is your choice and your opportunity to change your life's course. Your day is here—it has arrived. No more excuses. No more waiting for the "right time" or the "right circumstances." No more "Well, I've messed up—might as well stay like this." This is it. Your time for good health has come. Your time for the new you is here and now, so proclaim, "I used to feel trapped, **BUT** I'm getting a feeling in my heart that I can change…in fact I'm *going* to change!"

Get your gear on. Fix your gaze on a better quality of life. And let's press on!

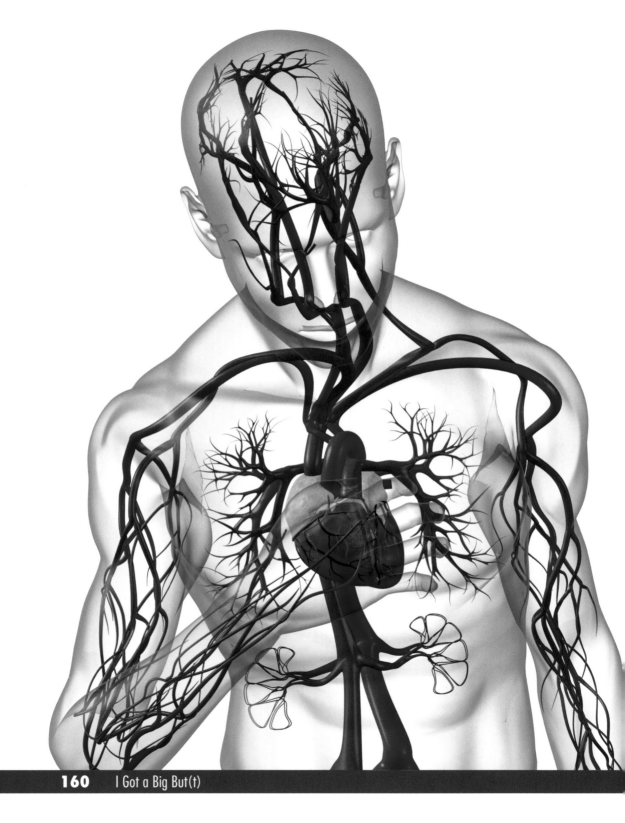

21 | BIG FAT DISAPPOINTMENT

Four months ago I opened up RB's right coronary artery by placing two stents. RB is in his forties and had multiple risks for coronary artery disease, including high cholesterol, smoking, and obesity (BMI 33). I had warned him about his smoking and weight. He slowly tapered himself off tobacco by placing a rubber band around his wrist and snapping it when he had the craving. For this I was thankful.

However, my patient, without seeking medical advice, somehow took himself off of his blood thinners for two weeks and binged on massive amounts of food. The next call I got was on a Friday night from the hospital regarding RB's condition. When I saw him on the table, I knew he was 30 seconds away from death. He was grimacing, his color was ashy blue, and he was sweating profusely.

The pictures showed an ominous clot in the previously deployed stents. By God's grace, I fixed the obstruction, transferred RB to ICU near midnight, then went to evaluate his status. There was peace on his face as his heartbeat danced steadily on the monitor. And for his own benefit, I raised my voice and expressed my thoughts.

"If you want to kill yourself, that's your deal," I said, "but here in my house, I need you to listen, pay attention, and get it done right. Lose weight, eat better, take your medications, stop killing yourself, and take care of your body. Either that or you'll need to find another heart doctor. You got it?"

My patient had nothing to say but, "Yes."

My nurses know me well, so they looked at me in shock as the compassionate Dr. Sam spoke in that manner. There is a time for everything; a time to laugh and a time to cry; a time for fun and a time for concern. And there is a time for a lecture—a special one delivered only after midnight hours.

Four weeks later, RB had an office visit. He weighed less, had been compliant with his medications, was eating vegetables, fruits, and nuts, and seemed happier than ever. RB, who had always been somewhat sedentary, was now exercising regularly; he had traded his rotten habits for the promise of a healthy future.

There is a lot of talk about which is better for your health, radical changes or slow, meticulous changes. Unlike RB, one of my patients, Robert, lost 38 pounds in three months as he won the "biggest loser" in his workplace. The bad news is, Robert gained the 38 pounds back, plus ten for good measure. He initially lost the weight by reducing his intake, but he also used laxatives and colon cleansing kits!

Whether it has been by means of gastric bypasses, lap bands, "biggest loser" contests, or mustering up points, I have seen patients lose weight, only to gain it back again—with a vengeance. Here's the deal, if you don't form a lasting, life-long habit, why bother? You really can't go around life saying, "Now honey, you know that's 7 points, or 5 points, or 3 points." Life is not about points; it's about choices on a day-to-day basis and even on a meal-to-meal basis.

Why disappoint yourself over and over again? If your means of losing the weight is only temporary, any positive results you get will not last. I'm not being ugly; that's just a fact. Habits are not formed over hours or days, but over months and years.

Dr. Sam's Insight

You can wire your mouth shut, surgically reduce your belly, ingest pills that will decrease your appetite, and eat specially packaged foods, but if you don't change your heart, you will gain your weight back. Losing weight in a few days or weeks may be quicker, and the weight loss may be undeniable, but the ultimate results for many will be a big fat disappointment.

Seriously now, do I have to take you into my cardiac catheterization lab so you'll get the point? Do you have to go RB's route to find out that high cholesterol will put you on the surgery table? I hope not. After getting multiple stents placed in his coronary arteries—each requiring a cardiac cath visit, and the last one almost costing his life—RB, the sleeping giant, has awakened. The secret to RB's success is that he has developed good habits that he can live with for a lifetime, and the results he has seen and felt have given him hope for a bright future.

One of the things that put RB on my table in the first place was cholesterol that had built up in his arteries. Cholesterol builds up as lipid pools within the artery walls, contributes to an inflammatory cascade,[46] narrows the arteries, decreases the blood flow, and causes a "traffic jam." When the arteries of the heart get clogged, they can't supply enough blood to the heart muscles, especially in stressful situations, and that can lead to a major heart attack.

What is cholesterol? Somewhat like fat, cholesterol is made in the liver and is essential for your body to make hormones, vitamin D, and build cell walls. But cholesterol is also found in foods.

Dr. Sam's Insight

Any animal that has a liver will produce products—including meat and eggs—that contain cholesterol.

You should have your cholesterol checked, and then follow up as planned by your physician. The lipid panel ordered by your doctor should include the following: total cholesterol, LDL (bad cholesterol), HDL (good cholesterol), and triglycerides.

- **Total cholesterol** is the amount of all the cholesterol in your blood. The higher the number, the greater the cardiovascular risk. A level less than 200 mg/dl is normal.

- **LDL** (remember **L**DL as **L**ousy, and you want to keep it **L**ow). This is the main source of cholesterol that blocks arteries. A level less than 100 mg/dl is normal.

- **HDL** (remember **H**DL as **H**appy, and you want to keep it **H**igh). This prevents cholesterol from building up in the arteries. Instead it carries serum cholesterol to the liver where it can be excreted. Men should have a level above 40 mg/dl, and women above 60 mg/dl.

- **Triglycerides** (TG) are stored in fat cells. Eating more calories than you burn leads to increased TG (by storing the unused calories). Hormones release TG for energy between meals. High levels are usually due to heredity, too much alcohol, too much fatty foods and fried foods, or "empty" and "easy" calories. Normal levels are below 150 mg/dl.

The formula to calculate total cholesterol = LDL + HDL + Triglycerides/5. For example if your LDL is 100, HDL is 40 and

Triglyceride is 120, the total cholesterol would equal 164. Let's do the math: $(100 + 40 + 120/5 = 100 + 40 + 24 = 164)$.

I have seen patients have great success managing and preventing high cholesterol by paying attention to the following foods and their impact on cholesterol levels:

- Most margarines, vegetable shortenings, deep-fried foods, fast foods, cookies, cakes, and pastries raise LDL, which is not good.
- It's the same with whole milk, butter, cheese, ice cream, red meat, chocolate, coconuts, coconut milk, and coconut oil—they raise LDL, and our goal is to decrease it.
- Olives, nuts (cashews, almonds), and avocados in controlled portions are excellent for you, because they raise HDL and lower LDL levels.
- Use canola, corn, olive, safflower, and soybean oils instead of butter and margarine.
- I've got to make sure you're with me on this—eat five servings or more per day of fruits and vegetables.
- Whole grains and cereal products—eat six servings or more per day.
- Have 2–4 servings of low fat milk.
- Have 2–3 servings of baked or grilled fish fish such as salmon lowers your LDL and raises your HDL.
- Enjoy a small amount of nuts and seeds daily.
- Be sure to plan for at least 30 minutes of activity five to six days a week. This will help raise HDL and lower LDL levels.
- See Chapter 47 for proper serving sizes.

Although I've touched on the different types of fat in several earlier sections of the book, I think this is a good place to sum these up for you again, in simplest terms. There are basically two main types of potentially *harmful dietary fats*—they are:

Saturated fat: This is a type of fat that comes mainly from animal sources of foods. These include cheese, pizza, grain-based desserts, sausage, hot dogs, bacon and ribs, fried white potatoes, candy, and ice cream. Other sources include lard, butter, coconut, palm and other tropical oils.

Trans-fat: Most of these are made during food processing through the partial hydrogenation of unsaturated fats. This process creates fats that are easier to cook. These include margarines, snack foods, and prepared desserts, such as cookies and cakes. Hydrogenation of fat occurs naturally in meats and dairy products.

The two main types of potentially *helpful dietary fat* include:

Mono-unsaturated fat (MUFA). These are found in a variety of foods and oils, such as olive oil, peanut oil, canola oil, avocados, poultry, nuts, and seeds.

Poly-unsaturated fat (PUFA). These are mainly found in plant-based foods and oils; vegetable oils such as safflower, corn, sunflower, soy, and cottonseed oils; nut oils, such as peanut oil; poultry, nuts, and seeds. Omega-3 (found both in cold water fish such as salmon, mackerel, and herring, and in ground flaxseed, flax oil, and walnuts) is an example of PUFA and is beneficial to your heart.

How much fat is healthy for you each day?

Limit your **total fat** intake to 25–30% of your daily calories, based on a 2,000-calorie diet; this is approximately 44–67 grams of total fat, daily. See how to calculate these figures in Chapter 47.

Limit your **saturated fat** to 7% of your total calories. Based on a 2,000 calorie diet, this is approximately 15.5 grams. If you choose to limit your saturated fat to 10% of the **total fat**, which is stricter, the amount decreases to approximately 4.4–6.7 grams daily.

Limit your **cholesterol** to less than 300 milligrams per day, and less than 200 if you are at high risk of cardiovascular disease. Sources of cholesterol include eggs, chicken dishes, beef dishes, hamburgers, dairy products, lard, and butter.[47]

Dr. Sam's Insight
**Fatty and fried foods may fill your fancy,
but the big bulging butt will break your back.**

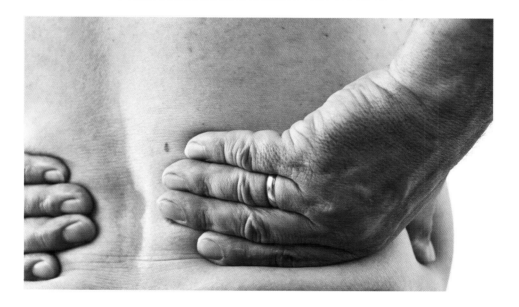

22 BUSTED

This may be one of the most controversial chapters in this book. Although I am not an expert on plastic surgery, I am a man of science, working on people's hearts, and have made key observations in my years of practice. One such observation is that many women who have had breast implants are complaining of cardiac symptoms, and are losing hope as they are plagued with the disheartening diagnoses of connective tissue disease, due to the breaking down of their immune system's foundation.

How have I made this discovery? Many women with unsuspected illnesses such as rheumatoid arthritis, lupus, and chronic fatigue syndrome have visited my office with a common complaint of palpitations—when the heart suddenly beats rapidly or skips a beat. The one thing I have found these patients have had in common is breast implants.

Certainly, we can find many patients who do not have breast implants who have rheumatoid arthritis, lupus, chronic fatigue syndrome, and palpitations. What's more, we can find women who have had breast implants and who have no physical ailments.

Interestingly, Lee and colleagues[48] sought clarification by conducting a study of the association of breast implants with connective-tissue diseases (CTDs), such as rheumatoid arthritis and lupus. Out of the 23,847 U.S. women who participated, 3,950 had breast implants and 19,897 did not. During follow up, women reported CTDs, confirmed by using a screening questionnaire and medical records. 77 out of 3,950 women with breast implants developed CTDs (1.95 percent), while 226 out of 19,897 women without implants developed CTDs (1.1 percent). According to the authors, "a reasonable conclusion is the lack of large increase in CTD risk (e.g. >2-fold) associated with breast implants."

Though there was a higher percentage of connective-tissue diseases in women with breast implants, the authors interpreted the results cautiously given the methods used to obtain the data. The association of connective tissue disease in women with breast implants is still unclear.

I wonder if this synthetic material is leaking, forming scar tissue, or causing havoc with a woman's immune system. Just as these implants have the potential for fibrosis (scarring) and contraction, they may also stimulate an "anti-self" response, leading to the development of autoimmune diseases, such as lupus, where the body "attacks" itself.

In 2007, Backovic and colleagues[49] identified inflammatory proteins on the surface of silicone implants that likely cause the fibrosis and contracture of the implants, and may cause the onset of autoimmune syndromes.

So, the question arises: is it the inflammatory proteins or the large scale litigations that are linking the association between cosmetic breast implants and connective tissue diseases?

Dr. Sam's Insight
When embellishing yourself, consider the risks and alternatives, and take caution.

To those who have implants or are considering getting implants, I ask that you and your family remain vigilant about your well being: look for any breech in your health, and have regular checkups and blood work done with your physician.

23 BIG-OL' UGLY ASHTRAY BUTTS

Several months ago during a particularly windy stretch of weather, I ventured out to my backyard to discover my basketball goal, once firmly secured in concrete, lay face down on the ground. Rainwater and moisture from the sprinkler system had seeped into the base of the pole over the years, corroding the steel, and allowing the wind to deal one huge knockout blow. The backboard that read "Shatter Proof" was in hundreds of pieces. Rust had undermined the integrity of the steel pole on which the manufacturers had proudly stamped, "Lifetime."

Because of my schedule, I didn't have time to clean up, but left to see my patients. The first patient on schedule for the day was Mr. H, a 64-year-old who had undergone a quadruple bypass surgery ten years ago. Recently, he had been playing golf out of state and smoking his cigars when he felt back pains. He ignored the symptoms, as he had for two months, finished the round and played another 18 holes. The next day, heading home, he felt ill. His friend who was driving him asked if he was all right. "No, you better stop." He got out of the car and collapsed on the road.

Mr. H was rushed to the hospital where he was diagnosed with an abdominal aortic dissection (tear in the biggest artery, causing internal bleeding). He was then rushed via air to a hospital that could handle an emergency of this magnitude. The surgeons found the problem and saved his life.

After his hospitalization, Mr. H visited me in my office. "Man, God surely smiled on you when He snatched you from death's zone and got you back into the land of the living!" I said. "You had about one percent—just one percent—chance of making it! This may sound insane, but there was a 99 percent chance of dying that day, and look at you now! You're alive! You're one blessed man!"

"Do you think I'll still be able to play golf?" he asked with a slight smile.

"You still smoking?"

Sheepishly, he said, "Yes, Dr. Sam…I know, I've got to quit."

I was so disappointed to hear him say, "Yes." He'd had his chest cracked open ten years ago, his aorta repaired a few months ago, almost left dead on the freeway, and he was still puffing away?

"Are you kidding me?" I said. "You're a walking miracle. You're going to stop today!"

I told him about the agents like water, moisture, and wind and how they had dealt my "Lifetime" basketball post and "Shatter Proof" backboard their final farewell. The nicotine was the nasty agent that tenaciously tore up his arteries and aorta, shattering his very life.

"You've got to get this. It's that nasty nicotine that's tearing away at your arteries. Hey bud, do you want to die before your appointed time?" This wasn't our first lecture about smoking, but I was determined it was going to be our last. "You're not leaving here until you shake my hand and agree you will quit this junk. I care for you too much to let this continue. It's not 'I'm going to try.' And it's not 'I've got to quit.' You're going to quit, *today*!"

The silence in the room was so audible, it was deafening.

"Okay Doc," he said with tears in his eyes. "I quit. I'll quit for you!"

"No bud, quit for your sake; honor yourself, honor your family, and honor your life!"

We celebrated life that day, and I was thankful that the "Lifetime" pole and "Shatter Proof" backboard offered insight in helping my patient live a life void of nicotine-drenched arteries. Mr. H visits me often. He still plays golf. He has kept his promise and his smile is now filled with hope.

Smoking offers you no hope. It causes nearly half a million (that's 500,000 people—a small city!) premature deaths each year, accounts for up to 30 percent of cancer deaths, and is the single most *preventable* cause of disease and death in the United States. One out of five U.S. adults currently smoke, and despite tobacco taxes and media campaigns, the prevalence of adult smoking is not decreasing.[50] Please recall from Chapter 1 that the two best ways to decrease mortality are to stop smoking and to lose weight if you are obese or overweight.

If you smoke, you are committing slow but sure suicide. You are killing yourself and everyone else around you. You think your children don't inhale your nasty fumes? You stick your cigarette out of your car window to save your pretty leather seats from ashes; forgive me for asking you this, but how about saving your brain from a stroke, or your heart from a heart attack, or your legs from cramping, or your lungs from lung cancer, or your colon from colon cancer, or your bladder from bladder cancer, or your joints from degeneration, or your kids from asthma, or your spouse from grief?

How do you stop smoking?

1. Seek your doctor's advice. Visit these websites and quit-line for help: www.surgeongeneral.gov/tobacco; www.smokefree.gov; www.cdc.gov/tobacco; or call 1-800-QUIT-NOW.[51]

2. Declare a quit date like Mother's Day, Father's Day, your birthday, or anniversary.

3. Tell your friends and family you **HAVE TO** quit (almost everyone "*WANTS TO*" quit; tell the ones who will hold you accountable that you **HAVE TO** quit) and allow them to hold you responsible. This is called "reframing," where a different perception will aid in the cessation of smoking.

4. Use nicotine lozenges and patches, if needed.

5. Ask about prescription medications such as Chantix® (designed to block nicotine in the brain) or Zyban® (an antidepressant).

6. Get a green rubber band and place it on your wrist. Snap it when you have the urge. The pain will help you understand that cigarettes are associated with pain and not pleasure. Why green? It represents life and that's what we're looking for: healthy living, filled with hope, no regrets, built on a solid foundation of smart decisions. If you can't find a green rubber band, get a blue one, and start snapping, so you can prevent a "code blue."

7. Put away lighters and ashtrays.

8. Throw out cigarettes and matches.

9. Clean your clothes to get rid of the hellish stench of smoke. What is so offensive to others will soon become offensive to you!

10. And pray for supernatural strength to quit!

Dr. Sam's Insight

Cigarette smoking is arguably the most significant cause of preventable morbidity (illnesses) and mortality (death) in the developed world.

As my favorite rap artist, Dr. Rap® says,
"Smoking causes cancer, nothing but disaster.
Smoking ain't the answer, it becomes your master.
You become its prisoner, heart attacks hit sooner.
Makes you die, makes you die faster."[52]

Testimonial #6

DAVID BEFORE

In January 2010, during my regular physical, an ECG indicated I had an abnormal result. My primary care physician recommended that I see a cardiologist.

I was seen at Dr. Kojoglanian's office where a stress test was carried out. Dr. Kojoglanian was kind, understanding and compassionate, and at the same time, emphatic that I needed to lose weight and start exercising.

I work for a large international firm and my position requires that I travel overseas regularly, so it is difficult to go on a controlled diet, and lose weight; in the past, this has been more than a challenge for me. In fact, it has been impossible. However, with Dr. Kojoglanian's support, I set about a determined weight loss program. In following his advice, I cut out all starchy foods, fatty snacks, my wine every night during dinner, reduced my portion size, and started walking more.

On a steady basis, I follow up with Dr. Kojoglanian, who continues to encourage me to persevere with my weight loss. When I first met the good doctor in 2010, I weighed 235 pounds with a BMI of 31.4. Two years later, I weigh 190 pounds with a BMI of 27. By losing the weight, my doctor has helped me get my blood pressure and sugar numbers back to normal.

Whether you travel or work locally, weight loss is a challenge. For me, it has to do with making good choices every single time I eat. Though difficult, it is worth it when I look at the benefits in feeling better and becoming healthier. My laboratory results will attest to that!

I am pleased to say that I have lost 45 pounds in the past two years, and attribute my success to the expert care and attention given to me by Dr. Kojoglanian.

—David Christie

DAVID AFTER

24 BAD BREAK, HEART ACHE

Mike is a 42-year-old father of two sons. He's healthy, doesn't smoke, and has normal blood pressure and cholesterol. About a year ago, he came to my office for a stress test and he walked 14 minutes on the treadmill. You might think 14 minutes is child's play, but less than 5% of my patients are able to make it to this stage, going 4.2 miles per hour at a steep 18 degree incline! It is one of the markers I use to determine whether my patients have healthy hearts. Mike got the green light that all was okay, and I asked him to follow up with me in six months.

Six months came, but Mike did not follow up.

The next time I would see him would be 12 months later in the hospital where, in an emergency procedure, a stent was placed to relieve symptoms of obstruction in a heart artery that had become 100 percent blocked. How could a youngster like Mike have so much disease that was not detected by a stress test? Our stress tests are at most 90 to 95 percent sensitive, and are not 100 percent accurate. But 14 minutes on the treadmill and no EKG changes, no symptoms and no ultrasound changes—and a heart attack a year later: that's uncommon!

As I spoke to my patient, I found out what led to the hospital admission. The past year had been "a living hell" for him. He had lost his job due to a poor "economic environment" after serving his company faithfully for 15 years. His wife had left him because she was "no longer in love" with him; she'd dumped him for a "young punk."

She left their two sons with him because they were "a burden." Mike broke down. He doused his heartache in alcohol and fell into the dark, jagged pit of depression. As depression turned to despair, the grieving expressed itself, not only emotionally, but also physically—in his heart.

This story is no soap opera—it's real life.

Dr. Sam's Insight
Resentment and depression will paralyze your soul and corrode your heart's foundation.

Recent literature has shown depression alone is not only an independent risk factor for cardiovascular events, but it is associated with doubling one's risk for cardiovascular events.[53] Patients with depression are more likely to have increased platelet reactivity—clumping of platelets, making a person more prone to have a heart attack by triggering the inflammatory cascade.

The American Heart Association has rightly recognized the effects of depression and has recommended that cardiac patients be screened for it by using the Patient Health Questionnaire (PHQ-2),[54] which is a two question survey: 1) During the past month, have you often been bothered by feeling down, depressed, or hopeless? 2) During the past month, have you often been bothered by little interest or pleasure in doing things? Since the questionnaire relies on self reporting, all responses should be verified and reviewed with your physician. Diagnosis and treatment may require further questioning and testing, only under your physician's supervision.

Circumstances are often cruel, unfair, and out of our hands. People are often careless and calloused, dealing us a bad hand. But ultimately, no matter what our pain and how deep the cut, choices have to be made. Even though we all have different stories, my attitude is a choice, your attitude is a choice and Mike's attitude is a choice. And it is our choices that will lead us to our prospective destinies.

As Mike relived his nightmare, he fumed with unbridled anger and succumbed to the ugly roots of bitterness; his soul cried out for answers. It will take time for Mike to heal. The good news is, he is beginning to realize that anger, bitterness, resentment and depression are not his advocates. He understands that his physical heart took a beating, but it has bounced back. Forgiveness may seem foreign at this point, but it will be essential to heal his weary heart and soul. I pray that he and those who are deeply wounded will one day be able to confront their dejected state, and say, "I'm hurting badly, **but** I have finally found lasting hope!" More on this in Section 3. Keep reading!

25 EMPTY SYRINGES AND BROKEN HEARTS

The syringe was found on the counter. Consider it carefree or careless, arrogant or apathetic, a cry for help or a disdain for life; whatever the intention, the blood-stained needle was now empty.

Rightfully suspicious, Joe's wife called me with his recent blood pressure readings. They were in the neighborhood of 190/90, which is elevated (normal is 120/80) and surprising. Over the years, Joe and I talked about him giving up smoking and he quit; we pulled him out of the obesity pool, and he's down to a good weight; we've laughed and reminisced about the doughnut munch-fests and he's now snacking on vegetables instead.

Joe called my office and asked me if he should increase his blood pressure medication, which we had gotten down to the smallest dose. Given his recent achievements, the plan had been to taper him off the medication completely.

"What's up Joe?" I asked. "What's bugging your heart, bud?"

"Not sure," he said.

"Tell me why we're increasing your medication dose, pal?"

"My blood pressure is up, Dr. Sam."

His weight hadn't changed, he wasn't smoking, and he had forgotten the number of the doughnut aisle at his grocery. After we spoke about the economy and the threat of higher taxes, I asked him to come in for a check-up. That's when he told me, "It's my son;

he's a good kid, but I guess he got into marijuana. One thing led to another, and now he's doing heroin. Dr. Sam, it's killing me; it's killing our family."

Joe had found the syringe and was devastated. The son had sworn the needle was not his. A week later, Joe found out that his son had stolen from his retirement fund. He threw his son out of the house. Joe's blood pressure got worse and he started having chest pains. We admitted him to the hospital and rushed him to my cardiac catheterization lab. He needed multiple stents, one for every major artery of his heart, each of which was 99 percent blocked.

Stress has a clever way of tugging at the heart, and it can rear its ugly head at any time. We don't even have to look for it; it seeks its opportune moment and strikes. If we allow it, stress will seriously strain our lives because it presents uncertainty and threatens to strip our security. I'm just laying it on the line. Stress can literally steal your peace and your health. For instance, when England lost their penalty shoot-out with Argentina in the 1998 World Cup soccer match, admissions for heart attacks in England increased by 25% on June 30, 1988 (the day England lost) and the following two days.[55] The daily numbers of deaths attributed to cardiovascular disease increased dramatically on the day of the Northridge, California earthquake in 1994, as contrasted with the same date (January 17) in previous years.[56]

However you want to define stress, Joe felt the shake and the aftershocks in his heart as he was vexed about his son. After dealing with a verbal shoot-out with him, Joe ended up on my cardiac catheterization table, getting stent after stent placed in his heart arteries.

I am convinced that Joe did well in surgery because of his rigorous and physically demanding line of work. The day after I placed the heart stents, he left for home a new man with brand new freeways in his heart!

Though Joe's son had been kicked out of the house, he will always be Joe's son—and Joe will always love him. After Joe saw the chaos the stress and anger had caused his heart, he decided it would be best to forgive his son, pray for his well-being, and hope for his son's healing. Forgiveness does not change the facts, it does not excuse or justify the wrong actions, and it does not demand amnesia; it simply sets the hurt person free!

Joe had found that healthy living is not only physical, but it is mental, and it is a matter of the heart! For that reason, Joe tossed unforgiveness to the curb. Not because his son deserved it, but because Joe deserved to care for his own heart.

What about you? Whether you find yourself in one of England's soccer stadiums, in one of California's earthquakes, in one of the Midwest's tornadoes, in Ted's kitchen (Chapter 1), in Joe's household, or in your own world of hurts, stress is no respecter of persons. Without being dramatic, it needs to be said that stressful news is one phone call or text away, and the future is truly uncertain.

If you are like a lot of my patients, you might be waiting for "the right time" to get started on healthy living.

The only right time is NOW.

You have no idea what tomorrow will bring—sorrow or joy, failure or success, hardship or goodness. So do yourself and those you love a favor—get off your comfy couch. It's time to do everything in your power to care for yourself, heal yourself, and prepare for your bright future.

Dr. Sam's Insight
Stress is inevitable, but getting a big butt is avoidable.

We may not be able to stop stress from visiting us, but we can control our big butts, our activity level, what we eat, and our unforgiving attitudes. It's time to face yourself. It's time to face the truth. If you have the big butt, big gut, and unforgiving heart, it's time to change. It's time to seek a better answer, and strive to accomplish the "undoable." Joe had all the reasons to drown himself in self pity and despair, **but**, as we'll see in Section 3, there is a better way. In fact, it is the only way.

No one can make this decision but you. Everywhere I go, people say the same thing, "Yes, I want to be slim, I want to look good, I want to lose weight."

No! Just wanting to do it is not the answer. It is not that you want to lose weight, BUT it is you **HAVE TO** lose weight. Your well-being is on the line. Are you kidding me? No, wait up, you're kidding yourself! It's not time for "just one more"; it's time for "one less." It's not time to sit and waste; it's time to walk and hope. It's not time to harbor hatred and resentment; it's time to forgive and love. It's not time for excuses; it's time for action. It's not time for the past; it's time for your now and your future. This is your life. Claim it back! This is your time. Rise up. Make your choice. Let's go…let's press on!

26 POTATO CHIPS AND NEW HIPS

I coined a term called GAP'S' which is an acronym for Gender, Age, and Parents. Obviously, we cannot control our gender or age, nor can we choose our biological parents. Therefore, the following risks are considered non–modifiable (unchangeable) risks.

Gender — Men are more prone to cardiovascular events than women. But in modern day America the incidence of heart related events in females is catching up to that of males, due to smoking, obesity, and enormous stress in the work force.

Age — As we age, our risk for cardiovascular events increases. The way to decrease risk is to stay active and eat sensibly. To further help in decreasing risk, a certain patient population who is at a higher risk for cardiovascular events should consider taking baby aspirin (81 mg)—but only with their doctor's consent and supervision. This simple step has proven in studies to reduce the risk of heart attacks in women over 65 years old[57] and in men over 50 years old.[58]

Parents — We cannot change our parents; we have no choice in the matter. They may be athletes, or they may be obese. They may be brilliant, or they may have average intelligence. They may be high achievers, or they may be dysfunctional. They may be successful, or they may be failures. They may abstain from the use of alcohol, or they may be alcoholics. They may be healthy, or they may be ill. Whoever and whatever they are, they are our parents.

Dr. Sam's Insight

What's that you say? You feel stuck?
It's not in your gender; it's in your determination.
It's not in your age; it's in your activity.
And it's not in your genes; it's in your heart!
BUT wait up; I've got great news for you…
How do you change yesterday's unchangeable?
By changing today's changeable!

One of my sweet patients, Peggy, who loves potato chips, has to have a hip replacement—again. It's her second within one year. Why so soon? It's not because she's 65. And it's not because the manufacturer is recalling their hip prosthesis. Peggy's mother and father were obese and diabetic, and she has always blamed them for her weight issues.

Five years ago, I warned Peggy about her weight. She was making horrible choices in daily life, including excessive eating and no exercise. She falsely relied on being of the "safer" gender, thinking women are not as vulnerable as men to heart disease.

Although we are still treating Peggy for high blood pressure, high cholesterol, and diabetes, I have taught her over the years that her choices can "trump" her genes. She is finally ready to lose weight, but is unable to move like she could five years ago. Back then her five-foot, six-inch frame weighed 170 and she had a BMI of 27.4; today she weighs 190 with a BMI of 30.7.

"It was so much easier then," she said. "Why didn't I just pay attention to you? You told me."

I didn't say a word as she vented her regrets.

"Is there anything you can do to help me now, Dr. Sam?"

"Well hon, let's get your surgery done, get through physical therapy, and then let's use your bionic hip to help us walk, one step, one block, one day at a time."

Peggy agreed.

"Now it's going to be 'one bite less' and 'one serving less' instead of 'just one more piece!' You've changed your heart; now we can change your life!"

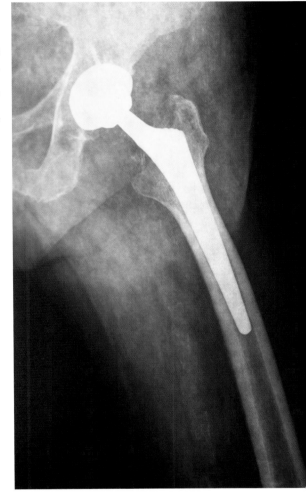

Testimonial #7

NIKKI BEFORE

Nikki is a nurse by trade, and when she first met me, I introduced her to Peggy's potato chip story with new hips. Nikki said, "No! That's not going to be me!" It's truly heartbreaking to see my patients face consequences that could have been avoided. That's why I strongly encouraged Nikki, my 52-year-old patient, to consider her future. A year and a half ago she weighed 200 pounds with a BMI of 33. Her EKG was abnormal, her blood pressure was out of control and she complained of chest pains.

I am so thrilled to have met Dr. Sam. My life is so different since then. Can one person have that much impact in your life? He said to me 'Nikki, I know you want to be well…you know you can change all this. You know you can change your choices. I know you've failed before, but with some instruction and accountability, you know you can get this, right?' I visited him regularly, and the last time we met, a year and a half later, I weighed 145 pounds with a BMI near 25. I walked on the cardiology treadmill for 13 minutes (difficult to achieve according to Dr. Sam, and more than I could have dreamed a year before), and I feel absolutely fabulous.

Dr. Sam showed me 'a picture' of my past—it was embarrassing. I then was shown 'a picture' of my future—it had disability written all over it with hip replacements, back surgeries, and heart attacks. So I said, "No!" I opted out. I changed my course. I simply ate less and walked more. If it weren't for Dr. Sam's instructions, encouragement, love, care, compassion, and prayers, I couldn't have made it.

NIKKI AFTER

Dr. Sam, thank you! It is because you care so much and because you honor your patients that I have become healthy. You're a Godsend and a light that shines with love!

Meet the new Nikki…I have no chest pains and no high blood pressure. I don't take any medications anymore! Hurray! As Dr. Sam says, I'm rocking my new jeans and defying my old genes, one choice at a time!

— Nikki Saucy

27 WRAP IT UP WITH DR. SAM'S TOP TEN FOODS

Often I hear people say that eating healthy foods is more expensive than what they are used to paying for their regular groceries. The *benefits* you gain from spending a little more money on healthy foods will make all the difference in the world to your health, happiness, positive mindset, physical well-being, and a rock-solid future. Plus, home cooked meals are less expensive than the frozen dinners, pricey for their convenience. By the way, try on expensive when the "inexpensive" or "convenient" foods escort you directly into the hospital! "Inexpensive" foods will lead to expensive medical bills while "convenient" foods will serve inconvenience into your future.

Dr. Sam's Insight
"Inexpensive" foods will lead to expensive medical bills. "Convenient" foods will serve inconvenience into your future.

The following foods are my top ten favorites for your body, heart and mind.

1– Almonds: Great source of fiber, magnesium, iron, vitamin E, protein, and calcium. Like all nuts, almonds provide plant protein, so you don't need to eat so much meat. Most of the fat in almonds is mono-unsaturated fat—good for your heart! One serving is about one ounce, or about 23 almonds and has more calcium than any other nut.

2 – Apples: Good source of pectin, a soluble fiber that can lower blood cholesterol and glucose levels. Apples are also a good source of vitamin C, an antioxidant that protects your body's cells from damage.

3 – Broccoli: Contains phytonutrients that may help prevent chronic problems, such as heart disease, diabetes, and cancer. Excellent source of vitamin C, because it protects the body from cell damage; and vitamin A, which preserves eye health. Good source of carotenoids,[59] Vitamin K, and folic acid.

4 – Organic blueberries: Rich in phytonutrients that may help prevent chronic diseases; can also improve short-term memory and promote healthy aging. This food is rich in fiber and Vitamin C.

5 – Red Beans: Good source of iron, phosphorus, and potassium. Excellent source of protein and dietary fiber. Also contains phytonutrients which may help prevent chronic diseases.

6 – Wild Salmon: Contains Omega-3 fatty acids, a type of fat that decreases bad cardiovascular events, such as heart attacks and strokes. Salmon is low in saturated fat, low in cholesterol, and a solid source of protein.

7 – Spinach: Jam-packed with vitamin A, vitamin C, and folate. This good source of magnesium can boost the immune system and keep hair and skin healthy. The carotenoids—beta carotene, lutein, and zeaxanthin—are found in spinach and protect against vision loss, heart disease, and cancers.

8 – Sweet Potatoes (not fried): Rich in the antioxidant beta carotene. An excellent source of vitamins A and C, and a very good source of fiber, vitamin B-6, and potassium. Also fat free. One large sweet potato has approximately 160 calories.

9 – Tomatoes (not canned): Contain lycopene, an antioxidant that may reduce the risk of heart attacks, prostate cancer, and possibly other types of cancer. Tomatoes are a rich source of vitamins A and C. Cooking tomatoes with a small amount of oil increases lycopene absorption into the body.

10 – Wheat germ: Found in the center of a grain of wheat, this germ contains thiamin, folate, magnesium, phosphorus, and zinc, enriching your heart and your body. The unprocessed germ also contains protein and fiber.

Wait a minute, you say you don't like these healthy foods? You would rather have your enchiladas, baby back ribs, biscuits and gravy, and top it all off with chocolate cake and cappuccino? You do have a point—those fat- and sugar-loaded foods have a strong appeal. But before you read any further in this book, you need to answer one question: Do you love your food more than your health, or do you love your health more than your food? Unfortunately, by the look of things, I think people care for their bellies and seek instant gratification over their health and their future well-being.

Dr. Sam's Insight
**Do you love your food more than your health,
or do you love your health more than your food?**

How you answer that question speaks volumes about the sturdiness of your foundation—and about your future. For your sake and those you love, I urge you, place a high value on your health and make the appropriate changes, starting today. You will taste sweet victory when you eat healthy and decline to eat fast foods and processed foods. You will see the pounds come off, safeguard your foundation, and move like you've never moved before!

This is it, it's time.

Get off your big butt, clean the junk out of your fridge and cupboards.

Claim the blame!

Speak the truth!

Exchange desire with discipline!

Exchange the big butt with a bigger but!

Go to the store and stock up on the living foods.

Start drinking your water—hydrate.

Get your walking shoes on—ambulate.

Get the measuring cup and the food scale out—tabulate.

Kick disease in the butt!

This is *your* house.

It is *your* foundation.

It is *your* choice.

And it is *your* time for all things to become new.

Press on!

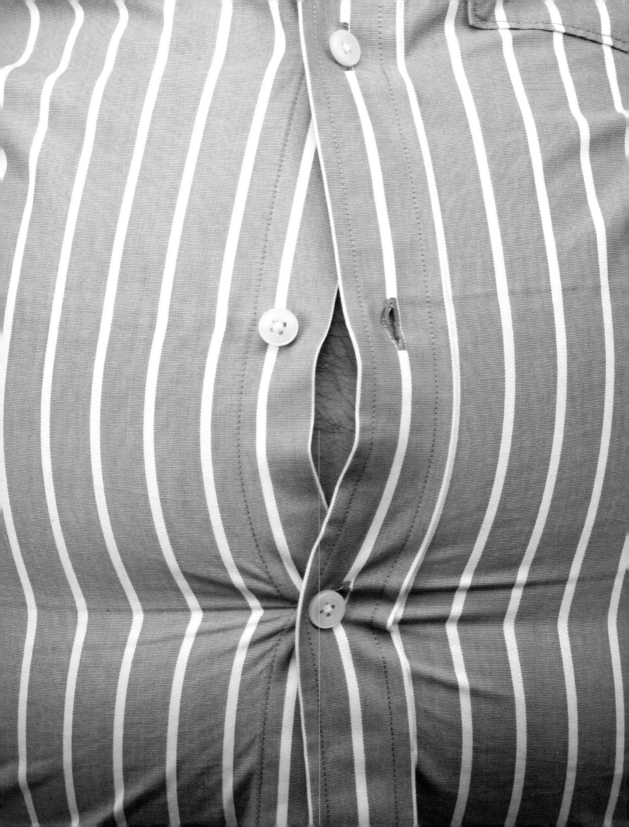

II.

UGLY IMAGE

The Psychological, The Problem

28 PORTION BIAS VS. PORTION CONTROL

As we've seen, a sturdy and healthy foundation is built on self-discipline and conscientious choices. When we understand the truth and the benefits of wise decisions, why do we consistently make unhealthy choices and chip away at our firm foundation? One thing that continues to amaze me is when my obese patients tell me, "I swear, Dr. Sam, I don't eat that much."

Recently, one of my patients swore he did not snack on anything.

"Anything?" I asked.

"That's right, Doc!"

"Anything…like candy or cake?" I asked.

He held his ground. When getting out of his chair, out fell bubble gum that was nicely wrapped in its yellow, red and blue wrapper.

"Hey, I know that gum," I said. "It has about five grams of sugar per piece. How do you think it got into your pocket?"

"Yeah, okay, Doc, you got me this time!" he sheepishly said.

Really, I don't wish to "get" my patients. I live to heal them!

After hearing their excuses or denials over the years, I rack my brain:

- Why do my patients do what they do?
- Why are they like they are?
- What influences them?
- What clouds their judgment?
- What force grips the central thinking process and lulls it to sleep?

- When do these influences begin?
- Why are they hopelessly stuck, slipping and sliding toward their silent death?
- What psychological forces weaken them and what emotional matrix fortifies a person to healthy living?
- How does a solid foundation that is conceived in hope become subject to these negative influences before any signs of deterioration begin to show?

Jan, a 50-year-old patient of mine, has shed much clarity on helping answer these perplexing questions. Jan weighs 295 pounds and suffers from arthritis of the hips and knees; she will soon face a total left knee replacement.

"Jan, I need you to level with me on something," I said. "Let me know one thing in the diet that's causing this weight gain. Why are we at 295 pounds?"

She hesitated. "I don't eat much at all, Dr. Sam, and I watch what I eat."

When a 295-pound patient proclaims she doesn't eat much, I force myself to remain silent for an extra long moment as I sit there bewildered by the enigma of eating very little and reaping a huge butt. There have been times when I've thought about saying, "Who are you kidding? Are you for real? Do you actually believe what you just said to me? Can you not see reality? Mirror, mirror on the wall, can you help my patient see their butt is big and not small?!" But compassion overrules. I hurt for my patients. And I desperately want to intervene and help them.

Dr. Sam's Insight
Herein lies the first major problem in losing weight: People consciously or subconsciously underestimate the amount they eat.

Call it what you will—denial, delusion, or dementia—but overeating will show up in the big butt and big gut, and no amount of lip service should convince us otherwise. *Portion bias* is called blindness, influenced by several factors including ignorance (not knowing the truth); suppression (knowing the truth, but silencing it); entitlement (embellishing the truth with a self-serving and self-deserving attitude); assimilation (casting away the truth by becoming accustomed to the new normal); or denial (refusal to face the truth).

Read that paragraph again. Meditate on it. Of which are you guilty?

Portion bias can also happen when we over-reward ourselves without thinking about it. You finish a task, get up, have a bite, and return to work. You finish the next task and repeat the behavior. You think, "I'm not eating much…I've had very small portions today." Doesn't happen? Ask your accountant what happens in the office during tax season!

Dr. Sam's Insight
Though each portion may be "small," many "small" portions repeated over time add up to one big butt!

Did you know envy could cause overeating? Sound absurd? Have you ever been in a restaurant and thought you were content with what you ordered, until you saw the waitress deliver someone else's platter? You say, "Oh man, I wish I would have gotten what they're having—it looks incredible!" I thought so…and I've been guilty of it!

According to the wisest man who ever lived, King Solomon, "The eye never has enough of seeing."[60] The unquenchable thirst and unending yet futile search for fulfillment turn into a food fetish that leads to the perception that, "Whatever I'm eating is just right for me, it fulfills me, and it's no one else's business." I beg to defer. It's your big butt's business, so put down that extra bite, stop the greed, and walk away before you get caught in the cyclone of a hopeless, broken foundation.

Know what else leads to overeating? Things like pain, unfulfilled dreams, scars of betrayal, heart wrenching hurts and memories, and feeling rejected—all leading to a depressed and dejected soul that is hungry for love. Why do people turn to food as a source of solace? Because we are beings who are searching for answers, rewards, and comfort; we long to fill the voids in our lives, to nurture the pain, to hoist our success, to foster our insatiable senses—not realizing that overeating will cause a breakdown of our foundation. **But** there is an answer. Yes, a surefire answer to all the emptiness and all the pain, soon revealed in Section III.

Dr. Sam's Insight

**While your pain lives off the food,
the food will never ease your pain.**

I continued to speak with my patient. "Jan, you came to see me about chest pains and we're going to get you help, but right now I need your help. Please, I'm your advocate, lend me a hand here. Just give me the one thing that's causing you grief in your diet?"

"Well, I really don't know."

"I think you know, Jan, and I need you to tell me, because your weight is putting too much of a burden on your heart.

"Is it bread?" I asked.

"No Dr. Sam, I don't eat bread."

"Okay, ice cream?"

She shook her head. "I rarely have it."

"All right, what about cheese?"

"Oh, I hate cheese."

There went my top three suspects.

"Are you eating or drinking too much of something?"

"No, I'm watching what I eat."

"Any sodas or diet sodas?"

"No, I drink water."

I'm thinking, "How can Jan possibly be drinking water when she's five foot eight, weighs 295, and has a BMI near 45—clearly above morbidly obese?"

"Jan, you can't gain weight with water—what else are you drinking?"

The truth began to seep out. "Could it be the milk?" she asked innocently.

"How much milk do you drink?"

"I thought it was a good source of protein," she said.

"It is," I said, "but how much are you drinking?"

"About, well…up to a gallon of 2% milk."

"In one day?" I hoped the shock didn't show on my stunned face.

"Yes, in one day."

"Okay." I tried not to make it obvious that I had to pick my jaw up off the floor. "Let's try something, let's try to cut this down to one eight ounce glass of milk a day. Milk is good, and an important source of protein and calcium, but too much is helping you gain more and more weight. You think we can cut it down?"

Jan agreed, but you need to understand that it took her many years to muster enough strength to seek help, and confiding in me was no easy emotional task. She later told me that it was only because she was disgusted with herself that she finally opened her heart to let someone see her torment. I didn't ask what she was eating *with* the milk at this point, because I did not want to overwhelm her.

So I drew a circle on a piece of paper and drew a line right down the middle. "You see the right side of this circle, Jan?"

"Yes."

"This represents half of your plate. I want you to fill it with vegetables like broccoli, carrots, salad, and cauliflower."

"Okay."

"Now, I'm going to take the left side of the circle and cut it in half, where we have one quarter and another quarter. You see that?"

"Yes, but we don't get a separate plate for the salad?" she said.

"Let's concentrate on this one plate first," I said. "That way, you have small portions. In this one quarter, you can place your proteins, like lean meat, fish, or chicken without the skin. In the other quarter you can place carbohydrates, things like brown rice, whole wheat pasta, and sweet potatoes. Now, if you want to eat salad all day long with lemons and vinaigrette, have at it, but none of the nasty blue cheese, ranch dressing, Italian, or Thousand Island. You can also use the light version dressings sparingly, got it?"

"Got it."

You know what? Just by cutting down on her milk and eating from one small plate with imaginary lines dividing one-quarter, one-quarter, and one-half, without having seconds, Jan has started losing weight. Instead of watching TV, she is riding her stationary bike, which is the only type of exercise she can do, given the pain in her knee. She is snacking on veggies and has stopped eating heavy meals after 6 p.m. I told her how proud I was of her. These are enormous steps for a patient who was entrenched in such bad eating habits.

Do me a favor. Go to your cupboard and grab the peanut butter. This happens to be one of my favorite foods. Flip the jar to the nutrition facts and look at the serving size. Can you read it? Mine says, "Serving Size — 2 Tbsp (tablespoons)." One tablespoon is approximately as big as your thumb. I dare say that most people will use more than two tablespoons for each serving. Now, that is what I call *portion bias,* where you *make up* your own portions and believe it is acceptable because it appeases your appetite.

Dr. Sam's Insight

When one has portion bias, one gets a big butt.
When one exercises portion control, one loses the big butt.

Portion bias is deceptive; pacifying you into taking another bite and another, until you feel guilty, and ill, and swear you'll never do it again—only to fall into the same trap four hours later. Once we see or smell the food, our senses usually overpower us, and we end up eating what we swore we wouldn't. Portion control, on the other hand, is disciplined. With portion control, you listen to counsel, logic, and the prudent voice of good health, and stop at the recommended serving size so you can enjoy your food, be guilt-free about what you are eating, and reap great health benefits today and tomorrow.

Why did portion control finally work for Jan? Because she was tired of the guilt and disgusted with her situation. She longed to feel strong again. She started loving her health more than she loved food! She discovered the truth—that yesterday's pain, guilt, entrapment, and failures could no longer keep her chained to the regrets and hopelessness of that past. She began to "*reframe*."

What's "*reframe*"? It's seeing the same thing in a different light, with a different perspective, and with a different goal in mind. It's saying, "I may have seen myself as a hopeless case, paying money to lose weight, gaining it back and even more, **BUT** now I see myself differently! I'm not a loser, I'm not hopeless, I'm not going to be caught with a disease-laden body. I care for myself, and I will, for the first time in my life, turn this thing around for good!"

This ain't no rocket science, ya'll. It's cardiology with compassion. It's about putting your big foot down, drawing a line in the sand, and declaring with everything in you—"I've been given another chance. I'm finding my way. I'm finding new hope. I'm finding the new me in a new framed picture. I've been down. I've been deceived. I believed the lies that you can do what you want and get away with it. **BUT** now I see. Now I'm beginning to understand. And now I will rise. This is my song. This is my war cry. This is my heart's voice being kindled by hope. This is my time. I no longer just desire, **BUT** I will do everything possible to make the changes and persevere for the sake of a much improved quality of life, starting today."

I'm in this with you.

I'm cheering you on.

You can do this.

You got this.
One choice.
Choice by choice.
Walk with me.
Together, we press on!

29 THE "CLEAN PLATE" SYNDROME

When you were growing up, did your parents insist you couldn't leave the table until you cleaned your plate? I grew up in a very modest home. My dad worked 16 hours a day, not to make more money, but to make enough money to take his family out of a small Armenian community in Jerusalem and bring them to another Promised Land known as America.

We arrived like the pilgrims, except we took a plane and set foot on the streets of a sweet place called Chattanooga, Tennessee. Although at first it was an unforgiving place where I was bullied, called a foreigner, and experienced bigotry like I'd never known before, it eventually became a home where kind-hearted people embraced us. At mealtime, I was told to clean my plate, because there were starving children who were not as fortunate as we were. I'm sure you've heard those exact words.

Jan was born in America and her parents told her the same thing—no leaving the table until everything was eaten. She was also lectured about the importance of drinking her daily cup of milk. Today, we live in a world where a plate of food costs us a pretty penny and, since we paid for it, you know darn well we are going to eat the whole thing! And if the bread they serve is "free," hold up ya'll, it's like receiving gifts at Christmas, so we're gonna devour the whole basket and have seconds, too!

It is in the "tabulating" phase that our mind's computer is lulled into the sleep mode. Why do we forget what and how much we have eaten? This question requires a multifaceted answer. The truth is that a "cleaned" plate translates into a fully satisfied belly. Because we are feeding ourselves, we feel it is imperative to care for, nurture, and do what it takes to gratify our desires and satisfy our cravings. Since we are creatures driven by our senses, and our eyes will never have enough, we are prepared to justify anything to satisfy everything.

Dr. Sam's Insight

Since we are creatures driven by our senses, and our eyes will never have enough, we are prepared to justify anything to satisfy everything.

The fact is, one out of three adults and children are obese, and the act of gluttony has become the new normal. Did I just refer to "overeating" or "emotional eating" as gluttony? Yes, call it like it is so you can do something positive about it! Not only is there a lack of control about overindulging, there is a lack of guilt. People are denying the illness and addiction in record numbers, and justifying their actions by comparing themselves to others who have even bigger butts than theirs!

There is also a lingering wish in people's hearts to cheat "just this time," and hopefully not have to deal with the consequences. The law of life, however, is that the truth always catches up—even if it takes awhile to reveal itself.

"It's in my genes," a patient will tell me, "and that's the reason I am the way I am." This gene game undeniably has its place, but it has become a huge cop-out and *must* change. To what? How about the truth? How about, "I am making harmful choices, lying to myself, hurting myself, justifying my health away, and I desperately need to change before my self-willed actions destroy my good health."

You recall that Jan was drinking a gallon of milk a day, right? One gallon is equal to 128 ounces, which is equal to 3,785 ml (milliliters), while a normal serving size is 240 ml. Since one cup contains eight ounces, Jan was drinking 16 cups of milk a day (8 ounces x 16 cups = 128 ounces).

How do people eat and drink so much? First, by doing it while watching TV, while their minds are occupied, and they are placed into a world of "unrealistic reality" shows. Second, by working on their computers, which for many, is their workstation. These two have become the greatest hypnotizers of the brain and handicappers of the body.

Dr. Sam's Insight

How do people eat and drink so much? By doing it while watching TV and working on their computer—two of the greatest hypnotizers of the brain and handicappers of the body.

Do you remember the cup of 2% milk I had before testifying in court? It had about 236 ml of fluid, which had 130 mg of sodium, 25 mg of cholesterol, 5 grams of fat, 10 grams of protein, and 13 grams of carbohydrates. Well, Jan was having 16 times that amount:

Sodium: 130 mg x 16 = 2,080 mg of salt, exceeding the 1,500–2,000 mg daily allowance.

Cholesterol: 25 mg x 16 = 400 mg of cholesterol, exceeding the 300 mg mark.

Fat: 5 grams x 16 = 80 grams. If we were to calculate the amount of calories, it would translate to 80 grams x 9 = 720 calories from fat. *Oh, no you didn't!*

Protein: 10 grams x 16 = 160 grams of protein. If we were to calculate the amount of calories, it would translate to 160 x 4 = 640 calories from protein. *Somebody help me, please!*

Carbohydrates: 13 grams x 16 = 208 grams of carbohydrates. If we were to calculate the amount of calories, it would translate to 208 x 4 = 832 calories from the carbohydrates. *I'm just sayin'!*

Calories: To tally all the calories for one gallon of milk, we add 720 + 640 + 832 = 2,192 calories, exceeding the 2,000 calorie mark in an inactive patient. And this is just the calories from milk! Milk does the body good, yes—in moderation. *You feelin' this?*

The first problem we faced was portion control. Here's the second problem: we may be eating or drinking healthy things, organic things, low cholesterol things, low fat things, and "healthy" fruit juices, but we are eating or drinking *way too much* just because "it is healthy," or because we have been trained to "clean our plates."

We ease our minds and stuffed guts with the comforting promise that the massive amounts we just consumed were "sugar free." We finish the plate or entire package, convincing ourselves that we have been given the license because it is "fat free." *Hello...you with me?*

Dr. Sam's Insight

Tragically, we seem to be oblivious to the truth, that "sugar free" and "fat free" have a "sour cost"—bad health!

The "clean plate" bias may be a behavior learned as a child, but that does not justify gluttony, greed, obesity, and lack of self-control. The ability to choose, the willingness to change and the commitment to live a better life are your choice and are in your hands. If the portions are excessive, the "clean plate" diet will lead to a foundation riddled with fractures. That leads to handicaps and disabilities. And that grinds a person down until they feel as if they are on a dead-end street with absolutely zero hope of turning things around.

Because we have turned off the voice of reason and have chosen to ignore its existence, we continue eating and drinking, cheating and hiding, consuming and overindulging—not facing the truth that sickness, disease, disability, and even death will knock our doors down.

Remember Dr. Sam's HAT Trick?

Hydrate.

Ambulate.

And, please, as you're digging into your food, make a conscience effort to *Tabulate!*

Your butt will thank you, and your loved ones will rejoice, because your good health brings them joy.

Testimonial #8

ROBERT BEFORE

When Dr. Kojoglanian (I affectionately call him Dr. K) told me about the "Clean Plate Syndrome," I knew exactly what he was talking about! My name is Robert Stuart, I'm 60 years old, a dad of three, and a grandfather of four, working in customer service for an insurance company. It's hard to say when I started getting big, but I was 350 pounds when I first saw Dr. K. I've always been embarrassed about my weight, and I've heard from others, "Bob, you have got to lose weight."

When I told Dr. K I was overweight, he asked me to first speak the truth, saying, "Bob you're not overweight, you're not even obese, you're morbidly obese and you're going to pay a huge price for it." I heard the truth, and now, I speak the truth. "I'm morbidly obese!" Wow, it hurt me to say it at first, but the truth is helping me make better choices.

I know I have to lose weight, but how? All the TV advertisements show superstars who advertise for programs they say I should join, because I'm worth it. Dr. K helped me see where I was heading: a place he calls, not

Disney Land, but "Disaster Land"—a body plagued with illness and gut wrenching disease.

Dr. K also helped me to "reframe" my thoughts. Instead of saying "I can't," he says, "I can." After hearing his encouragement, I began to believe that I was able to lose this weight! He wants me to have a BIG BUT! The word BUT is actually a simple tool that works…I've messed up in the past, BUT I'm now a different person. I understand I have to change, and because I am well informed, I am able to overcome. I used to think I had to have a clean plate, BUT now I use a smaller plate, and eat smaller portions! I finally got it. It's not in a diet. It's not in a pill. It's in my choices…every time I eat. Dr. K was right…it's hard at first, but it's simple and it gets easier, especially when you see the results.

People are starting to notice and want to know if I've got the lap band after my 50 pound weight loss. No lap band for me. Just eating less, and walking more. I have occasional slip ups, but that's allowed under Dr. K's plan because he dislikes extremes. I have my pizza, but not all the time. And if I have splurged today, that's okay, but I won't have it tomorrow. I'm eating healthier, making wiser choices, and I'm moving more. I'm not on any of those diets I tried in the past.

My total cholesterol has gone from 250 to 150…that's a hundred point drop! You should have seen Dr. K's face when he looked at my lab numbers…he was beaming with joy for me, and

ROBERT AFTER

congratulated me with a huge hug! That's the thing about my heart doctor. He inspires me. He cares for me! Though I may be upset at myself, wanting to lose more weight, he'll say, "Bobby, you used to be 350 pounds, look at you now, you're working wonders, you are losing weight steadily without the roller coaster ups and downs!" That's my doctor—he always sees the good.

My blood pressure has fallen from 140/100 to 110/80, and Dr. K is getting ready to taper off my medications. I want to let you know about my car handicap plaque. I used to struggle to walk and parked my car just next to the store door. Now I've gotten rid of the plaque. I park further and walk! No need for the elevator. I'm using the stairs. My life is so different. I feel so much better! I want to be there with my grandkids and I want to enjoy them!

Dr. K holds me accountable for my weight and we have our weigh-in sessions. I've not looked back since. I've taken off the weight. Pressing on like Dr. K wants, and my life has changed for the better, for the good, and forever!!

— Robert Stuart

30 CULTURE BIAS

I am convinced people are at their happiest when they are surrounded by food. Oh, you can argue that happiness is at its highest when people are doing their hobbies, or spending the holidays with family, or enjoying a special date, or cheering on their favorite sports team. But I have seen it time and time again—when food is present—a person's very demeanor changes.

A friend told me about a grouchy nurse in her 30s who used to work with him at a dermatologist's office in Tennessee. Although she was a tyrant, she was a diligent, hard worker, helping with front and back office, as well as with skin biopsies. She would snap at the manager, snap at patients, and even seem to snap at herself at times. But when food appeared at the office, hold the phones, ya'll! She would sing, put on her happiest face, turn on the Southern charm, and become friends with everyone.

Dr. Sam's Insight
Food changes people's attitude, food changes people's behavior, food changes people.

Think about it—weddings, parties, family gatherings—they are all centered around food. If you want a bunch of doctors to come and hear another physician speak, you may lure a handful of intellectuals to come. But child, if you want the whole hospital to attend, even if you're talking about toe fungus, just let the people know there will be food and the place will be packed!

Much of what we eat and drink is fed to us via a culture that is being blitzed by magazines, movies, television shows, and TV commercials. One of our "biggest" problems is that we sit down and eat in front of the television. Once this happens, we lose focus of how much we are eating.

One of my patients eats just once a day, at night. He will have five tuna sandwiches, along with a 10-ounce bag of chips. Sure, tuna is healthy, but eating five sandwiches for one man at night is erroneously distorted. The bag of chips says it has zero grams of trans-fat, but wait up, he just ate the *whole bag*, and that's at least 1,500 calories! He just consumed an enormous amount of fats (100 grams or 900 calories), carbohydrates (150 grams or 600 calories) and "harmless" salt (1,800 milligrams, which exceeds the daily allotted 1,500 limit).

Eating out can be extremely deceptive. As we watch TV, we are enticed with commercials that tell us we're hungry and that we need to visit the incredible restaurant around the corner, because it has everything to make us happy. Not that you didn't notice, but did you see the slim, happy and beautiful people on the commercial? That's a part of our culture: pretty people getting paid to act happy so they can persuade us to be "happily fed and fulfilled."

Once we're seated at the restaurant, we are greeted with the bottomless basket of bread and butter, which hardly can be ignored. We are asked if we would like an appetizer first, which, at times, contains as many calories as the main meal. Do your well-being a favor: skip the appetizer! For the sake of being healthy, we order the salad, but we tend to drench the nutrients with thick dressing, croutons, and bacon

bits. And then the main course arrives, deep-fried, sautéed in butter, flavored with rich sauces, or covered in gravy. Oh and, by the way, "Would you please refill my beverage and bring us some more bread? Thank you!"

To ease our consciences, we consider the diet soda a reasonable companion to all this fatty food. But diet sodas are even worse than regular sodas because they give us the false license to eat and drink more, and they contain ingredients that are wreaking havoc on our bodies.

Another cultural bias is being raised up in a family that encourages eating because of previous hardships. My grandparents survived the Armenian genocide of 1915, when 1.5 million out of 3 million Armenians were heartlessly and savagely slain by the Turkish people. I grew up with an Armenian neighbor in Jerusalem whose parents drilled it into his head, "Your grandparents were beaten, slain, and stripped of all dignity; they were starved to death in the desert by the Turks who raped and killed our people! You are too skinny my boy, eat, eat, eat!" And eat he did. Today his BMI classifies him as morbidly obese.

While some families may compensate for previous tragedy by eating in excess, not all families operate this way. In fact, many people around us, from all backgrounds, with or without tragedy, overindulge simply because they love to eat. To them, food has become an impassioned hobby, something they look forward to with unbridled gusto.

What is the first question people often ask when they speak to someone who is losing weight? Without considering the person's feelings, they come straight out and ask, "Are you sick? Is everything okay?" Though the question may be due to concern, in some cases, I believe it stems from envy. The answer is, no! They are not sick. They are trying to become healthy, to move a little quicker, to weigh a little less, and to reduce the size of their butt and gut to the point where they look and feel like a healthy human being again!

Although the passion people place in food is not completely empty, as it is essential for survival, it can be immensely deceiving. It is when people come to consider meals or snacks as "comfort" that food will end up betraying them.

Dr. Sam's Insight
The comfort that too much food offers today will confront you tomorrow with the cold reality of betrayal.

Every choice is an important choice. There are no insignificant choices when it comes to our health and our eating habits. Each decision adds to the healing road of healthy living, or to the breaching of our foundation. Each meal, each snack, in fact, each bite, offers us a decision. Just one more, or simply one less—all intertwined by yesterday's influences and today's cultural beliefs. All of these outside forces can easily manipulate our thoughts, opinions, and appetites—but we are the ones who ultimately make each and every choice. And we the ones who wear our health on our own skins.

Dr. Sam's Insight
Culture is impossible to escape,
but unhealthy decisions will be impossible to ignore.

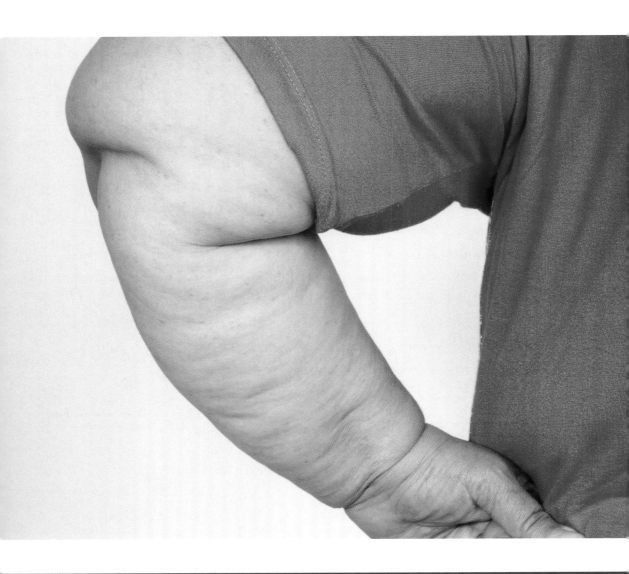

31 MIRROR, MIRROR ON THE WALL...

Jan wasn't always so big. Once upon a time, she weighed 130 pounds. But that was a while ago, when she was a teenager. Over the years, Jan really put on the pounds, but the odd thing is, she never considered herself overweight—until that dreaded trip when she returned home to Kentucky for her thirtieth high school reunion.

One remark was all it took. One mean, brainless comment, spoken by "an old friend."

"Jan, what did you do to yourself?" the friend asked. "You look fat!"

I am not kidding you, those were her exact words. It was a nasty hit, spoken unwisely, and without an ounce of care for Jan's feelings. Jan was devastated. She ran out of the banquet hall and found herself lost in the hallways where she used to walk 30 years earlier. When she saw her image, reflecting back from a glass case that held some of her trophies from the past, she said, "Oh my God, I am fat..."

Jan came to my office asking for help about two years after the reunion. Her friend's words had haunted her ever since. Sometimes it only takes a few words, sometimes it takes many years, and sometimes it takes an unwelcome and devastating stroke or heart attack to drive the point home—you're too big, and it's killing you.

I hope you are wise enough to let my words sink in deep right now. I hope you are seeking the truth, and not trying to hide from it.

I hope you are determined to embrace the new and healthy you right now—not tomorrow!

Yesterday's failures and disappointments were just that—yesterday's—not today's nor tomorrow's. That's the main thing with this book and you. You look in the mirror and if you dare speak the truth, you'll see a frame around you: framed overweight or obese. We take that frame with you in it and project it into the future: if you're still in the truth, you'll see the evils of high blood pressure and high sugar levels stealing your health and years. But we have learned by now that we have a simple tool; it's the word "*BUT,*" helping us "reframe" our thoughts and approach.

You can object all you want to. Some will say, "What's in a word, a simple word anyway; are you pulling out this 'positive' thinking on us? Say it, believe it, and it will happen?" Believe me, you'll need more than words to lose weight, but words spoken by the tongue have much power. According to King Solomon in Proverbs 12:18, "Reckless words pierce like a sword, but the tongue of the wise brings healing." Speak a word; it can cause great pain or bring healing and hope.

As you continue to look in the mirror, I need for you to use one more frame. Break the frame of the past and the frame of consequences. We will introduce a new frame: "I see what I've become. I'm very sorry about my situation. I don't like it and I now understand that it is causing me harm. *BUT* I am going to change. I'm going to start making wiser choices. It may be hard, *BUT* it is simple! I will eat less, and I will walk more. This is my new frame of mind and viewpoint. I have been deceived, *BUT* no longer. Hold me accountable, because this time I give my word, and I *will* become healthy!"

How do you like your big **BUT** now?

This might surprise you, but many seriously overweight people still have an image of themselves when they were younger, faster, brighter, slimmer, and had a full head of long, curly hair, without a hint of one gray strand. Call it denial or survival—the truth is masked, swept away, ignored, covered, coated, and purposely or inadvertently overlooked. I call this *image bias*.

When Jan gave me permission to use her story, she told me she viewed herself as "perhaps slightly overweight," but never obese or morbidly obese. Since weight gain is usually gradual, and in the average adult, two pounds per year, I believe many people don't even realize who they have become, what bad habits they have developed, and in what rickety condition their foundation rests.

It is time to gently lead you to the mirror. And, please, forgive my boldness, but I want you to take a long, hard, realistic look at your unsightly waistline, look at your bulging hips and thighs. It's probably not your imagination, your face *is* widening, you may have fat jowls and a *big, baggy, bulging butt*! There may be some hope in having an image bias, but it is false hope, unable to leady you to a healthy foundation. The key is to see the truth, speak the truth, and pursue the truth so that you stop wasting your precious life away.

Dr. Sam's Insight
Stop saying, "I'm a little overweight." If you are obese, speak the truth, and say, "I am obese, BUT I am about to change my ways!"

Image bias or not, this is your time to live. This is your time for health. This is your time for honor, strength, and stability. This is your time to regain the hope you have lost. Don't just sit there, feeling sorry for yourself, worshipping at the feet of self-pity. Get up, look in the mirror, call a spade a spade, stop buying empty calories that tempt you, lace up your walking shoes—and press on baby, *press on!*

32 SO FAR FROM BEING A TRACK STAR

Many of my patients were former superstars in various sports, whether as NCAA speedsters or pro standouts. It is not unusual that these former athletes become obese. Why? When they stop training as full-time athletes they continue to eat as if they were as active as ever.

Most of us are not athletes, but we act like we are still teenagers. Teenagers bounce off walls, expend energy, and many can often afford the calories they consume. But most adults become sedentary, and still eat like they are teenagers. So what, you say? So, the big butt, that's what!

Jan's high school hallways boast trophy cases filled with reminders of the glory days when she was a track star. That day when she saw the trophies again with her true reflection, she cried about who she had once been, and the person she had become. She had continued eating a lot despite the fact that she had quit running; but in her mind, she still considered herself an athlete. I call this *athlete bias*. Well, this athlete would be leaving her reunion soon, heading toward her home in California, where she was scheduled to have a total left knee replacement. In her case, it wasn't the sports injuries that caused her knee to deteriorate; it was careless eating choices, which had been made one choice at a time over many years.

Have you lived a similar life? The choices made 20 years ago seem so remote, so far away. As you get older, the years seem to go by faster and faster. Each choice is a building block placed atop the foundation you've built. What is the condition of your walls? How is your foundation? Is it standing tall or about to fall? The truth can be rejected or it can be denied, but it will always be the truth. And the truth will either catch up with you or run over you!

Dr. Sam's Insight

The truth can be rejected or it can be denied, but it will always be the truth. And the truth will either catch up with you or run over you!

I have seen enough overweight and obese patients who have turned their lives around to tell you, it is *not* too late for you. But here's the deal—if you are going to eat in excess, you are going to need to walk. By the way, many of my obese patients exercise at the gym, but still cannot control their portions. Exercising does not give you the license to overeat. Similarly, changing channels on the TV and walking to the fridge do not count as adequate exercise.

Dr. Sam's Insight

Drop the TV, detach your fingers from the computer key, listen to me, and declare yourself FREE.

Let's drop the TV. Let's detach ourselves from the computer. If you make your living at the computer, then force yourself to take breaks and get up, stretch, walk and then go at it again. Go ahead, admit you are addicted to Facebook which consumes so much of your life. Not addicted? Can you let it go without touching it for 7 days? I thought so. Let's say no to the *extra* cookie. If we've got to have a heavy dressing, let's have a small portion and dip into it or choose a light version and use

it sparingly instead of drowning the food with it. Let's get our running shoes on, baby! I'm not looking to make anyone unsightly skinny, and I will not get everyone down to a BMI of 25. But I'm here to deliver the truth so you can have a hope-filled life, so you can save your health and really know what it feels like to *live!*

Don't give yourself any excuses.

This is all about making wise choices.

Don't just bring me the desire to lose weight.

Desire in itself doesn't determine your fate.

I'm asking you to bring discipline to the table.

I'm asking you not to settle.

It's not time for you to speak; it's time for you to *do*.

Cast the guilt behind you.

Forgive yourself for yesterday—it's past due.

Embrace the hope that is new.

Find someone who will hold you accountable; ask a friend.

Throw your shame to the wind.

Stop the lies.

It's time to rise.

Testimonial #9

BARRY BEFORE

To my friends and family, I offer strength through guidance, consistency and calm when the waters are stormy. I am Barry Schwartz, urbane in deportment, steadfast in friendship, generous, funny, and kind.

But when I'm alone, away from the reflections of the man I see in my loved ones' eyes, I am anxious and fragile and so often afraid. I am uncomfortable and self conscious and fundamentally unhealthy in a longevity-lessening kind of way. I am consumed with guilt and self absorbed. I am fat. Or at least I used to be.

A man came to me with a hammer in his hand. His head was bloodied and bruised. He struck his head repeatedly with that hammer and called out to me for help. "My head is killing me," he cried. "What should I do?" I told him to stop hitting himself with that hammer he held in his hands. Months later he came back to me with that hammer so tightly gripped in his hand, his head far worse than the time before. "My head, sir," he again cried, "It hurts worse than ever! Please help me—what can I do?" "You simply need to drop the hammer, my friend," was all I could say.

My cardiologist, Dr. Kojoglanian, came to me one day as I was being discharged from the hospital after a four-day visit for a heart related incident that I had suffered. It was the third such event that year, and the eighth or so within the last five. I was 54 years old and weighed 303 pounds—all 5-foot, 8-inches of me. He told me in no uncertain terms that if I didn't find a way to drop the hammer, the hammer would soon be dropping me. I wonder if you can be devastated and inspired at the same time? I was. Dr. Kojoglanian's words, delivered with love, landed more forcefully than a hammer's blow.

Maybe a gastric sleeve might do the trick, or some kind of by-pass surgery. I've seen the commercials and everyone looks great. They drink through a straw for a couple of weeks, they gum broccoli mush for a month or so, then eat a thumb size portion of food once a day for another month and BAM, they've lost 45 pounds and are cured! Then the little pouch of a stomach some surgeon built for them starts to expand. Soon a small taco from Taco Bell will fit … soon a couple will, and before you know it, like most of us, you find yourself in the garage. It doesn't take long to find that hammer you left there just a few months ago.

BARRY AFTER

So I decided to drop it. I knew I needed to. I was going to get around to it sometime soon anyway, right? I'd needed to drop it practically all my life. It was a situation that I knew so well. I'd lived with it. It was a part of who I was. It defined me. I carried that bloody hammer with me everywhere

I went, and everyone I knew and everyone I met, saw me for who I was. I was the funny, sweet, smart, cool guy with a bruised and bloody hole in his head, and a hammer in his hand. So I dropped it. I dropped it and I kicked it to the curb.

I lost weight. I lost a lot of it. Ninety pounds of it as of today: I weighed 303 pounds in 2008 and 213 pounds in 2012. And guess what? I'm still funny and kind and generous. And do you want to know what else? My knees don't hurt anymore when I walk up stairs. And my hips don't hurt anymore when I walk the aisles of Costco (and I didn't even know I had hips that hurt until the pain went away!) And my back doesn't hurt when I get up in the morning or out of the chair I sit in when I work. I can walk for miles now. I honestly feel like I'm maybe 15 years younger! I wear clothes that fit and I look GOOD. And I feel really good. And I'm proud of myself. No gimmicks, no tricks, no self-loathing, no anxiety—nothing took the place of the hammer.

Dear reader, if you're still here with me, please allow me to share what I know to be the truth of all truths: if you could walk in my shoes for just one minute, you'd never take them off. Please don't wait for Dr. Kojoglanian to tell you that you have heart disease or diabetes. And if you already have it, don't wait for him to tell you it is getting worse. Drop the hammer and live your life. Do it once and for the last time. You should see the look in my son's eyes. He's so proud of me. Best feeling in the world. Put on these new shoes, you won't believe the feeling…toss the hammer…and save your life!

— Barry Schwartz

33 DOUGHNUTS AND PIES THROUGH CHILDHOOD EYES

Can you imagine being on a winning kid's soccer, baseball, swimming, or football team—or any other winning kid's team—and the coach yells, "That's my team! I'm so proud of each and every one of you; you went the distance and you gave it your all. Time to celebrate the champ in you!" Then he breaks out the lettuce, beets, broccoli, carrots and celery sticks!

Not gonna happen.

In this scenario, kids are used to chips, ice cream, crackers, packaged cakes, pizza, soda, chocolate chip cookies, apple pies, flavored drinks, and Krispy Kreme® doughnuts. These are the foods they look forward to—the foods we all consider to be happy, rewarding, festive foods. They are "comfort me" foods. Often, the "yuck" factor we associated vegetables with as children still lingers in our psyche as we grow older. This is what I call "childhood bias."

Dr. Sam's Insight

Often, the "yuck" factor we associated vegetables with as children still lingers in our psyche as we grow older. This is what I call "childhood bias."

If junk food is so bad for us, why in the world does it tastes so good? I think it's the tantalizing smell, the undeniable good taste, and the pleasure it brings. But if we don't recognize and can't even pronounce the words on the label, we should back off, and understand that moderation with "reframing" will lead us to decrease our total intake.

My point in this chapter is that, sure, kids are going to eat their share of fun, junk foods. But the key is to ensure that they grow up with a steady diet of fruits, nuts, and vegetables as well. A bag of raw almonds and a bag of carrots and celery sticks make excellent snacks. Hot vegetables at mealtime should be a regular. And kids need plenty of water, just like us adults; in fact, I believe water is what they should get in the habit of drinking most of the time.

What about you, Dr. Sam, do you ever break the rules?

You know I do. I love my Kit Kat® bars and In-N-Out® Double Doubles, popular burgers on the West Coast. Just the other day my family and friends got together to go to the Krispy Kreme® doughnut shop. The rains had battered Southern California all week long, and on this particular Sunday, the sun came out, the breeze blew, and everyone in the village, it seemed, must have hopped in their vehicles to go to the Krispy Kreme® shop.

I didn't have my sunglasses or my cap, so I seriously prayed like a mad man, "Oh my God, please don't let any of my patients see me in this place!"

I sat down like a little kid, laughed my head off, and enjoyed a half of a banana cream-filled doughnut and half of a chocolate glazed cream-filled doughnut. The verdict is in: no broccoli will ever taste that good, no sweet potatoes will ever ring so sweet, and no salmon will ever melt in the mouth like those doughnuts did! Oh, that was good! And all in all, I had one doughnut.

We had an absolute blast and, just in case you wondered, the good Lord answered my prayers—not one of my thousands of patients witnessed the event!

34 | IT'S TO DIE FOR

Man, we can lose all control, can't we? We think of food as being so grand, so wonderful, such a milestone in our day, so "to die for," that when we smell it, pull up to the table, see the delicacy set before us—we lose all self-control. Unfortunately, many also routinely eat on the sofa, standing up in the kitchen, in front of the refrigerator, in front of the TV and in their beds. Food is glorified and all discipline goes out the window. Because food is equated with pleasure, it is not associated with consequences. We focus solely on eating as much as we can, until buttoned pants are changed to the stretchable type. "Stretchable" is a synonym for pantry raiding, fridge scavenging, and harmful decision making.

Dr. Sam's Insight
Because food is equated with pleasure, it is not associated with consequences.

When it comes to food, poor choices are not considered harmful, but as a sweet reward. As we are enticed by the smells and drawn by the possibility of eating the "best food I've ever tasted," we give no thought to the discomfort we will face today or the cost we will pay tomorrow. For many people, the craving for food becomes overwhelmingly addictive, yet deceitfully exaggerated; I call this *exaggerated bias*. Self-control slowly slips away. King Solomon, the wise ruler, said, "Put a knife to your throat if you are given to gluttony."[61] Otherwise, the big butt gets bigger. The foundation gets weaker. And hope for the future becomes darker and bleaker.

Dr. Sam's Insight

King Solomon, the wise ruler, said, "Put a knife to your throat if you are given to gluttony."

An unforgettable example of overindulgence with a bittersweet bite dates back 4,000 years. There were two brothers, sons of Isaac: Esau, the firstborn, and Jacob, his younger brother.[62] The elder son enjoyed the birthright, which gave him the honor of a double portion of the inheritance and exalted position over any of his siblings. Esau was the brawny sports-hunting type while Jacob was more of a chef and indoors-man. One day the latter, Jacob, had cooked up a delicious stew when Esau returned from a long hunting trip—he was famished. He smelled his brother's delightful stew and asked for a bowl.

Little brother Jacob might have said, "Hey Esau, I got your back, big bro. I'll serve you this stew—made it just for you! But there's just one minor thing I need for you to do—exchange your birthright for my stew."

Dumb proposition, right? Unlikely to happen. Why would Jacob even try to make such a deal fly? But listen up, Esau was famished. He was so hungry that he said, "What good is my birthright when I'm about *to die*. Give me the stew. Have your birthright!"

Wait up. Did you hear him? He said, "I'm about to die." He wasn't going to die, but hunger changes perception. And the words "to die for" become an action.

Bad decision. Downright stupid. How could you give up your birthright, your honor, your life, your future—for a bowl of stew, Esau? I guess it's the same as when a man or woman gives up his marriage, family, and future for a one night affair. I guess it's just like when people give up their honor and good name for tax evasion. My goodness, I suppose it's like when a person stuffs himself silly with hidden grease, salt and sugar in exchange for his good health tomorrow.

The bottom line is that one bowl of stew was all Esau thought about in that moment. Everything else around him—the priceless future possessions, a crown of blessings, the splendor of hope, joy, and comfort—were blurred, ignored and forgotten as he hyper-focused on one bowl of stew, and his appetite screamed for immediate gratification.

I doubt the stew could have been that good, and even if it were, it could not have been worth the troubled and tragic future for which he exchanged it. Esau went on to lose the blessings of his father, lose his position of honor, and constantly hear that his God was the "God of Abraham, Isaac, and *Jacob*"—rather than the "God of Abraham, Isaac, and *Esau.*" Short-lived decision? No, to this day, the way millions worship and call on God's name is due to a decision made by Esau over a bowl of stew…millennia ago.

There are many deceptive faces of the exaggerated bias. They emerge when food is presented in such a way that it comes across as "a must have," "you will miss out big if you don't grab this now," and "you have never experienced such goodness before!" We tend to smell, salivate, and bite in, thinking this pleasure will last forever. The seductive delight is only temporary, while guilt that follows overeating is relentlessly cruel.

Dr. Sam's Insight

We tend to smell, salivate, and bite in, thinking this pleasure will last forever. The seductive delight is only temporary, while guilt that follows overeating is relentlessly cruel.

I often ask my patients, "Is food really that good?" "Is it really 'to die for'?" "Is it worth your heart attack and ICU visit?" "Is it worth being placed in a wheelchair while others care for you, because you can't care for yourself?" "Is it worth destroying your joints?" "Is it worth tasting your own bile when the reflux strikes?"

I guess, at that moment, just like Esau with his stew, or a businessman trading his wife and children for a relationship with his co-worker, it *seems* good at the moment. We have an insatiable appetite. We want immediate gratification. We demand portions that are too big for us. Our eyes are fixed on things we are led to believe will bring pleasure. That's when all sacred beliefs, steadfast honor, future victories, and good health are recklessly cast by the wayside.

How about you?

Would you like that rare or medium?

Or would you like to start a new life—today?

35   I GOT A BIG BUTT, BUT...

I used to let my patients say things like, "I just can't do it," "It's impossible," and "It's no use, I'm not going to be able to do this!" What I've learned over time is that spoken words are powerful, as we discussed in Chapter 31. Articulated words are not mere verbiage; what is spoken mirrors the condition of one's heart. Once a person says something, they tend to track those words until they are fulfilled. What you say has a way of shaping your future; that's what I call *word bias*.

When we constantly say we can't stop eating fatty, greasy, sweet foods, and can't reduce our portions, can't stand vegetables, and don't like to drink water—we will ultimately prove ourselves right. We don't like being wrong, so we end up ultimately doing what we said we would or wouldn't do. Then, when we can't lose weight, we say, "See, I told you so. I told you I couldn't get it done!"

Instead, we must speak positive words, and speak the truth in advance. Now, I am not suggesting we sit around on our big butts all day, reciting, "I'm skinny, I'm tiny, me and my hinny—everybody say it with me—don't I look pretty!" Getting a smaller behind will take effort and require persistent positive thoughts that encourage us to action.

Dr. Sam's Insight

The truth is always the truth, and no lie will change it, but the truth will only change you if you are willing to accept it.

The tongue has the power of life and death.[63] You must stop saying, "I can't do this." Why? Because you can't allow—nor can you afford—the word "can't" to rule your life.

Many people tell me, "I *don't feel* like I can lose weight and get healthy, so saying that 'I can' would feel like a lie." You must speak words of healing, even if you don't *feel* it.

We have to reframe the frame!

Say, "I know I got a big butt, ***BUT*** I am willing to work at it diligently so I can be lighter and happier!"

"I know my knees are shot, ***BUT*** I'm going to take Dr. Sam's advice and get healthy!"

"I have failed all my life, ***BUT*** this time, I'm bringing much more than desire. I'm determined and self-disciplined. Not only am I going to lose the weight, ***BUT*** I *will* keep it all off!"

"Don't care much about exercise, ***BUT*** I do care about my health; watch me do my walk—ambulate!"

"I love my sodas and my meals, ***BUT*** I will drink water—hydrate, and eat smaller portions—tabulate!"

"I have said I'll never make it, ***BUT*** this is my time, this is my life, this is my health, and this time *I AM* going to make a positive and lasting impact, now and for the rest of my life!"

By saying such things, often you will begin to transform your words into a lifestyle. At first, you may not believe it, but with repetition, you will *become* it! Many times in life we must declare and pursue an action *before* we *feel* like it.

This brings up a very important aspect of losing weight. Having positive people around who will encourage you and cheer you on is critical on this journey. We need to be accountable to someone. Even if you can't find that person, get a journal and write down your goals, hopes, and dreams, and write down how you are going to pursue and accomplish them. Create a detailed record of everything you eat and drink for a four-week period. Record your weight and physical activity each day. See Dr. Sam's simple journal in Chapter 50. The person lost in today's greasy pit has no vision of tomorrow's pitfalls. ***BUT*** the person who identifies the greasy pit can climb out of it and change his future. Re-visit the journal weekly, note your progress, be accountable, be positive, and be healed!

Dr. Sam's Insight
The person lost in today's greasy pit has no vision of tomorrow's pitfalls. *BUT* the person who identifies the greasy pit can climb out of it and change his future.

Here are some words my patients speak. See if you can identify with them:

- *"I swear to you, I don't eat that much!"* Lies. Better to speak the truth, and set yourself free.
- *"I had lost 20 pounds, but I just got back from my cruise."* Hope the bowl of stew was worth it.
- *"I can always start tomorrow."* Your heart and joints may give out tomorrow—start today. One out of two people who dies suddenly has no previous warning. They are too busy

nurturing their big butts. But the big butt will bite you. Set your cookie down, turn off that TV, and get walking!

- *"Food comforts me."* It can also kill you—don't kid yourself.
- *"I'm cutting back."* Make sure you don't do what some stores do—increase the price by 50 percent, then have a 30 percent off sale!
- *"I blame it on my genes. My father had it, my aunt had it, and now I have it!"* Blame them all if you want to, but(t) the truth is staring at you in the mirror.
- *"I'm not as large as they are!"* They're not the one with your health problems, now or in the future.
- *"I messed up already, so I might as well give up."* Stop! You are one decision away from healthy living! You are one step away from building a sound foundation! And you are one breath away from saying, "I will love myself back to health!"
- *"You don't know what I'm going through."* Eating your way through it will only lead you into darker valleys.
- *"I can't. I've tried, I've failed, I'm so discouraged—what's the use of trying again!"* You are precious, and you are worth the effort—again and again!

Don't give up on yourself! This is your life. This is your time for health. This is your season for goodness. Get up, even if it's just to take a few steps, get up! Even if you can't go outside or you're too embarrassed to do so, get up and start walking in place, in your own room. We can't have today's guilt rule you. Let's use today's strength—however little it may be—to build tomorrow's healthy promises. We've got no other choice. Let's press on; yes, let's *press on!*

Testimonial #10

ROBERT BEFORE

I'm Robert Fischer and I met Dr. K in 2009, when he opened up one of my heart arteries. He pleaded with me to change my ways, which meant decreasing my portions, decreasing my salt, decreasing my alcohol intake, and increasing my walks.

I'd heard this all my life, and had ignored it. It wasn't the opening of my heart artery that "scared me" into changing my ways. It was Dr. K's compassion that motivated me to change my life!

Now it's two years later, I am 40 pounds lighter, and I am so much healthier.

ROBERT AFTER

That's what someone with passion, love and encouragement can do for you! Thanks Dr. K!
— Robert Fischer

36 A BITTER ROOT

Jan is as sweet as can be. It is difficult to believe she could get angry at anyone, until you talk to her about her father. He was a drunk who loved alcohol more than he loved his family. His rage broke the very spirit of Jan's family, including her tender heart. Jan's mother spent many days nursing the bruises and wounds she sustained from nightly brawls with her husband. Jan can hardly talk about it, but she was deeply hurt by her father, who molested her when she was just a child.

Over time, Jan grew more and more distant to her father. Eventually, her fear of him turned into anger, which grew into a raging bitterness, as she watched him verbally and physically abuse her mother, and tasted the shame of abuse on her own skin, and in her own soul. She vowed that she would never be abused again, and that she would never abuse anything or anyone.

Jan found that she could run away from her anger on the track field and that she could comfort herself by feeding her shattered spirit. I call this *bitter bias*. The pleasure of eating took over her life and she kept on feeding her pain, emptiness, loneliness, and bitterness with food— long after she hung up the track shoes.

Although food masked Jan's pain for a little while, her 295 pounds was working a number on her joints, back, and heart, causing medical problems that were not foreseen, and were not the central topic on her mind, as she took the next bite.

Dr. Sam's Insight

Emotional pain is inevitable, but most hip and knee replacements are avoidable.

Have you weighed the people who have these operations? I have. They are usually obese, unless they faced accidents or physical trauma. As pain tears at the heart, obesity tears at the joints, causing limping. Limping favors the good limb. And then the good joint tears down because of overuse.

And that's part of life?

No, that's taking away from life.

Watch your pain, and seek help. Food is not the answer, as it further suppresses the sorrow of your heart, because the pain is not confronted. The sorrow will somehow manifest itself one day and cause greater pain, because it was unattended to.

Watch what you put in your mouth. Don't feed your sorrow with food coated with self-pity. Sorrow is like a leech that is never satisfied. Excess food is a deception that never nurtures completely. Food is not your friend, it is never "to die for," nor can it be a suitable substitute for happiness. Understand the purpose of good food: it is essential for strength and survival. Jan understands that now and is finally speaking about her past. She is also finding that speaking the truth is much healthier than drowning the pain with food.

37 | WHAT GOLDEN YEARS?

Most people plan on living healthy lives right on into their golden years, but what I have observed is that the sheer wear and tear on the human body will only allow this weary temple to go so far. Often, the years that were "supposed to be" filled with rest and relaxation are, instead, plagued with doctor visits and hospital stays. For many, the "golden years" consist of a black appointment book packed with the names of doctors, surgeons, and specialists.

Having a big butt will catch up with you—quicker than you think. I have known many people who have finally determined it's time to lose weight, but wait—they can't move like they did before, their knees and hips are so shot that they can't even exercise. I call this the *golden year bias*. Jan can attest to it, even though she is only 50 years old.

I do hope you are listening. If you know you are overweight, *now* is the time to act. Don't wait another day. I've seen too many of my patients get on a vicious cycle of thyroid pills, steroids, high blood pressure medications, and anti–inflammatory drugs.

Dr. Sam's Insight

Injuries occur unexpectedly. Surgeries are scheduled unwillingly. And our years pass rapidly.

Many get to a point where they want to lose weight, but their foundation is so broken that their bodies will not cooperate with the will of their minds, as they once did.

Sandy, 35, is a waitress who has been raising two kids on her own. Her heart began fluttering not long ago, and that's when she made an appointment to be seen in the office. I suggested she cut out the caffeine, reduce her chocolate intake, increase her water consumption, and get her thyroid tested. We spoke about her weight, and she said, "I know I'm overweight."

"Sandy, hon, you are only 10 pounds away from being what is considered 'morbidly obese,'" I said.

"Obese?" she was stunned.

"No, *morbidly* obese. Your body is going to break down, it's going to give up, you're going to start getting all kinds of illnesses if we don't turn this ship around."

She looked down, then around the office. "I'll manage somehow," she said.

"Yes, but Sandy, how about your little ones? Who's going to manage them?"

After a long pause, Sandy broke down. The tears flowed.

I let her get it all out and when she calmed down, we continued to talk.

"Tell me the truth, Dr. Sam, what's going to happen to me?"

"Okay, let me introduce you to Sandy," I said. "She is a

35-year-old mother who loves her children. She is 10 pounds shy of morbid obesity. No medications are needed at this point. By the time Sandy hits 40, she'll be limping because of premature arthritis, and taking medications to decrease her blood sugars because she's diabetic. When she's 45, she'll get a left hip replacement because bone on bone doesn't work so well. When she's 50, she'll be on insulin for diabetes, two pills a day for high blood pressure, two for cholesterol, and one for reflux."

Though her eyes gazed at me sadly, her demeanor begged for the truth.

I felt she was giving me the license to continue, so I did.

"Sandy will likely have her first stroke around the age of 50. Although she will desperately want to continue taking care of her family, she will physically be unable. She will then be willing to change, but reality has slowed her down. She will beg to take back her bad choices, but will be unable to."

Sandy was down as low as she could get, and it was time for a lift, time for a change, and time for a new hope.

"But the Sandy I know did not get to that point." I smiled. "She went to her doctor, she listened, she heard, she cried her tears, she understood, she saw, and she changed. She made it to her doctor's visits, and in one year, she lost 30 pounds. She no longer has palpitations, and she will continue losing weight. Because, this is the Sandy I know. This is the Sandy I believe in. This is the Sandy I am speaking to right now."

Sandy stopped crying. She looked as if someone had breathed new life into her. She was grateful for the truth. She left my office with a thankful heart, and in one year, Sandy had lost 35 pounds! We have only just begun, and she is a different woman with a new found hope and a very bright future.

Sandy hit many plateaus while losing weight, but kept on working, walking and believing. When you hit a plateau and are not able to lose weight, don't be discouraged—be encouraged; this is a time for you to celebrate the work you have done, to congratulate yourself on staying the course, and to savor the fact you are pursuing healthy living. For some, this period may be weeks, for others it may be months. Once you gear up for the next level by increasing your activity even further and counting your calories, you will once again see the weight come off.

Move before you can't. Get up before you're stuck. Press on before the golden years become nothing more than a painful death sentence and your black book full of doctor names becomes your closest companion. Whether you are Jan, Sandy, Peg, Jim, Tom, or Hank—your time is *now*. The decision is yours. What in the world are we waiting for? It's time to march onward and upward. It's time to kick this thing in the butt!

III.

TRANSFORMING TRUTH

The Spiritual, The Promise

38 FEED ME THE TRUTH, THE WHOLE TRUTH, AND NOTHING BUT THE TRUTH

I applaud you for successfully completing the first two sections of this book! If you adhere to the truths, facts, and wisdom found there, you will be successful in your weight loss goals established with your doctor's supervision. Why? Because insight guides you, strengthens you, inspires you, and changes you to pursue and attain healthy living.

Now we are about to begin the section that will mend your soul. Since this section focuses on the spiritual aspect of your being, you might be tempted to bail out…

BUT…

…If you have been looking for answers to some important questions and want to finally grasp the meaning of your existence; if you've sought peace and contentment and have fallen into anxiety's deadly grasp; if you have lost your joy and desperately want to reclaim it; if you have been seeking unmerited grace that will erase all your regrets, guilt and failures; if you want to sink your teeth into unending hope that will sustain you in every circumstance, and acquire an unbreakable foundation that will keep you secure forever; if you want supernatural power that will help you lose weight; and if you long to find the purpose of your life—read on.

Dr. Sam's Insight

**I don't know a lot of things about you.
BUT I definitely know one thing about you…
You want to experience lasting hope, joy, peace and love.
That's why you can't afford to miss this entire section!**

Although this section falls toward the latter half of the book, it is *not* a byproduct of the book or an afterthought. In fact, it is where the idea for the book *started* and where the title, *I Got a Big But(t),* was conceived!

Have you noticed the price of gold lately? As this book goes to press, gold has soared to levels once unimaginable. The price of gold is so important that it makes the front page of *The Wall Street Journal*® each day. But there is a commodity even more precious than fine gold. It is sweeter than honey straight from the comb. It cannot be found on the New York Stock Exchange, nor is it sold on NASDAQ. The means of acquiring a commodity more precious than gold is so simple that a child can grasp it, but so profound that a scholar can miss it.

Dr. Sam's Insight

The means of acquiring a commodity more precious than gold is so simple that a child can grasp it, but so profound that a scholar can miss it.

This commodity prolongs life, brings health to the body, gives peace, offers contentment, delivers wisdom, surrounds you with security, helps you sleep well, protects your mind, infuses abundant and abiding joy in your life, and guards your heart. It is not found in the produce aisle or where the doughnuts are prominently displayed.

Even though all of these promises and all of these advantages are within our reach free of charge, we tend to neglect them, gravitating towards the temporal things that easily disappoint us, and latching onto anything or anyone to help us fill an eternal void that resides in the very heart of our souls.

Just look around. You'll find people who are angry, lonely, discontented, bitter, depressed, scared, suicidal, confused, insecure, and unsure who they are and what their purpose is. You can find them in Hollywood mansions or Hollywood alleys. Money and fame don't feed the soul, nor do they feed a person's well-being. The tragic deaths of Michael Jackson and Whitney Houston can attest to that. On a global basis, look at the unrest in the Middle East, the turmoil in Europe, the fear in America. Who is secure? Who is at peace? Who has the answers?

We try to fill these voids and insecurities with many different things that we see, smell, taste, hear, touch, and bring home with us. We run to food, which *does* satisfy—for the moment. Some latch onto drugs, only to find out that the drug latches on to them even tighter, refusing to let go until it demands its user's life. Some run to relationship after relationship, only to find that people can disappoint to the bitter end. Some long to be entertained through sports, movies, TV shows, Netflix®, only to wake up, hungry and thirsty for more, and still manage to feel void of any joy and contentment. I believe everyone thirsts for the truth, and when they find the truth they are surprised to discover that it is pure and simple and their minds were just too preoccupied, their hearts too burdened, and their souls too proud to accept it.

What then is the answer to this uncertain mess we live in?

Are there many answers or just one?

Are there many ways or just one?

Are there many speakers or just one?

What is the source of real hope?

What is the one true "commodity"? Is it silver, gold or platinum?

Can we find it in cash, "things," or moving up the proverbial ladder of success?

Can we find it in a best-selling "how to" book or in a message delivered by an eloquent, inspirational speaker or guru?

Can we find it in our dream house, cars, jobs, or family?

This commodity will not save you from hardships.

But it will carry you *through* hardships with peace.

So where can we find it?

I believe one king of old gives us the answer.

The king is David.

The time is 3,000 years ago.

And the *truth* hasn't changed since then.

Dr. Sam's Challenge

If you will, if you dare—set aside
your preconceived notions,
your pride, pain, biases, well earned diplomas, toys,
trophies, failures or great accomplishments—and join me
in the following chapters on a life-changing adventure.
Unless, that is, you're too preoccupied or
possibly too prejudiced to stomach the truth.

39 IRREFUTABLE TRUTH

The previous sections of this book were written with the hope that they would guard and strengthen your physical foundation. This chapter goes beyond your weight and was written with the hope that it will secure your spiritual foundation. This is the section and chapter you've been waiting for! It will certainly offend some, and you are welcome to skip it. It will, however, heal many souls, and help us get a glimpse of an eternal realm and foundation that we tend to ignore or resent at this transient moment, but will be unable to avoid after our days on earth are spent.

Part I: Finding Pleasure

Many people remember David slaying the giant Goliath, or plunging into adultery with the beauty Bathsheba. Although David was the second king of Israel, credited with writing some of the most reassuring words known to man in the book of Psalms, there are many things people don't know about him—things that can change our lives in the here and now.

David had innumerable enemies who hungered, thirsted and *lived* to witness his demise. He not only was a man after God's own heart, but he was a man of many heartaches. At times his life was a living hell, despite our perception that his was a life of success, popularity and glamour. David shares his troubles with us in Psalms, Chapter 13:

> *1 — "How long, O Lord? Will you forget me forever?*
> *How long will you hide your face from me?*
> *2 — How long must I wrestle with my thoughts and every day*
> *have sorrow in my heart? How long*
> *will my enemy triumph over me?*
> *3 — Look on me and answer, O Lord my God.*
> *Give light to my eyes, or I will sleep in death.*
> *4 — My enemy will say, 'I have overcome him,'*
> *and my foes will rejoice when I fall."*

I wonder if that sounds like your heart's cry. Perhaps you are trying your best to get ahead or just to stay afloat. Maybe you have tried with all your might to do good, to leave a bad habit behind, to escape the grasp of a cruel past, or to be released from your present hell—only to be faced by people who oppose you, bring you down, ridicule you, hurt you, and even want to sabotage you.

I believe with all of my heart that each and every one of us comes to a place in our lives when we realize that we are not as great as we thought we were. We realize we are inadequate, that we cannot save ourselves, and that we need help beyond what man can give. If we refuse to water down this important truth, we'll begin to understand that man-made inspiration cannot give us the breath of real contentment, true love, lasting peace, and abounding joy.

Today, you may find yourself in a rut, feeling hopeless and overwhelmed. The demands of life may simply have engulfed you with worry, anxiety and a broken heart. At times, there seems to be no end to the bad news, the lack, the loss and the betrayal. Even if you have seemed to have "conquered the world" with your diplomas, trophies, job title, accomplishments, possessions and ever expanding business—you know deep down at the core of your being that none of these things is making you whole, complete, or satisfied.

Like David, you might be on the verge of breaking down and giving up on life for good. But I've got another message for you—better than any dish you've ever dug into, any paycheck you've ever received, and any precious accolades man has ever laid on you.

These words—these following verses—reveal the very answer to life. Read them carefully. In these words, you will find unadulterated truth, the secret of fulfillment, the love for which you have been longing, and the hope you have been holding out for. It is the *only thing* that will fill the eternal void and eclipse your every possession, pleasure, position, or lack thereof:

> *5 — "BUT I trust in your unfailing love;*
> *my heart rejoices in your salvation.*
> *6 — I will sing to the Lord, for he has been good to me."*

Hold up, I know what you're thinking.

"That's it? That's the so-called secret to life? You have got to be kidding! You had me so pumped—and that's all you got? How is *that* going to help me today? How is *that* going to pay the mortgage? How is *that* going to help my family? How is *that* going to stop the tears? How is *that* going to halt the divorce or stop my spouse from walking out on me? How is *that* going to bring back my kids? How is *that* going to erase my shattered past? How can *that* eclipse my accomplishments? And how in the world is *that* going to help my big butt?"

First, notice that David too had a **Big "BUT"**! It's true—he transitioned from a heavily burdened life of hardship to a life of eternal hope by using the word, **"BUT."** This word and this fifth verse from Psalm 13 have had a remarkable impact on my life: "**BUT** I trust in your unfailing love; my heart rejoices in your salvation." Hang with me here.

Do you know what David said when he met Goliath? You may have missed it, so let's take a closer look.

"You come against me with sword and spear and javelin, *BUT* I come against you in the name of the Lord Almighty, the God of the armies of Israel, whom you have defied." (1 Samuel 17: 45)

Do you see the *"Big BUT"*?

David never denied the truth of Goliath's strength and stature, but because Goliath was mocking God, he had to be dealt with. Everyone else was afraid to take on this giant, including King Saul. What made David great was that God was *real* to him, and he trusted in the Being who was higher than himself—God the Creator, the Sovereign God, the very source and Author of Life. What helped

David survive and overcome his heartaches, trials, hardships and betrayals was taking his eyes off himself and placing his trust in his Sovereign God.

You may say you don't believe in the Creator. I think that most people do believe. Some call Him Father God while others have coined the term "mother nature." I often remind myself that if I were given a handful of dirt, I couldn't breathe life into it. As an interventional cardiologist, I cannot dispense chemotherapy or perform a colonoscopy. I am, at best, limited, and my limitations testify to a source greater than I. But there is a God who is all knowing, all present, and all powerful. His "weakness" is stronger than man's strength and His "foolishness" is wiser than man's wisdom. Being intellectually honest allows me to admit that there is a force greater than myself. Not only is God unlimited, but His love for you and me is limitless.

Dr. Sam's Insight
Not only is God unlimited,
But His love for you and me is limitless.

While the whole army of Israel placed their hope in themselves and in their weapons—and fell short—David placed his trust in God's unfailing love. He had skills, but he knew the source of his skills and the God who could sharpen his talents.

I believe people are desperately searching for an answer today. I think you'll agree that we are facing many challenges in our attempts to *purchase* pleasure, secure happiness and experience lasting love. Some are plunging into drugs, and facing the dire fallout. Some are fixating on foods, and facing the big butt and the big gut consequences. Many are placing their trust in themselves, "things," and other people, only to be left more disappointed than ever.

The only true answer to anyone's needs is God's love.

In trying to help you experience the life-changing force I've experienced in my life, I am going to pose three questions in Part II of this chapter that you may be asking right now—plus the answers to each.

Part II: Finding Perspective

Question #1

If God is so good, why does He allow evil people to hurt others?

How could a God of love allow people like Phillip and Nancy Garrido to roam the earth? They abducted a precious 11-year-old girl, Jaycee Dugard, locked her up, raped her, impregnated her twice, imprisoned her for 18 years—and tormented the very souls of her family for almost two decades. It was a captivity worse than slavery, a hell on earth that most could not bear. Though Phillip Garrido was sentenced to 431 years in prison, how does that bring back Jaycee's 18 lost years?

I have come to understand that it grieves God when His creation acts in such evil ways.[64] While many of us may be quick to judge, God is compassionate and gracious, slow to anger and abounding in love.[65] He is patient, gives us the freedom to make the right choices, and longs for us to embrace His truth. If he didn't give Adam and Eve a choice or doesn't give you and me a choice, than that's forced love, which is no love at all. We want justice when it comes to others, but mercy when it comes to us. We want God to take others out, but forgive us. God continues to be patient, longing for us to turn to His truths. He will punish or discipline in time, but His thoughts and ways, not to mention timing, are higher than ours.[66] No matter what, His grace abounds!

Though we are limited beings and unable to explain many circumstances, we are teachable and, without a doubt, responsible. The lack of felony charges does not make us righteous. If we are brave enough to admit it, our insatiable cravings are not willing to be silenced, our pride is not willing to bow, and our greed is not willing to give in. When our pleasures take center stage, we lose the perspective of honoring God and serving others, and rather serve our thirsts. That's when we end up hurting others and hurting ourselves.

Dr. Sam's Insight
God is slow to anger and abounding in love.
Perhaps that's why He allows evil to occur.
No matter who we are, and no matter what we've done,
God is patient with you and me, and loves us unconditionally.

Question #2
Why do people who claim to know God act so ungodly?

Why do self-proclaimed "Christians" act like hypocrites? Why do church-goers look and act like non-church-goers? Why do so many pew-sitters have such a big butt? I believe it is because we are so self-absorbed with our problems, possessions, personal promotions, and pleasures that many times we forget the true source of contentment, goodness, and love: God.

He pleads with us to serve, but instead, we want to be served.

He asks us to put others first, but we want to be first at all times.

He instructs us to give, but we hoard and want more—calling it "savings"—and saturate our pleasures until our cup runs over.

Since He is love, and loves all people, He asks us to love our neighbor as we love ourselves. I think it's safe to admit that we miss the neighbor part of the deal many times over.

When culture and entertainment influence us more than God's word, then our perspectives and actions reflect it. What we fail to realize is the fact that he who searches for "life" in perishable, temporal things, will lose his life,[67] and he who finds God's wisdom will find life in abundance.[68]

Even those who know this truth tend to gripe, gossip and gorge. In turn, our testimony sheds a dark light; this in turn promotes cynicism, empowers critics and fuels resentment. Going to church doesn't make anyone a follower of Christ, unless he has met God, confessed, asked for forgiveness of sins, and received an "angioplasty" or cleansing of his soul's arteries, if you will.

True followers live "my life for Christ and others" instead of "my life for me." True followers forgive. True followers are here as telescopes and microscopes. If God is far off somewhere for others, true followers are to be telescopes, to "bring Him closer" so that others may see Him as He is, abounding in love, mercy and grace. If God is minuscule to others, true followers are to be microscopes, to "magnify Him" so that others may see His heart, which longs to bring healing to weary souls.

Truly, non-Christians also say one thing and do another.

They want world peace, but they have no inner peace. Some fight for tolerance, but are fueled with unquenchable hatred and are most intolerant to followers of Christ. They get so agitated because an offering plate is handed out in church when souls are being fed, while they have no problem paying a restaurant when their stomachs are being filled. They say they won't go to church because of hypocrites, but if you break your leg, are bleeding, and are sensible, you would go to the hospital, right? Well, the church is a spiritual hospital where the tax evaders, liars, adulterers and addicts are admitted.

You've got the ER, ICU, Cardiology Unit and Step Down Unit in a functional hospital. Same with the church: some who attend are critically ill, some are improving, some don't want to get well, and some float in and out. But just as there may be "bad" medicine or malpractice in a hospital, there can be inadequate ancillary care in the churches or "bad doctors" who are wolves in sheep's clothing. Unbelievers also call followers of Christ "narrow-minded" while they focus only on what is seen—the now, the physical—and miss out on the spiritual realm and eternity with God. And what's mind-boggling is that unbelievers reject God or God's Son, Christ, when they are alive, but want to go to heaven after they die. When hypocrites call others hypocrites, they too are hypocrites.

But God abounds in grace and mercy. His love triumphs over our inconsistencies and hypocrisies. No matter who we are, we are still responsible for our actions. The irony of it all is that whether we are church-goers or club bouncers, none of us are righteous. God loves us *despite* ourselves, longs to heal us of our past, and yearns to provide us with hope on our journey.

Dr. Sam's Insight

Whether we are church-goers or club bouncers,
none of us are righteous.
God loves us despite ourselves,
longs to heal us of our past,
and yearns to provide us with hope on our journey.

Question #3
How could a kind God condemn people?

God does not want to condemn anyone. The prophet Ezekiel proclaimed God's words in Ezekiel 18:23: "Do I take any pleasure in the death of the wicked?" declares the Sovereign Lord. "Rather, am I not pleased when they turn from their ways and live?" God does not condemn; He saves.

We have all gone astray, and have all fallen short of God's glory; He is not sending us to eternal death, we're going there on our own accord, and by our very nature; He is saving us from eternal death to give us eternal life and secure our eternal foundation.[69]

**A loving God is faultless in dispensing justice.
But His heart bleeds with grace and forgiveness.**

He is offering us hope in the midst of hardship and heartaches. His word, the Bible, is the only source that provides relevant answers for today's problems. Nothing in all creation is hidden from God's sight. He will never be outdated even in our progressive world. He has created progression; He can handle yesterday, today, and even tomorrow all in one setting![70]

Remember what David said in Psalm 13:5? "My heart rejoices in your salvation." Despite his horrible circumstances, David still rejoiced. Why? How? Because he had found salvation. Where can we find salvation?

Should we not first seek internal strength and salvation within ourselves, and then search for an external being? Would that not give us more credibility as we arrive with our own wits and strength, creating our own destiny? We can search within ourselves, but a quick glance in the mirror will reveal our imperfections and will either lead us to dismay, lies, or pride. Trusting in God does not give us the option to neglect the pursuit of excellence; but no matter how skilled we are, we cannot create or find salvation within ourselves or our accomplishments. An honest reflection reveals, at best, a heart of fear, festering wounds, irrefutable envy and endless frailty.

So what is the answer? Where is salvation found? It is found in God's love.

If we are facing our Goliaths alone and believing in our own strength, we will soon find that we've ignored the very God who loves us and gives us strength, ability, intellect, opportunity and life. David knew where to turn and who to trust. He states in Psalm 20:7, "Some trust in chariots and some in horses, **BUT** we trust in the name of the LORD our God."

In Psalm 62:1 David states, "My soul finds rest in God alone; my salvation comes from Him." Salvation comes from God and it means that He saves us. From what? From our mortal selves, from our greed, from our insecurities, from our pain, from our past, and from our sinful nature—which leads to eternal death, hell and separation from God.

The mere denial of God does not make Him disappear. He is very much involved in our lives and His grace gives us the breath to carry on and endure. Some believe in heaven but not hell. Some believe there is nothing beyond the grave. But truly, life runs in parallels. For instance, we have light and we have darkness. We have hot and we have cold. We have small and we have big. We have short and we have tall. We have good and we have evil. We have God and we have Satan. We have heaven and we have hell. If we can't stand the thought of hell, we are not given the privilege to "cancel" it out. God is not in the business of orchestrating our admission to hell; He has graciously provided us the gift of salvation which will save us from hell.

I guess many people have a hard time believing that a holy God truly loves them. For many, the guilt of the past brings uneasiness, resentment, and even an excuse to reject Him. How can the gap be fixed between a holy God and greedy, unholy, messed up people like us? What is the answer to this enigma? It is found in the gift of God's Son, His love, His Salvation, His answer to our prideful hearts: Jesus Christ, who gave His life freely on the cross, and rose to conquer sin, death, and pain on the third day. Why Him? According to the Bible, He is the only Way, the only One, who can take our guilt and sin and place it on Himself, and in return take God's holiness and grace and place it on us. That is the only way of redemption. Not through man— we're all sinners—but only through Christ.

According to the prophet Isaiah, "He was pierced for *our* transgressions. He was crushed for *our* iniquities; the punishment that brought us peace was upon Him and by His wounds we are healed."[71] Isaiah further states in 53:6, "We all like sheep have gone astray, each of us has turned to his own way, and the Lord has laid on Christ the iniquity of us all." Three hundred years before death by crucifixion was even invented, King David prophesied in Psalm 22:16 that Jesus would have His hands and feet pierced. And in the death of Jesus Christ we were given an eternal gift, where a sinless man, Jesus, God's Son, humbled himself and died for sinful man, us, in order to reconcile us to a Holy God, so we may enter into heaven.[72]

According to the Bible, "Whoever believes in Christ shall not perish but have eternal life."[73] It is not through our good behavior or good deeds or lack of a murder rap sheet that we will get to heaven; otherwise, who would decide exactly how much good we would have to do? And how many mission trips should we go on? And wouldn't we be boasting about our goodness and stating that we earned our way into heaven?

One good person's goodness is not weighed out against the bad he's done, in hopes that his good deeds, generous gifts, and helping hand overshadows and outweighs his bad deeds and thus gets him into heaven. It's not the murderer or rapist or "bad person" that's got an automatic admission into hell; *all* of us are born in sin. Our very nature separates us from God, and no matter what our status, achievements, earnings, disposition, beliefs, actions, upstanding citizenship, generosity or "goodness," the consequences of sin are eternal death and hell. But there is a way of forgiveness, salvation and reconciliation, and it is not man-made or manipulated by man. The Bible states that it is *by grace through faith*—and this not from ourselves—it is the gift of God, not by works, so that no one can boast.[74]

Dr. Sam's Insight

God is not "in the business" of
unrelenting condemnation.
He is "in the business" of soul resuscitation—
and securing our eternal foundation.

Part III: Finding Purpose

God created mankind in order to have a loving relationship with us. Satan, who was a beautiful and blameless angel, became prideful, tried to ascend above God's throne and overthrow God, and then was cast out of heaven with the angels he influenced—one-third of the angel population in heaven. Satan "infected" the hearts of man, Adam and Eve, with the virus of pride. This virulent sin of pride contaminated the souls of mankind. As man multiplied, sin abounded, manifesting itself through malice, hatred, rebellion, murder and every kind of evil.

God gave His laws, the Ten Commandments, through Moses so we would know how to love God and love our neighbor. Israel was chosen to carry God's light to the world, but fell short. God asked the Israelites to slaughter a lamb so when He witnessed the blood of the animal He would forgive them for their sins; according to Leviticus 17:11, the life of a creature is in the blood, and because sin required atonement, the blood of an animal like a lamb had to be spilled.

Despite rules, rituals, judges, priests and prophets, man was unable to devote himself to God or save himself. And since our sins lead to eternal death, God sent His Son, Jesus Christ as the perfect and sinless lamb, who came to die on the cross, spill His blood, place our sins on Him, take our punishment on Himself, and impart His holiness to us. Because His own rejected Him, the Word and gift of salvation went out to the entire world for all people. There is no more need for animal sacrifice. Our debt was paid once and for all through Christ! That's an unfair substitution, that's unmerited grace, and that's unending love. He is the only God who died for us; He is the only God who rose from the dead for us; and Christ is the only way to eternal life.

Today we find ourselves at a crossroads, whether to accept the fact we are sinners and in desperate need of a Savior or to go on thinking that we—mankind—can save ourselves. Only pride, the same sin that originally deceived Satan, will hold us back from making a commitment.

Christ is coming back again to, first, claim those who have accepted Him and, second, defeat Satan. No man knows when He is coming back, but He won't be riding on a donkey, or present Himself with humility this time. He is coming as a Conqueror. If we accept the fact that we are sinners and respond to His act of love on our behalf, His blood will wipe away all our sins, and we will be indwelt and guided by His Spirit.

If we reject God's way of salvation, then we will die in our sins. There are two places to go after death: heaven or hell, both of which are forever. In a split second we will make a choice. That choice will not only last a lifetime here on earth, but an eternity in heaven or hell. God doesn't force us. He simply loves us and longs to walk with us. It is too late to make a decision after we die. He will extend his grace even up to our very last breath. The time to choose is *now*. Today. Christ's followers will reunite with God in heaven eternally, but Christ's rejecters cannot unite with God. Satan will ultimately lose, and be thrown with the souls of all Christ's rejecters into eternal hell. That's Satan's goal: to steal, kill and destroy. Christ will rule in a tear-free, sick-free, and sin-free heaven with all His saints forever and ever. That's God's heart: to love, to heal and to give life abundantly.

How can you be sure He's for real? Prophecy fulfilled over the centuries verifies it! Six hundred years before His birth, it was prophesied that the Messiah would be born in Bethlehem, and the government would be on His shoulders; He would be betrayed for 30 pieces of silver; He would enter Jerusalem riding a donkey; and He would be crucified. All were fulfilled. Now let's look ahead to the future. For every prophecy regarding His first coming, there are eight prophesies about His second coming. You can bet the farm that He is coming again!

It is all by God's love; it is all by Christ's obedience unto death; and it is all by the Spirit's indwelling power. He saves our souls.

But God is a gentleman. He gives us a choice. If we don't want Him, we shouldn't be mad at Him. If we reject God and His Son in our fleeting years, we cannot "gain access" to heaven after we die, because we would be "miserable" living with God and His Son in our eternal years. One way or the other, it's a choice all of us make. Make your choice as if your eternal life depends on it... because it does! Remember, He sees us as who we are and what we've done, and He loves us anyway!

Dr. Sam's Insight
This uncompromising set of statements will be viewed by some as absolute or relative; either way they're right— it is absolutely essential and irrefutably relevant.

Christ rose from the grave on the third day and sent His Spirit to live in those who have accepted Him. What joy, peace, and life He gives—not only here on earth, but the eternal life to come! If we confess with our mouth, "Jesus is Lord," and believe in our hearts that God raised Him from the dead, we will be saved.[75] To accept God's gift by confessing and believing in Him results in eternal life. But to reject Him results in eternal death.[76]

"That's bogus," you say! "That's exclusive and intolerant." The Bible makes it clear in John 3:16 that Jesus is *all* inclusive: for God so loved *the world*, the entire world, that He gave His only Son, Jesus, that whoever believes in Him will not perish but have everlasting life.

Can't I get to God and heaven by myself, any religion, any path, any savior, or any other way? All other man-invented ways are a belief that we can elevate ourselves to God by our own accomplishments, somehow achieving access into heaven by being a good person; all these paths have subscribers who are unsure of their final destiny until after death. Following Christ is a belief that God, instead of elevating Himself, humbled Himself unto death, loves us despite our past, accepts us as we are, and gets in the mire with us and lifts us out; it gives us the assurance of abundant life to enjoy today and an eternal life after death in heaven with Him.

Think of it this way—Jesus came not to start a religion but to restore a relationship between a holy God and unholy man that had been broken by sin. There is no love like God's. Through His Son, He wipes out our past mistakes by forgiving us. There is nothing we can do that makes Him love us more, and there is nothing we have done or are doing that can make Him love us less. We struggle with this concept because we are achievers, having gained our status in life by hard work and overcoming obstacles. For many, it is difficult to perceive that we cannot "achieve" salvation nor can we "clinch" God's love on our own merit. God simply loves us! Once again, it comes down to a choice whether or not we accept this wonderful gift.

Dr. Sam's Insight

There is nothing we can do that makes God love us more, and there is nothing we have done that makes Him love us less!

God helps us in our troubles, heartaches, shortcomings, and difficulties by walking with us through the storms. He wipes away our tears and gives us great hope for tomorrow by promising to be the light in our darkness, today. Though our actions have consequences in the form of discipline, divine retribution is not the source behind our pain. Nothing we have said or done—nothing—can separate us from the love of this compassionate God. Looking for unmerited grace and immeasurable mercy? Looking for *real* love? Looking for supernatural strength to overcome your present circumstances? Looking for answers? Looking for the strength to overcome the sins that have mastery over you? Looking for your purpose in life? God is waiting for you! In Matthew 11:28, Jesus said, "Come to me all you who are weary and burdened, and I will give you rest." That's the deal of a lifetime!

Dr. Sam's Insight

Deal of a lifetime and beyond...

Substitution: Christ took on our sins and died the death that belonged to us.

Redemption: Christ paid the price for our sins and atoned for us.

Forgiveness: God does not hold our past sins against us.

Justification: God declares us no longer guilty.

Reconciliation: Christ brings us back into fellowship with God.

Sanctification: God, by His Spirit, sets us apart so we can bring Him glory.

Glorification: When the last breath is taken, we'll be ushered into God's glory.

"How can you ask me to give up everything?" you may ask. Securing "life" on earth can be a pursuit that lasts as long as we do—50, 70, perhaps 100 years; then it ends. By surrendering your life to Jesus Christ, you will discover your purpose, enrich your life, find immense peace, experience great joy, and secure a life that will last an eternity, with God, forever.

Why should we give up our dreams and life to Him? Because He will enrich our dreams, give us a vision beyond our own limitations, and give us the strength to accomplish the impossible. He doesn't strip us of our purpose. He *gives* us a purpose: to serve Him and others with a compassionate heart. He's not a dream killer. He's a dream giver and dream maker! If you were forced to make a decision against your will, that would not be love. God is love, because He is the only God who has given us the freedom to choose.

Dr. Sam's Insight

Salvation is the only means to secure our eternal foundation.

Will we have constant success, prosperity and goodness when we walk with Him? No, we'll face plenty of problems and taste many tears and sufferings, like King David, but the Sovereign God of love will be our strength, shield, salvation, song and our very present help in times of trouble.[77]

How did David make it? By looking at what God had done and what Christ was to do.

How can we make it? By looking at what Christ has done and what God is going to do!

Seriously, you can pray right now, making the most important decision of your life. The thief on the cross simply said, "Jesus, remember me when you come into your kingdom."[78] It's not the words or the length of the prayer; it's the *heart* behind the words and the prayer.

I don't have a formulated prayer, but you can say something like this: "Father, I want a relationship with you. I want you to be my God, Savior and Lord. I accept the fact that I'm a sinner, and that Jesus, who had no sin, became sin for me and made me righteous by dying on the cross and paying the price for me. I've done things that I'm not proud of, and have kept them secret. I thought I had to be 'clean' or 'right' so that you'd accept me. I thought you hated me. I thought you didn't believe in me, so in turn, I didn't believe in you. All of that doesn't matter anymore. I come to you as I am with all my sins and ask you to wash it all away by the blood of Christ, the risen Savior. God you are now my friend. I'm blown away. I'm not perfect, but I am forgiven!

"Because of your grace you love a person such as me. I'll likely mess up again, so I ask that you teach me your ways and empower me by your Holy Spirit to guide me and counsel me. I'm still blown away that you won't hold my sinful past against me. I am yours. I belong to the King of Kings! I am set free, bonds are broken, I'm finally liberated, justified, a new creation, and reconciled to you! I understand my purpose in life. It is to bring honor to you by serving you and others with the talents you have given me. It is to choose joy despite my circumstances. It is to rely on your strength and wisdom in all things. And it is to give you praise all the days of my life. I am so humbled and ever grateful. Take me and use me for your glory. In Jesus' precious name I pray, Amen and Amen!"

Dr. Sam's Insight
Choices are made every day. Let your choice in this matter be a wise one.

If you earnestly prayed the above prayer, welcome to a life of peace beyond understanding, strength beyond yourself, and joy beyond measure.

40 BENEFITS OF THE BIG BUT

Right about now you may be thinking, what's God got to do with my weight? God not only gives strength to the weary and restores them, but He also gives supernatural help and guidance to those who find themselves trapped, yet who call on His name.[79] Occasionally life reaches a boiling point where it becomes almost unbearable. King David once again helps us find the way to the truth: "I lift up my eyes to the hills—where does my help come from? My help comes from the Lord, the Maker of heaven and earth."[80]

God helps you "reframe" life. That's not a cop-out for working hard, achieving, training, sharpening your skills, struggling, going beyond expectations or completing the task. In fact, followers of Christ should work harder, be more joyful and be more humble because they understand their destiny!

Today I stand only because of God's grace. Yes, I still face setbacks, disappointments, failures and betrayals, *BUT* "I am more than a conqueror through Him who loves me."[81]

Yes, I face many foes, detractors, and people who want to see me go down hard, *BUT* "If God is for me, who can be against me? The Lord is my light and salvation, whom shall I fear? The Lord is the stronghold of my life, of whom shall I be afraid?"[82]

Yes, I am at times puzzled and troubled about my hardships, tears and God's silence in my unanswered prayers, *BUT* "I know that *in all things* God works for the good of those who love Him, who have been called according to His purpose."[83] Hardships are inevitable, but they don't dictate my joy or peace. Despite hardships we press onward, work, pray, and choose thankfulness and joy!

Yes, I am hard pressed on every side, **BUT** "I am not crushed; I am perplexed, **BUT** not in despair; I am persecuted, **BUT** not abandoned; I am struck down, **BUT** not destroyed."[84]

Yes, I have come close to my breaking point, and have often told God, "I thought you would only give me what I could bear, **BUT** 'His grace is sufficient for me, for His power is made perfect in my weakness.'"[85]

Yes, I am faced with the impossible when it looks like there are no solutions, **BUT** "I can do all things through Him who strengthens me."[86]

Yes, I am overcome with trouble, and hardship upon hardship, **BUT** "Even though I walk through the valley of the shadow of death, I will fear no evil for you are with me; your rod and your staff, they comfort me."[87]

Yes, I am unsure, and at times uncertain and insecure, **BUT** "My God will instruct me and teach me in the way I should go; He will counsel me and watch over me."[88]

Yes, at times I am lonely and scared, **BUT** I hear Him say, "Do not fear, for I am with you; do not be dismayed, for I am your God. I will strengthen you and help you; I will uphold you with my righteous right hand."[89]

Yes, I am attacked, **BUT** "I am victorious."[90]

Yes, I am sinking, **BUT** "He lifted me out of the slimy pit, out of the mud and mire; He set my feet on a rock and gave me a firm place to stand. He put a new song in my mouth."[91]

Yes, I am overwhelmed, **BUT** "I have been given a great purpose by God."[92]

Yes, I am hurt, **BUT** "I trust in God's unfailing love."[93]

Yes, I am beat, **BUT** "I have a refuge."[94]

Yes, I am falling, **BUT** "I am sustained."[95]

Yes, I was lost, **BUT** "I am found."[96]

You can take the ***Big BUT*** with you everywhere. You don't need to compartmentalize God's word. You need to exercise your privileges and rights as a child of God. A ***Big BUT*** looks at a situation, stares reality, depression, despair, disappointments, dejection, and failure in the eye, reframes the scene and states, "You thought you had me, **BUT** I will overcome by God's grace!"

A ***Big BUT*** looks at a big butt and says, "Man you have defeated me all my life, **BUT** no longer. I will overcome by God's power in me!"

In the same way, a ***Big BUT*** looks at an impossible situation and says, "I am down and in the pit, and I don't see a way out, **BUT** my God will help me, deliver me and sustain me! It is not by might, it is not by power, **BUT** by the guidance and indwelling of the Holy Spirit in me, I will prevail!"

Even Jesus understood the power of a ***Big BUT*** in John 16:33 by saying, "In this world you will have trouble. **BUT** take heart, I have overcome the world." Do you see how He can catapult us from a grungy natural level to a supernatural level?

Is God my crutch? No, God is my source of life, strength, hope, joy, peace, contentment and salvation. He is my power source. No amount of money, charisma, strength or prominence can ever generate such power, and will ultimately fall short on all counts. No matter what life deals me, including victories, losses, betrayal, suffering, failures, hardship or unanswered prayers, my God carries me through. In no way does that exempt me from aspiring, equipping, working, training, achieving, or serving my fellow man. I am who I am solely by the grace of God, and I was born to mend hearts and heal souls! Crutch? No, He is the Rock upon which I stand—the Rock of my Salvation—who enables, equips and empowers me to rock your very planet!

What about you? Have you turned to this magnificent God for your salvation, for your sure help in time of need? He is calling out to you this very moment . . .

Here I am!
I stand at the door and knock.
If anyone hears my voice and opens the door,
I will come in and eat with that person, and they with me.[97]

Whatever your past—good, bad or simply unmentionable. Whoever influenced you or hurt and crushed you—family, a "trusted" family friend, or an outsider. Whatever your present—you may have loaded pockets or holes in your pockets. Wherever you found your fortune or misfortune. However you got yourself in the world of success or the cyclone of failure. You may have filled your belly with much in order to feed your cravings or bury your sorrows. You may have filled your walls with diplomas that would put a rocket scientist to shame. Or you may have filled your heart with anger, resentment or fear. No matter what, you need a Savior. You need healing from the past. And you need to start thinking about where you are going to spend eternity. None of this will benefit you if you don't accept Christ's love for you as the Savior of your soul.

Come as you are and come with what you've got. You are loved no matter what. No worries. When God sent His Son, He slept in a stinking manger not a shining mansion. That alone tells you who He is: a gentle and humble Spirit who loves you no matter what your story. You are loved no matter what you've said or done. He is not in the business of judging you; He loves you and longs to heal your wounded heart. It's time for you to realize that just as you feed the body with good food, you need to feed the soul with the truth as was revealed in the previous chapter.

If you have already accepted Him, and cannot seem to get out of the grunge of life including habits like overeating, your God has not abandoned you. He longs to help you with the power of His Spirit. The battles we face on earth are not overcome by our might, power or intellect, but by the Spirit of the Living God.[98]

The root of failure is the love of self, the love of pleasure and the desire to feed the bottomless pit of self-gratification. In II Timothy 3:1–5, we find that men will be lovers of pleasure and without self control. But there is endless hope in Christ as we find in II Timothy 1:7, "For God did not give us a spirit of timidity, but a spirit of power, of love and of self discipline." The author, Paul, is instructing young Timothy to be bold as he proclaims God's Word. But the same power and self discipline can be and must be applied to every aspect of our lives. The spirit of self discipline is already given to us; it is our choice to accept it and put it to use.

To help you focus on the journey, I am providing you with some tools. You have your earthly physical body, **but** perceiving this body as God's temple is absolutely essential. I Corinthians 3:16 reads, "Don't you know that you yourselves are God's temple and that God's Spirit lives in you?" When we embrace this and the fact that God's temple is sacred, we'll start caring for it and respecting it with great honor. This is a matter of stewardship: We are responsible to God, we are accountable to God, and we are to honor God. We are given only one temple, and we need to have a deep longing to handle it with great care. Please consider this, not out of guilt, but out of service and *obedience* to the Lord.

Solomon is a bit more graphic in Proverbs 23:2: "Put a knife to your throat if you are given to gluttony." It's true that you want seconds, you want one more doughnut, you want one more scoop… **but** if you recall that God has given you the power of self-discipline and your body is God's temple, you can "put a knife to your throat" (speaking only figuratively), stop eating, and continue on your journey with a bigger smile, a smaller frame and a healthier you.

Dr. Sam's Insight
Simply put, the desire to honor God's temple must be stronger than the desire to feed, serve and worship the cravings of the belly and the body.

In your struggle, do not give up. If you fail, press on. Continue to hope. Continue to work. And continue to pray. Prayer should be an integral part of losing weight, not used as a "crutch," but as fuel, to receive supernatural power in helping you overcome the desire to eat in excess.

You can even pray now by saying, "Father, I belong to you, and I have been washed by the blood of the Lamb, Jesus Christ. I don't understand why I can't trump my eating habits. I tried praying, confessing, fasting, and begging—and still feel defeated. Please empower me by your Spirit to conquer my compulsions. You bear the wounds, I experience the healing. I trust in you and want to bring you honor in all that I think, say, and do. I am yours, and I ask that you cleanse me, wash me, deliver me, and sustain me, for I am made new in Christ.

"Holy Spirit, guide me and help me to be obedient unto God. Help me to be aware of the power you have given me, and empower me to use that gift of self-discipline in order to bring honor and glory to your temple. In all my difficulties and hardships, I am more than a conqueror in Jesus Christ who loves me! I am going to overcome and press on with your might! The past can stay in the past. Today, I am renewed, empowered and set to prevail by your Spirit so I can bring you the glory. In Jesus' precious name I pray, Amen and Amen!"

You're not a body that has a soul and spirit.

You're a soul and spirit that has a body.

Understand who you are.

Know what is sacred.

Feed your soul with God's Word, the Bible, for it will encourage you to triumph.

Feed your spirit with God's abounding love, for it will give you the strength to endure!

Cast off the past, stand tall and press on!

Testimonial #11

NICOLE BEFORE

Hi. My name is Nicole Cruz and I am 38 years old. This story begins when I was about 33. My husband and I were trying to conceive a baby, but were not successful after one and a half years, so we began the infertility process. Going through that process was very taxing on my body. I gained 10 pounds just from the hormones. After 4 rounds of infertility treatments, we are happy to say that we have 2 beautiful children now—twins! Of course carrying twins means carrying around a lot of extra weight. I am 5 feet tall, and when I delivered my babies I weighed 200 pounds. I quickly lost about 40 pounds, but the rest seemed like it would never come off.

After having the twins, I started to develop shortness of breath. I went to the doctor and after going through a variety of tests, the results came back that I was suffering from anxiety. One of the tests however was an ECG, which showed that I have left ventricular hypertrophy— which, if you Google anything on the Internet about it, says you are going to die. I was terrified. I needed to be around for my children! I inquired about a couple of cardiologists in the area and was referred to Dr. Kojoglanian by my grandmother. She said how amazing he was and called him the "Mender of Hearts."

Boy was she right!

When I first met Dr. Kojoglanian I was 36. He had me perform a stress test and after reviewing everything, he said I was basically healthy, but that I needed to lose weight. Of course every woman wants to hear that, right? He showed me where I was for my BMI; and for my height and weight, I was considered obese. Really? It was that bad?

Dr. Kojoglanian prayed with me and something in me transformed. Prayer changes a person's life. I thought about my kids and how young I was and decided I needed to change something. But what? I had tried diets before and never really lost all that much weight. Dr. Kojoglanian helped me believe that I could do this with God's strength, and without pills, programs or "diets." After changing my lifestyle and eating habits, cutting back my portions, and incorporating exercise into my routine at least 3 times a week, I am happy to say that I have lost 40 pounds! I am down to my high school weight, and went from a size 14 to a size 4! I have never been a 4 in all my life!

It took work to get here. It took discipline. And it takes work to stay here, but it's worth it. It gets easier to say "no" to too much food! My stomach has gotten smaller and I don't have the need to keep on filling myself; in fact, I feel full faster now than ever before!

If it weren't for Dr. Kojoglanian and how inspirational he is, I would still be considered obese and on the road to having other cardiac and blood pressure

NICOLE AFTER

problems. And guess what? My anxiety is gone as well. I believe being overweight was causing the anxiety in my life.

I visited Dr. Kojoglanian this year for a stress test. I had better numbers this year than last year, and feel so much better about myself, my life, and most importantly, I am around to watch my children grow up.

Thank you, Dr. Kojoglanian, for being a huge blessing in my life. God's hands are on you, and you truly do mend hearts— physically, emotionally, mentally and spiritually.

— Nicole Cruz

41 | BUILDING TO CODE

After Hurricane Andrew dealt its immense devastation to the Miami area in 1992, a reporter interviewed a man whose house withstood the storm. "Sir, why is your house the only one standing?" the reporter asked. "How could it have been the only one in this area to escape the damage of the hurricane?"

"I built this house myself," the survivor said. "I built it according to the Florida state building code. When the code called for two-by-six roof trusses, I used two-by-six roof trusses. I was told that a house built according to code could withstand a hurricane. I did, and it did! I suppose no one else around here followed the code."

We have spoken much about healthy living and building our lives on solid foundations. We have seen that the consequences of "breeching the code" bring debilitating harm and havoc to our bodies. Likewise, as we live our brief lives here on earth, each of us is confronted with a choice—will we build our eternal futures and the destiny of our souls by God's codes, or by our own codes? Will we walk in His ways or say, "I'll do it my way?" The choice cannot be ignored—it will determine where we spend eternity.

In Luke 6:46–49, Jesus told the parable of two men building houses for their families. I suppose they both loved their families, but the first man must have been lacking foresight, because he hurriedly built his house on sand. The second man wanted his house to last; he was thinking of the future, so he laid the foundation on solid rock. When the torrents of rain came, the floods rose, and the winds blew, the house on the sand washed away, but the house on the rock withstood the storm.

Though maybe not apparent at first glance, this story is about you and me and every person who ever lived. Some of us will choose to build our lives on sand: on *our own* accord, by our own rules, in our own strength, with our own beliefs, using our own resources and reasoning, and standing on our own accomplishments.

Others will build on the solid Rock, Jesus Christ, who tells us to take heart because He has already overcome the world.[99] When life turns to dust and breath is no more, the person who built his life on any foundation other than Christ the Rock will find that his man-made foundation has no substantial value; he will live forever in torment, separated from God. Meanwhile, the one who built his life on the solid Rock will meet his Maker after death and his life will be secured eternally in heaven.

Christ is the cornerstone, the very breath and life of the building, body and soul. According to the Bible, salvation is found in no one else, for there is no other name under heaven given to men by whom we can be saved.[100]

The Bible is the only book that cannot be refuted—archeologically, historically, or prophetically. Any attempt to explain its contents away is intellectually dishonest. And if you were to try to explain it away without reading it first, how open-minded or scientific is that? Any attempt to ignore its contents is spiritual suicide. Once we have tasted failure or success, betrayal or loyalty, loss or gain, sadness or happiness, we must realize there is a yearning deep within us, for comfort, acceptance, assurance and redemption. When we are alone and face the lonely night hours, the desperate fears, and the trying heartaches, if we are willing to tell the truth, we will begin to verbalize our desire for help, hope, and honor, which can only be found in the Solid Rock.

Unfair?

What about those who have never heard God's Word, you ask?

His Word is written in each person's heart, and no one is without excuse.[101] It would be unfair if we didn't have instructions, if we didn't have the "code." Each person is responsible for his own thoughts and actions. Not only is His Word written on our hearts, but the skies speak of God's glory in every language, tribe, and nation:

> *The heavens declare the glory of God;*
> *the skies proclaim the work of his hands.*
> *Day after day they pour forth speech;*
> *night after night they display knowledge.*
> *There is no speech or language*
> *where their voice is not heard.*
> *Their voice goes out into all the earth,*
> *their words to the ends of the world.*[102]

It comes down to making a choice, but it's your choice to make. People will search their entire lives to fill their empty, anxious and fearful hearts, coming up with one temporary solution after another. They look to fill the void with food, success, education, drugs, money, possessions, alcohol, restaurants, relationships, travels, trophies, cars, houses, gold, sports and entertainment.

But if each of us searches deep within, we will still feel the emptiness. We will still say, "I have lived life as fully as I could, and this is it?" There is nothing wrong with riches and possessions, with accomplishments and accolades, and the many pleasures God has given to us, unless they become our gods and the very codes on which we build our lives. If these are what our hopes are built on, then our foundation is made of sand, and our condition is spiritually bankrupt.

How sure is your eternal foundation? I truly hope and pray that you build your soul on the Solid Rock. Your eternity depends on it.

42 | THE BREAD OF LIFE

Okay, by now you might be asking, "What are you saying, Doc? I thought we were talking about weight loss and now we're talking about 'buts' and 'rocks'? Do I have to walk with God to lose weight?" You can lose weight with or without God, and you can certainly live your whole life with or without Him. But here's something to chew on—the temporary body we are given belongs to God and we are given the responsibility to care for it with honor and to cultivate it with goodness, health, and a servant's heart.

People who place their trust in Christ realize and come to appreciate the knowledge, "That you yourselves are God's temple and that God's Spirit lives in you."[103] If you've accepted God's gift, His Son, then the Spirit of the living God dwells within you! There is human strength and there is *supernatural* strength; the Spirit of God gives us supernatural strength to control all addictions, including the cravings for food.

We bring God glory in many ways: through our thoughts, our actions, our motives, our attitudes, and our bodies. Keeping God's commands in our hearts is the way of wisdom, for the Bible says His ways "will prolong your life many years," and fearing Him will "bring health to your body and nourishment to your bones."[104] Each time we eat, we should first thank our God for His provisions and then curb our appetites for His glory, for we are His temple.

As we saw in Chapter 40, the Bible speaks clearly and calls things as they are. Again, "Put a knife to your throat if you are given to gluttony," means back off, stop treating your cravings and belly like a god, and bring discipline to the table…every time! Don't let your stomach be your god; let your God be your God!

Dr. Sam's Insight

**Don't let your stomach be your God—
Let your God be your God!**

One way to "dethrone" the god of our stomachs is to take part in a temporary fast. Though it is mandatory in the practice of medicine prior to certain procedures and surgeries, fasting can be a voluntarily spiritual observation. It entails abstaining from food for varying lengths of time, and indicates the desire to deny oneself and to seek a more intimate relationship with God. This can be done for one meal or more, and should be done only with the consultation and supervision of your physician.

Fasting can deliver physical benefits, like detoxifying our bodies from the many preservatives we've ingested; it can also lower blood pressure, cholesterol, and sugar levels. The spiritual benefits of fasting are many, and include a time of drawing near to God, a time of reminding us that we were born to serve others, and a time to seek God's face, will, favor, anointing, strength, direction, victory, wisdom, freedom from sins, and miracles. The 58th chapter of Isaiah encourages us to fast, not to make noise and boast about it, but to untie and break every yoke.[105] I ask you…have you got any untying to do?

We've already talked about bread being one of the three main foods that are causing obesity, along with cheese and ice cream. However, there is bread that I recommend for daily consumption. In John 6:35 Christ declared, "I am the Bread of Life. He who comes to me will never go hungry, and he who believes in me will never be thirsty." According to God's word, man does not live on bread alone, but on every word that comes from the mouth of the Lord.[106]

Dr. Sam's Insight
Are you searching for the meaning of your existence? Nothing will make sense, satisfy or sustain you without the Bread of Life— Christ is the Author of Life and the only one who can bring fulfillment in your life.

Unfortunately, in today's progressive society—and I use the word 'progressive' cautiously as I see the character of man degenerate more and more—many people indulge on the physical bread alone, much more than they spend time with God's living Word. Therefore, many people who sit in the church pews across our land are physically obese, yet spiritually anorexic. Oh, don't get me wrong; we can be slim physically, and be equally as godless.

We should encourage one another, striving to have the attitude and lifestyle found in Job 23:12, "I have not departed from the commands of His lips; I have treasured the words of His mouth more than my daily bread." You and I will reap immeasurable benefits if we cut down on the bread for life while we maximize our hunger for the Bread of Life, Jesus Christ, the only true food for the soul and spirit.

In the Book of Proverbs, wisdom calls out from the highest point in the city, "Let all who are simple come to me. Come, eat my food and drink the wine I have made. Leave your simple ways and you will live, walk in the way of understanding." The "food" that our God offers us is His Word, His wisdom—and it is sweeter than honey and more precious than gold![107]

The great prophet Isaiah also encourages the reader to eat the Bread of God, the living Bread, the life-giving Bread: "Come, all who are thirsty, come to the waters; and you who have no money, come, buy and eat! Come buy wine and milk without money and without cost. Why spend money on what is not bread, and your labor on what does not satisfy? Listen, listen to me, and eat what is good and your soul will delight in the riches of fare. Give ear and come to me; hear me that your soul may live."[108]

And if you are searching for the best fruit for your appetite, no worries, I found it for you, nicely arranged in the Galatians Section, Aisle 5:22–23, "But the fruit of the Spirit is love, joy, peace, patience, kindness, goodness, faithfulness, gentleness and self-control." You say, "Yeah right, I wish, but I don't have any of this, especially self-control!" No, you're mistaken; it's already done because as we read in Galatians 5:24, those who belong to Christ Jesus have crucified the sinful nature with its passions and desires. We need to be aware of that, understand it, accept it, and by the power of the Holy Spirit, keep in step with it.

It all depends on you, with God's abiding help. The goodness of God lies before you. Remember, there is *nothing* you can do that makes Him love you more and there is *nothing* you have done that makes Him love you less. It has all been done, for if someone dies for you as motivated by divine love, what more can you do?

What no bank or money can do, Jesus can do. What no church or pastor can do, Jesus can do. What no institute or rituals can do, Jesus can do. What no law enforcement or prison can do, Jesus can do. What no hospital or physician can do, Jesus can do. What no college or diploma can do, Jesus can do. What no business or business person can do, Jesus can do. What no chef or food can do, Jesus can do. He accepts, forgives, heals, redeems, justifies, and sanctifies.

The only thing that stops anyone from coming to Christ is pride. Pride is the cyanide that ravages the soul. It may not kill the person in his prime, but when the last breath is taken, that soul will face eternal separation from God.

Dr. Sam's Insight
Pride is the cyanide that ravages the soul.

I urge you to seek the Bread of Life. If your convictions, intellect, training, reputation, and self respect demand another explanation, think on this: there will never be anyone else who knows you, loves you as you are, and has the power to change your eternal destiny. God will accept you with open arms and carry you, heal you of your broken past, and give you the power to stand firm. Come as you are, and enter through the door that will change the course of your life. Come and eat of the Bread that gives you hope. He is the *only* Bread you cannot do without!

IV.

TOMORROW'S TALE

The Reality, The Future

43 | HEART PORTFOLIO

Today's timely choices will greatly influence tomorrow's tales. The best way to take care of tomorrow is to take care of today. The best way of healing you tomorrow is to take steps toward healing you today. And the best way to secure a strong foundation tomorrow is to attentively work on your firm foundation today. Don't ignore today—it will dictate your tomorrow!

Throughout this book we have read stories of obese patients who weighed more than 200 pounds. Bo is a 52-year-old male, who is five-feet-ten-inches tall, weighs 194 pounds, with a BMI of 28. As you recall, a BMI of 18.5 to 25 is normal, 25 to 30 is overweight, and above 30 is considered obese. Bo is not obese, but he is overweight, which describes the majority of our population.

Bo's primary physician sent him to see me because he had an elevated blood pressure of 140/100. Upon glancing at his lab work, I noted that the blood sugar level was high and his cholesterol was elevated. Being a financial advisor, Bo sits in front of a computer for hours without exercising. Upon reviewing his history, I noted that his father suffered a heart attack in his fifties. Within one minute, we identified seven risk factors Bo had for heart disease: age above 50, male gender, family history, high blood pressure, diabetes, high cholesterol, and a sedentary lifestyle.

An ultrasound of his heart revealed two leaky valves, an enlarged chamber, and a stiffened heart. "Bo," I said, "do you want to know what your heart portfolio looks like?" Since it was about his "portfolio," Bo, the financial advisor, was very interested. He tuned in as I described how his "market" was going to crash in the near future if he didn't make some immediate "wise investments." Since we spoke in stock terms, Bo was analyzing every word, crunching the numbers, and realizing that he had bought some bad stocks.

"Bo," I said, "why is it that we secure everything from house insurance to health insurance, but we don't place a conscious effort to secure a most precious commodity, our health?"

"I guess we never think something bad will happen to us," he said.

And he was right. But Bo's health portfolio will crash in a heartbeat tomorrow if he continues in his ways today.

"Hey Bo, do you know one sure way to diversify and solidify your health portfolio?"

"No," he said.

"Lose weight," I said. "How about you lose six to nine pounds in the next three months, by the time you come for your next visit. We'll have to start you on medications for your blood pressure, but I have a hunch that we can get off that if you lose a good 15 to 20 pounds in the next year. I know you got this!"

Bo reached out his hand and we shook. "I got this!" he said.

We'll repeat Bo's lipid profile in several months. He will take his blood pressure readings daily. And, after he embraces Dr. Sam's HAT Trick, the 3 Steps to Healthy Living, he will be doing plenty of hydrating, ambulating and tabulating!

Dr. Sam's Insight

The best way to take care of tomorrow is to take care of today.

Testimonial #12

BRIAN BEFORE

I'm Brian Barnett, and I would like others to know how Dr. Kojoglanian, my cardiologist, has helped improve my heart and overall health.

In July of 2010 I was diagnosed as needing triple coronary bypass surgery. Prior to this surgery I had been moderately overweight, did not worry about what foods I was eating and did not exercise enough. I was also a Type 2 diabetic whose diabetes was controlled. After the surgery I wanted to find out what I could do to avoid further surgeries or heart disease. Dr. Kojoglanian and I discussed this and he recommended two goals: losing about 20 pounds and starting on an exercise program.

I began to understand that the patient is the pilot and the doctor is the navigator and together they form a team. The doctor can set goals, make recommendations and write prescriptions. The patient, in this case me, had to have the self discipline to follow recommendations, take prescribed medicines as directed, learn as much as possible about proper diet and exercise, and keep the doctor informed of both progress and problems encountered.

BRIAN AFTER

I started to keep daily records of what I ate, how much I exercised and my blood pressure and pulse readings. I averaged everything over each month. When I had appointments with the doctor I provided my charts and he had a better picture of how well medications were working and what I was doing to maintain my health. He had information to make recommendations about things I could do to improve my exercise program, such as raising my heart rate during exercise to a higher, but safe, level.

I tracked the following information:

Diet on a daily basis: *Total calories, total fats, saturated fats, cholesterol, trans fats, protein, sodium, carbs, body weight.*

Exercise: *Minutes per day walking, number of steps, resting heart rate, resting blood pressure, maximum heart rate, maximum blood pressure, and weight/ resistance exercises.*

When I see Dr. Kojoglanian, I bring charts that have all the data listed above into monthly averages. In a very short time he can see how I have been maintaining my diet and exercise goals. The navigator can see if the ship is on course. Small corrections can be made to avoid a large preventable health issue.

In the past year I have lost over 20 pounds and am maintaining my desired body weight. My cholesterol and other blood tests are all in the normal range. My A1C (diabetic level) has gone from 6.9 to 5.3 (I'm no longer a diabetic)! My *good cholesterol has gone from 40 to 58 and my bad cholesterol has gone from 120 to 70! That is the reward for staying disciplined. But without my navigator, I would be off course somewhere. I thank Dr. Kojoglanian for his medical skills and seeing that there is a person inside the patient.*

—Brian Barnett

44 | RISK PORTFOLIO

What's your risk of developing a heart attack or stroke? Do you know? The best-known risk assessment tool in cardiology uses information from the Framingham Heart Study[109] to predict a person's risk of developing a heart attack or death from coronary disease in the next ten years. I have simplified the process by generating "Dr. Sam's Mender of Hearts Risk Profile,"[110] which you will find in this chapter. Though this risk profile was not composed through a prospective randomized trial, it will serve as a practical guide for you in setting goals and modifying risks with the supervision of your physician. It will also be your guide as you heed warning signs that the "bridge is out."

To assess your own Mender of Hearts Risk Profile, simply circle the score under each risk that pertains to you. Add the points you have circled to achieve your final score. That number will identify you as "high risk," "at risk," or "ideal cardiovascular health." The higher your score, the higher the risk for cardiovascular events. I have not given a score for gender differences as cardiovascular disease is the number one cause of mortality in both sexes. Also, other risks dictate whether or not one will have cardiovascular disease (for instance, an obese female does not have an advantage in her risk profile compared to a normal weight male).

Of all the risk profiles available, I believe Dr. Sam's Mender of Hearts Risk Profile is the only one that rewards you with "minus points" for healthy habits. This assessment should not replace the care and attention you should give to yourself; it will hopefully encourage you to curb your appetite and inspire you to start walking. Go at it!

Dr. Sam's Mender of Hearts Risk Profile

RISK	*RISK SCORE*
AGE	
40–50	1
51–60	2
Greater than 61	3
FAMILY HISTORY OF HEART ATTACK / STROKE	
No	0
Yes	1
HIGH BLOOD PRESSURE	
Top # (SBP) < 129, or Bottom # (DBP) < 84	0
SBP 130– 139, or DBP 85–89	1
SBP 140–159, or DBP 90–99	2
SBP >160, or DBP > 100	3
HIGH CHOLESTEROL	
Total <200	0
Total 201–240	1
Total >241	2
HDL <40, or LDL > 150	2
HDL 41–49, or LDL 101–149	1
HDL 50–59, or LDL < 100	0
HDL > 60, or LDL < 70	–1
HIGH BLOOD SUGAR	
No	0
Yes	4
	TOTAL SCORE THIS PAGE:

RISK (CONTINUED)	RISK SCORE (CONTINUED)
TOBACCO	
No	0
Yes	4
PHYSICALLY ACTIVE (heavy work outs at least 5 x week)	
No	2
Yes, moderate work outs 3–4x/week	–1
Yes, heavy work outs 5–6x/week, or walking 30 min daily	–2
BMI	
18.6–19.9 (BMI below 18.5 is considered anorexic)	0
20–24.9	–1
25–29.9	2
30–38.9	4
>39	8
HIGH STRESS	
No	0
Yes	2
DEPRESSION	
Optimistic, content, enjoying life, people, and work	–2
No depression	0
Yes, depressed	2
HIGH FISH, FRUITS, VEGETA-BLES, OMEGA-3 IN DIET	
No	2
Yes, sometimes	0
Yes, daily and multiple servings	–2
	TOTAL SCORE THIS PAGE:
	TOTAL SCORE BOTH PAGES:

YOUR RISK	TOTAL RISK SCORE
IDEAL CARDIOVASCULAR HEALTH	6 OR LESS
AT RISK	BETWEEN 7–10
HIGH RISK	11 OR HIGHER

High risk: a greater than 20% risk that you may develop a heart attack, stroke, or die from coronary disease in the next ten years. This can be reduced by addressing and managing your risk factors with the help of your doctor.

At risk: a 10–20% risk that you may develop a heart attack, stroke, or die from coronary disease in the next ten years. Once again, this can be reduced by addressing and managing your risk factors with the help of your doctor.

Ideal risk: less than 10% risk that you may develop a heart attack, stroke, or die from coronary disease in the next ten years. Visit your doctor regularly to assess your risk and manage your risk factors by being diligent.

Dr. Sam's Insight

Please remember, the top two ways to lower your risk of dying from cardiovascular disease:
1) **Stop smoking**
2) **Lose weight**

Also note that the presence of *any risk factor,* including family history, requires attention. Why? Because, a single risk factor that is ignored can place a person at high risk of developing cardiovascular disease in the long run, even if the ten-year risk does not appear to be high.

**Any "small" risk can place us "at risk"
if not properly monitored and modified over time.**

Obesity racks up many points, because when a person is obese, killers like high blood pressure, high cholesterol, diabetes, and heart attacks are soon to follow!

**Just in case you missed the boat...
Your weight is the "epicenter" of your physical being.
From it comes the high blood pressure, high cholesterol
and high sugar. And from these "highs" come
the "lows," like heart attacks and strokes.**

You are one bite away from changing your risk. You are one step away from building a solid foundation. And you are one decision away from turning your health around—for a lifetime. Each choice, each meal and each bite matters.

This is it. Your time is *now.*

Not tomorrow, today!

It's time to press on.

45 LIVING PORTFOLIO

Just the other day, a man died in my office. He had walked ten minutes on the treadmill. As we spoke about life and the obstacles it presents, neither one of us could ever imagine what was about to transpire.

T.C. stepped off the treadmill and lay on the examining table. Post-stress echocardiogram (heart ultrasound) images were obtained. He denied chest pains, but his EKG showed otherwise. He said he didn't smoke, though the odor on his clothing and breath testified differently. T.C. denied being diabetic, but his 250-pound frame contradicted that claim. And he denied hypertension, though the sphygmomanometer screamed of dangerous levels.

T.C. was sitting up during the recovery phase of his stress test when he suddenly went silent. His eyes shut, his head flopped, and he tumbled to the floor. I quickly glanced at the monitor and saw fast ventricular tachycardia—a rhythm not compatible with life. We quickly laid him on his back, I got on my knees and said, "Lord Jesus, I'm gonna need your help!" We phoned 911, CPR was started, the patient's chest was thumped, and he was turning bluer by the second.

How did a seemingly well 55-year-old man just slip out of my hands, and pass through the putrid iron gates of death? How did a normal EKG turn into a terrifying rhythm? Though this was our first encounter together, didn't I have warning signs? He must have kept the whole story from me, including the severe chest pains that had to have come with the exertion.

But none of it mattered now; all that mattered was someone was alive and was now dead.

A thousand things scream through your mind when a man is dead on your floor, with no breath or pulse. Chest compressions? You bet, this ain't no time to sit and watch! Let's roll! My technician secured his airway while I continued to compress his chest, trying to get blood flow to his body.

This is when a few seconds feels like a lifetime. We prepared the automatic defibrillator and placed the pads on our patient's chest. The shock was delivered within seconds and my eyes scanned for signs of life.

By God's grace, we brought the dead back to life! T.C. was rushed to the cardiac catheterization lab. I saw two 99 percent blockages in his main artery, unclogged them with stents, and sent him home completely intact within 48 hours. That right there is one of my miracle patients.

T.C. visited us in the office several days later. His diet had changed and he had quit smoking. Life was different now—because of death. I had prayed for him when he was dying, and I prayed with him now that he was learning to live again.

Indeed, there are times when a person must die in order to live. Though our time on earth may seem eternal, it can vanish like a puff of smoke in the blink of an eye; and not all warning signs are obvious.

I want to call out the dead among the living and ask… "If not now, when? If not you, who? What in the world are you waiting for?"

Dr. Sam's Challenge

What in the world are you waiting for?

Stop complaining—now.

Stop smoking—now.

And start hoping—now.

Take care of yourself—now.

Eat and live healthy—now.

Pray—now.

And love—now.

The past is over—leave it.

The future holds your hope—reach for it, today!

46 SIGN UP FOR TOMORROW'S PORTFOLIO, TODAY

Before you begin your journey, I want you to take a moment to read and sign this contract:

I, _____(your name),

have made many mistakes in the past. I have made choices that have brought me harm.

I used to say, "I am going to indulge, just this once…one last time."

But that was yesterday. Now, I'm building for a different tomorrow, a *better* tomorrow, today.

"Just one more bite," I would say.

But that was yesterday, and now I am protecting my tomorrow, today.

"Just a few more sips today."

No! I drank that yesterday and yesterday is gone. I'm reinforcing my tomorrow, today.

"I can't take another step," I would say, or, "No, I didn't exercise today."

But all that's changed now; I'm "reframing" and fortifying my tomorrow, today.

In the spirit of building a sound foundation for tomorrow, I am starting something new today.

I am going to walk more and eat less, today.

The past is the past, and all I have is today.

Watch for me, because in a little while, you will not recognize me.

I am embracing Dr. Sam's challenge of healthy living with joy and excitement—today.

This is my life. This is my time. This is my health. Today and forevermore.

This is how I press on, today!

Your signature:
Witness's signature:
Date:

May the failures of yesterday be forgiven and forgotten as you journey with me on the road of healthy living for tomorrow, today. May one good choice lead you to another good choice, so that you will form strong and healthy habits for tomorrow, today. May your hope for a sound tomorrow provide the motivation to change your behavior, today. May you find yourself in a better place tomorrow, with a smaller butt, a *"bigger but,"* and a much grander smile, because you did the "undoable," today. And may all of us help and serve one another in love, compassion, and truth for a better tomorrow, today.

Bon appétit.
Dr. Sam
Mender of Hearts

Testimonial #13

NANCY BEFORE

I started seeing Dr. Samuel A. Kojoglanian because I was experiencing shortness of breath. After having a stress test, Dr. Kojoglanian talked to me about the results, and what needed to be done. The bottom line was I had a leaky valve which was placing too much pressure in one of the chambers of my heart and my lungs due to the extra weight I was carrying. It's almost surreal when a doctor sits you down and tells you the truth: I was not just "carrying extra weight," I was not overweight or obese; I was morbidly obese with a BMI of 39.

NANCY AFTER

Dr. Kojoglanian talked to me with passion and sincerity about how important losing weight was for my heart and other parts of my body. This wasn't just another doctor rushing his patient out. At the end of our consultation, he asked if he could pray with me. No health care professional has ever asked me that. I said yes, and the words of the prayer touched my entire being.

I started on a program to lose weight, eat less, and walk more per Dr. Kojoglanian's advice. When I came back to see him at the end of the year, I was no longer morbidly obese, and he was so pleased with me. We did an echocardiogram on me and at that time the leaky valve and the 'pulmonary pressures' had improved.

Within two years, at my April 2012 visit, Dr. Kojoglanian checked my weight and I have lost over 60 pounds. I will never forget seeing the images of the leaky valve before and after losing the weight, and how happy the doctor was. The pressure within the heart was now normal and the leak was what Dr. Kojoglanian called 'physiological,' meaning I was healed.

I can't say enough to everyone about the Mender of Hearts, Dr. Kojoglanian, because of his compassion for me as a person and his knowledge as a doctor. Because of his approach, I looked at myself to lose the weight because of the importance of a healthy heart. As a result, not only is my heart valve better, I am no longer taking type 2 diabetes medication. My blood pressure is great, and

Dr. K said I am no longer considered obese, having obtained a BMI of 28. I can breathe with ease now and don't have shortness of breath when I walk or exert myself. I don't have sleep apnea anymore and that has made a big difference for my heart's healing.

Many ask me if I had the lap band or gastric bypass, especially if they see my driver's license picture. I smile and say no. As my heart doctor says, "Nancy, we can change your stomach, but that only lasts a short time. If we change your heart and mind, we can change your life!" Many ask me how difficult it was to lose the weight and keep it off. I tell them that it gets easier as you see the results and know you are conquering something that has conquered you. I feel so much better in so many areas of my life.

Thank you again, Dr. Kojoglanian, for being a wonderful, caring, physical and spiritual doctor.

—Nancy Williams

47 | DR. SAM'S 7-DAY COOK OUT

Before getting started, use the following information as a guideline for your eating plan. Remember to check with your physician regarding calorie intake before starting any weight loss diet.

Fat intake guideline: less than 30% total calories from fat. This is how to calculate the amount of fat grams allowed each day when consuming a 1600 calorie diet:

1600 calories x 30% (or less) from fat = 480 fat calories, divided by 9 calories/gram = 53g fat per day, max.

Saturated fat intake guideline: less than 7% total calories from saturated fat:

1600 calories x 7% (or less) from saturated fat = 112 calories, divided by 9 calories/gram = 12.5g saturated fat per day, max.

Sodium intake goal: less than 1500 mg per day. If you are on a restricted sodium diet, adding additional salt to food is not advised. Should you choose to add salt, here is a reference chart from the American Heart Association to help you calculate how many milligrams of sodium you are sprinkling on:

SALT	SODIUM
¼ tsp.	600 mg
½ tsp.	1,200 mg
¾ tsp.	1,800 mg
1 tsp.	2,300 mg

Tips to using Dr. Sam's 7 day menu:

1. Make substitutions as needed due to food preferences/tolerances and seasonal availability, but be sure to compare calories, fat and sodium of the foods you are substituting. There are many free online resources to look up food items, including www.caloriecount.about.com.

2. Be aware of portion size when looking up nutrient content.

3. Tracking daily intake is also available at the above website as well as calculating the nutrient content of your own recipes.

4. Eating times are approximate. Adjust as needed.

5. If you weigh more than 210 pounds, start with an 1800 calorie diet by adding 200 calories/day to the sample menus either by increasing portion size or by adding foods. For 1800 calories/day, the fat intake goal would be less than 60g fat/day and saturated fat less than 14g/day.

6. Weight loss should not exceed 2–3 pounds/week. If this occurs, increase your calorie intake by at least 200 calories/day. If not losing 1–2 pounds/week after 3 weeks, consult with your physician regarding reducing calories to 1500/day or increasing activity.

7. Using 1 tsp. of honey in each cup of tea is optional. One teaspoon of honey contains 20 calories and 5 grams of carbohydrate. Should you opt to not use honey in your 3 cups of tea, you may add 60 calories to your daily total. (Freshly brewed iced tea may be used during the summer months). Unheated raw honey is preferable.[111]

8. Invest in a one pound scale for accurate portion control, especially for weighing meat.

9. Once you have achieved your weight loss goal and your BMI is less than 25, consult with your doctor and/or registered dietitian regarding your caloric intake for weight maintenance. Your calorie level may need to be increased.

10. Some food products, such as light mayonnaise, are allowed in order to make food more palatable and the cookout practical for you.

11. If you are eating out, remember to decrease your portions, avoid fried foods, and ask to see the menu contents, such as calories and salt.

12. Instructions for "drive thru" options and substitutions—remember 3 things: no mayo, no fried foods, and no supersizing. Also, watch the cheese and the buns!

Fruits: One serving contains approximately 60 calories and 15 grams of carbohydrates. Measure fruit out in the beginning for items like grapes, melon balls, strawberry halves, etc. to get an idea of what a serving size looks like, then place the fruit in a dish you would normally eat from. You will then have a visual reference in the future. If allergic to one fruit, try another.

Apple	1 medium=80 cals
Applesauce, unsweetened	½ cup=50 cals
Apricots, fresh	3 medium=50 cals
Apricots, dried	6 halves=50 cals
Banana	½ medium=55 cals
Blueberries	¾ cup=60 cals
Cantaloupe★	1 cup=60 cals
Casaba melon★	1 cup=45 cals
Cherries, raw	12 or 2/3 cup=60 cals
Cranberries, raw, unsweetened	1 cup=45 cals
Cranberries, dried	¼ cup=100 cals

Dates, dried (no sugar added)	3=70 cals
Figs, medium, raw	2=75 cals
Grapefruit, large	½=55 cals
Grapes (seedless red or green)	1 cup=60 cals (about 35 medium)
Guava	1 medium=45 cals
Honeydew★	1 cup=65 cals
Kiwi	1 medium=45 cals
Mandarin Oranges (packed in juice)	½ cup=80 cals
Mango	½ medium=70 cals
Nectarine	1 medium=70 cals
Orange, navel	1 medium=70 cals
Papaya	½ medium=60 cals
Peach	1 medium=40 cals
Pear	1 small=80 cals
Plums	2 small=60 cals
Pineapple, fresh	1 cup=80 cals
Pomegranate	½ medium=55 cals
Prunes	3 medium=60 cals
Raisins	1/8 cup=60 cals (2 Tablespoons)
Raspberries	1 cup=60 cals
Strawberries	1 cup halved=50 cals
Tangerine (Clementine)	1 med=40 cals
Watermelon★	1 cup=45 cals

★*A one cup serving of melon is equivalent to about 14 melon balls or 14 1" cubes. For melons such as cantaloupe and honeydew, this equals about 1/8 of a medium to large melon.*

Juices: One **4 oz.** serving of fruit juice contains approximately 15 grams of carbohydrate and about 60 calories. Many people do not have "juice" glasses at home, so measure ½ cup of juice and pour it into a drinking glass to visually see what one portion looks like. If you choose to have an 8 oz. portion of juice, make sure you calculate it into your total calories for the day.

Apple Juice (100% Juice)	4 oz.=60 cals
Apricot Nectar	4 oz.=60 cals
Cranberry Juice (100% Juice)	4 oz.=65 cals
Cranberry Juice Cocktail	4 oz.=70 cals
Grape Juice (purple or white)	4 oz.=80 cals
Grapefruit Juice (100% Juice)	4 oz.=50 cals
Orange Juice (100% Juice)	4 oz.=55 cals
Pineapple Juice (100%)	4 oz.=70 cals
Prune Juice	4 oz.=90 cals
Tomato Juice	8 oz.=50 cals (680 mg sodium)
V8® Vegetable Juice	8 oz.=50 cals (470 mg sodium)

Vegetables: One serving of vegetables (½ to 1 cup) contains approximately 25 calories and 5 grams of carbohydrate.

Artichoke, steamed	1 medium=55 cals (no sauce)
Artichoke Hearts, canned	2 pieces=30 cals (check sodium)
Arugula (Lettuce)	1 cup=6 cals
Asparagus, steamed	5 spears=25 cals
Avocado (technically a fruit)	¼ medium=70 cals, 6 gm fat/1 gm SF★
Bamboo Shoots (sliced, canned)	½ cup=25 cals
Bean Sprouts (canned)	½ cup=25 cals (270 mg sodium)
Bean Sprouts (raw)	1 cup=25 cals
Beets (canned)	½ cup=35 cals (290 mg sodium)
Beets (raw)	½ cup=35 cals
Bell Peppers (green, red, yellow, orange)	1 cup chopped=30 cals
Broccoli Florets (cooked)	1 cup =25 cals
Brussels Sprouts	½ cup=30 cals
Cabbage (green, red)	1 cup=25 cals
Carrots (raw) (66 mg/sodium)	3 oz or 10 baby carrots or 1 med=35 cals
★ SF = saturated fat	

Cauliflower (cooked)	1 cup=25 cals
Celery	2 medium stalks=20 cals (100 mg sodium)
Corn (fresh or frozen)	½ cup or 5˝ cob=75 cals
Cucumber (peeled)	½ medium or 1 cup =20 cals
Eggplant	1 cup=30 cals
Green Beans (fresh or frozen)	½ cup=20 cals
Jicama	½ cup=25 cals
Kale (raw or cooked)	1 cup=35 cals
Lettuce (all)	2 cups=15 cals
Mushrooms (raw)	1 cup sliced=20 cals
Okra (chopped raw or cooked)	1 cup=30 cals
Olives (black or green)	6 small=25 cals (180 mg sodium)
Onions (brown, red, white)	½ cup=30 cals
Peas (frozen)	½ cup=60 cals
Pea Pods (snow peas)	1 cup=60 cals
Potato (russet)	1 small or ½ cup=110 cals
Radish	7 medium=15 cals
Spinach (raw)	2 cups=15 cals
Spinach (cooked)	½ cup=20 cals
Squash, Acorn	½ cup=55 cals
Squash, Butternut	½ cup=40 cals
Squash, Spaghetti	½ cup=25 cals
Squash, Yellow & Zucchini	1 cup=20 cals
Sweet Potato (fresh: mashed or roasted)	½ cup=80 cals
Tomato (raw)	1 medium or 1 cup cherry=25 cals
Turnip (cooked)	1 cup=35 cals
Water Chestnuts (canned)	½ cup=40 cals
Yams	½ cup=80 cals

Sample 1600 Calorie Diet for Weight Loss/ Weight Maintenance

DAY 1: BREAKFAST (7:00 AM)

FOOD ITEM	SERVING SIZE	CALORIES	FAT / SF★	SODIUM: mg
Whole Grain Cereal	1 cup	150 (average) check label	1–2g / 0–.5g check label	200 (average) check label
1% Milk	½ cup	65	1.25g / .75g	80
Orange Juice	4 oz	55	-	-
Banana	½ medium	55	-	-
Hot Tea	1 cup	-	-	-
Honey— optional	1 teaspoon	20	-	-
Pure Water	2 cups	-	-	-
TOTAL		345 cals	3g / 1g	280

DAY 1: MORNING SNACK (9:30 AM)

Almonds: no salt	23 each	170	15g / 1g	-
Fresh Blueberries	¾ cup	60	-	-
Pure water	2 cups	-	-	-
TOTAL		230 cals	15g / 1 g	-
★ SF = saturated fat				

DAY 1: LUNCH (12:00 NOON)

Salmon Fillet	4 oz	285	18 / 3.3	160
Tossed Salad — light dressing	2 ½ cups	80	3g / –	170
St. Broccoli	1 cup	25	–	20
Strawberries	1 cup	50	–	–
Hot Tea	1 cup	–	–	–
Honey—opt.	1 teaspoon	20	–	–
Pure Water	2 cups	–	–	–
TOTAL		460	21g / 3.3g	350

DAY 1: SNACK (3:00 PM)

Apple (sliced)	1 medium	80	–	–
Pure Water	2 cups	–	–	–

DAY 1: DINNER (5:30 PM)

Vegetable Stir Fry with Chicken or Pork	¼ recipe	290	7.5g / 2g	160
Brown Rice	½ cup steamed	110	1.5g / .3g	–
Hot Tea	1 cup	–	–	–
Honey—opt.	1 teaspoon	20	–	–
TOTAL		420	9g / 2.3g	160 mg

DAY 1: SNACK (8:00 PM)

Low-Fat Yogurt	6 oz	150	1.5g / 1g	75
DAY 1 TOTAL		1605 Calories	49.5g fat / 8.6g	865 mg Sodium

DAY 2: BREAKFAST (7:00 AM)

FOOD ITEM	SERVING SIZE	CALORIES	FAT / SF	SODIUM: mg
Oatmeal—Plain	½ cup dry	150	3.0g / .5 g	10
1% milk	½ cup	65	1.25g / .75g	80
Raisins	⅛ cup	60	-	-
Cinnamon	⅛ teaspoon	-	-	-
Sugar—optional	1 teaspoon	16	-	-
Cranberry Juice	4 oz.	65	-	-
Hot Tea	8 oz.	-	-	-
Honey—opt.	1 teaspoon	20	-	-
Pure Water	2 cups	-	-	-
TOTAL		376	4.25g / 1.25g	90

DAY 2: MORNING SNACK (9:30 AM)

Hard Boiled Egg	1	70	4.5g / 1.5g	65
Watermelon	1 cup	45	-	-
Pure Water	2 cups	-	-	-
TOTAL		115	4.5g / 1.5 g	65

DAY 2: LUNCH (12:00 NOON)

Tuna Salad	1 serving / 5 oz.	207	6g / .5g	410
Whole Wheat Bread	2 slices (34 gm/slice)	180	3g / 0g	300
Lettuce/Tomato	2 pieces/slices	5	-	-
Baby Carrots	10	35	-	66
Hot Tea	1 cup	-	-	-
Honey—opt.	1 teaspoon	20	-	-
Pure Water	1 cup	-	-	-
TOTAL		447	9g / .5g	776

DAY 2: SNACK (3:00 PM)

Strawberries	1 cup sliced	50	–	–
Pure Water	2 cups	–	–	–

DAY 2: DINNER (5:30 PM)

Grilled Chicken	4 oz.	176	1g / .5g	128
Baked Potato	1 small	110	–	8
Light Sour Cream	2 Tablespoons	40	2.5g / 2g	25
Steamed Peas	½ cup	60	–	58
Fresh Orange	1 medium	70	–	–
Hot Tea	1 cup	–	–	–
Honey—opt.	1 teaspoon	20	–	–
TOTAL		476	3.5g / 2.5g	219

DAY 2: SNACK (8:00 PM)

Mozzarella Cheese Stick	1 oz. stick (part skim)	80	6g / 3g	190
Applesauce	½ cup	50	–	–
DAY 2 TOTAL		1594	24.25	1340

DAY 3: BREAKFAST (7:00 AM)

FOOD ITEM	SERVING SIZE	CALORIES	FAT / SF	SODIUM: mg
Toasted Whole Wheat Bagel	1 whole: 94 gm	240	2g / .5g	400
Peanut Butter	1 tablespoon	95	8g / 1.5g	75
Orange Juice	4 oz	55	-	-
Hot Tea	1 cup	-	-	-
Honey—opt.	1 teaspoon	20	-	-
Pure Water	2 cups	-	-	-
TOTAL		410	10g / 1.5g	475

DAY 3: SNACK (9:30 AM)

Honeydew	1 cup	65	-	-
Pure Water	2 cups	-	-	-

DAY 3: LUNCH (12:00 NOON)

Greek Salad	2 cups	239	18g / 6g	525
Lean Turkey Burger	4 oz	150	7g / 2g	80
Pear	1 small	80	-	-
Hot Tea	1 cup	-	-	-
Honey—opt.	1 teaspoon	20	-	-
Pure Water	2 cups	-	-	-
TOTAL		489	25g / 8g	605

DAY 3: SNACK (3:00 PM)

Fig Newtons®	2 squares (31g)	110	2.5g / 0g	115
Pure Water	2 cups	-	-	-

DAY 3: DINNER (5:30 PM)

Grilled Swordfish	4 oz	239	12.2g / 2.3g	149
Tossed Salad — light dressing	2 ½ cups	80	3g / 0g	170
String Beans	1 cup	40	–	–
Sweet Potato	½ cup baked	80	–	32
Hot Tea	1 cup	–	–	–
Honey—opt.	1 teaspoon	20	–	–
TOTAL		449	15.2g / 2.3g	351

DAY 3: SNACK (8:00 PM)

Grapes	1 cup (35 med)	60	–	–
DAY 3 TOTAL		1593	52.7g / 11.8g	1546

DAY 4: BREAKFAST (7:00 AM)

FOOD ITEM	SERVING SIZE	CALORIES	FAT / SF	SODIUM: mg
Veggie Scramble	2 eggs (1 yolk)	153	9.4g / 2.2g	139
Whole Wheat English Muffin	½	75	1g / 0g	125
Heart Healthy Tub Margarine	1 teaspoon	30	3g / .8g	30
Apple Juice	4 oz.	60	-	-
Kiwi	1 medium	45	-	-
Hot Tea	1 cup	-	-	-
Honey—opt.	1 teaspoon	20	-	-
Pure Water	2 cups	-	-	-
TOTAL		383	13.4g / 3g	294

DAY 4: SNACK (9:30 AM)

Peanuts—no salt	1 oz (about 28)	170	14g / 2g	-
Pure Water	2 cups	-	-	-

DAY 4: LUNCH (12:00 NOON)

Turkey/Avocado Sandwich	1 whole	321	14g / 2g	733
Cherries	12 ea. (⅔ cup)	60	-	-
Radish	7 medium	15	-	14
Hot Tea	1 cup	-	-	-
Honey—opt.	1 teaspoon	20	-	-
Pure Water	2 cups	-	-	-
TOTAL		416	14g / 2g	747

DAY 4: SNACK (3:00 PM)

Cantaloupe	1 cup	60	–	–
Pure Water	2 cups	–	–	–

DAY 4: DINNER (5:30 PM)

Chicken Kabob	2 skewers	237	9.8g / 1g	70
Corn—not canned	¾ cup or 7″ cob	112	.75g / 0g	–
Hot Tea	1 cup	–	–	–
Honey—opt.	1 teaspoon	20	–	–
TOTAL		369	10.3g / 1g	70

DAY 4: SNACK (8:00 PM)

Low–Fat Yogurt: any flavor	6 oz	150	1.5g / 1g	75
Raspberries	1 cup	60	–	–
TOTAL		210	1.5g / 1g	75
DAY 4 TOTAL		1608	53.2g / 9g	1186

DAY 5: BREAKFAST (7:00 AM)

FOOD ITEM	SERVING SIZE	CALORIES	FAT / SF	SODIUM: mg
Multi-grain Pancakes: from mix or frozen	3 each (4 inch) (105g total)	240	7g / 1g	370
Light Syrup —optional	⅛ cup	50	-	75
Orange Juice	4 oz.	55	-	-
Blueberries	½ cup	40	-	-
Hot Tea	1 cup	-	-	-
Honey—opt.	1 teaspoon	20	-	-
Pure Water	2 cups	-	-	-
TOTAL		405	7g / 1g	445

DAY 5: MORNING SNACK (9:30 AM)

Cashews— no salt	18 each	160	13g / 3g	5
Pure Water	2 cups	-	-	-

DAY 5: LUNCH (12:00 NOON)

Turkey Chili	1 cup	247	5.0g / 1.1g	150
Reduced Fat Cheese— shredded	1 oz (¼ cup)	90	6g / 3g	180
Tossed Salad — light dressing	2 ½ cups	80	3g / 0g	170
Pineapple	½ cup fresh	40	-	-
Hot Tea	1 cup	-	-	-
Honey—opt.	1 teaspoon	20	-	-
Pure Water	2 cups	-	-	-
TOTAL		477	14g / 4.1g	500

DAY 5: SNACK (3:00 PM)

Artichoke	1 medium	60	.4g / .1g	72
Pure Water	2 cups	–	–	–

DAY 5: DINNER (5:30 PM)

Lean Sirloin Hamburger 96%	4 oz	140	4.5g / 2g	85
Whole Wheat Bun	1 each (43g)	120	2g / 0g	190
Ketchup/ Mustard	1 tsp. / 1 tsp.	20/–	–	53/55
Light Mayo	2 tsp.	30	2.7g / .2g	63
Lettuce/Tomato	1 leaf/2 slices	5	–	–
Onion	2 slices	10	–	–
Crispy Spiced Potatoes	6 wedges (1/2 potato)	97	2.4g / .4g	7
Asparagus	5 spears	25		
Hot Tea	1 cup	–	–	–
Honey—opt.	1 teaspoon	20	–	–
TOTAL		452	11.6g / 2.6g	453

DAY 5: SNACK (8:00 PM)

Peach	1 medium	40	–	–
DAY 5 TOTAL		1594	46g / 10.8g	1475

DAY 6: BREAKFAST (7:00 AM)

FOOD ITEM	SERVING SIZE	CALORIES	FAT / SF	SODIUM: mg
Low-Fat Yogurt: any flavor	8 oz	225	2g / 1.3g	114
Granola— sprinkle on yogurt	⅓ cup	140	3.3g / .3g	20
Banana	½	55	-	-
Hot Tea	1 cup	-	-	-
Honey—opt.	1 teaspoon	20	-	-
Pure Water	2 cups	-	-	-
TOTAL		440	5.3g / 1.6g	134

DAY 6: MORNING SNACK (9:30 AM)

Unsalted Pistachios	47 each	160	13g / 1.5g	4
Pure Water	2 cups	-	-	-

DAY 6: LUNCH (12:00 NOON)

English Muffin Pizza	2 halves	327	12.1g / 6.3g	864
Cauliflower	1 cup steamed	25	-	18
Watermelon	1 cup	45	-	-
Hot Tea	1 cup	-	-	-
Honey—opt.	1 teaspoon	20	-	-
Pure Water	2 cups	-	-	-
TOTAL		417	12.1g / 6.3g	882

DAY 6: SNACK (3:00 PM)

Figs or Plums	2 medium	75	–	–
Pure Water	2 cups	–	–	–

DAY 6: DINNER (5:30 PM)

Chicken Fajitas	¼ recipe	199	6.6g / .7g	69
Tortilla 8˝ Whole Wheat	1	130	3.5g / .5g	120
Tossed Salad — light dressing	2 ½ cups	80	3g / 0g	170
Salsa	1 tablespoon	10	–	105
Hot Tea	1 cup	–	–	–
Honey—opt.	1 teaspoon	20	–	–
Pure Water	2 cups	–	–	–
TOTAL		439	13g / 1.2g	464

DAY 6: SNACK (8:00 PM)

Grapefruit	½ large	55	–	–
DAY 6 TOTAL		1586	43.4g / 10.6g	1484

DAY 7: BREAKFAST (7:00 AM)

FOOD ITEM	SERVING SIZE	CALORIES	FAT / SF	SODIUM: mg
Low Fat 2% Cottage Cheese	½ cup	90	2g / 1.5g	380
Mixed Fruit	1 cup variety	75	–	–
Cranberry Juice	4 oz	65	–	–
Hot Tea	1 cup	–	–	–
Honey—opt.	1 teaspoon	20	–	–
Pure Water	2 cups	–	–	–
TOTAL		335	2g / 1.5g	380

DAY 7: MORNING SNACK (9:30 AM)

Unsalted Sunflower Seeds	¼ cup	170	14g / 1.5g	–
Pure Water	2 cups	–	–	–

DAY 7: LUNCH (12:00 NOON)

Spinach Salad	1 ¼ cup	92	6g / 1.2g	87
Turkey Waldorf Pita	½ pita	315	6.3g / .7g	255
Mango	½	70	–	–
Hot Tea	1 cup	–	–	–
Honey—opt.	1 teaspoon	20	–	–
Pure Water	2 cups	–	–	–
TOTAL		504	12.3g / 1.9g	342

DAY 7: SNACK (3:00 PM)

100 Calorie Pack Cookies	1 pack	100	3g / 1g (check label)	75 (check label)
Pure Water	2 cups	-	-	-

DAY 7: DINNER (5:30 PM)

Mostaccioli with Turkey Meatballs	1 cup/ 2 meatballs	400	8.2g / 2.2g	635
Squash	½ cup	40	-	4
Hot Tea	1 cup	-	-	-
Honey—opt.	1 teaspoon	20	-	-
Total		460	8.2g / 2.2g	639

DAY 7: SNACK (8:00 PM)

Baby Carrots	10	35	-	66
DAY 7 TOTAL		1604	39.5g / 8.1g	1502

Use the following as an additional reference for a 1600 calorie diet plan. These are the suggested amounts of food to consume from each food group for a 1600 calorie diet provided by MyPyramid (USDA).

Suggested Servings/Portion Sizes 1600 Calorie Diet

Fruits	1.5 cups/day
Vegetables	2 cups/day
Grains	5 ounce equivalents/day
Meat & Beans	5 ounce equivalents/day
Milk/Dairy	3 servings
Oils	5 teaspoons
Extras	Approximately 132 calories—your choice

Lunch Day #1

Wild Salmon Fillet with Mustard Glaze *(Serves 4)*

Ingredients:

- *16 oz. salmon fillet (4 oz. = 1 serving)*
- *2 Tbsp. Dijon mustard*
- *1 Tbsp. olive oil*
- *1 Tbsp. honey*
- *¼ tsp. grated lemon peel*
- *1 Tbsp. lemon juice*
- *parsley sprigs*
- *lemon wedges*
- *pepper to taste*

Directions:

Rinse salmon fillet and pat dry. Line 9 x 13 inch pan with aluminum foil, then spray with non-stick cooking spray. Place fillet on foil, skin side down. Mix the mustard, oil, honey, lemon peel, and lemon juice together in a small bowl. Brush fillet with the mustard mixture.

Broil fish about 5 inches from heat just until it looks slightly translucent and wet in thickest part (cut to test), about 9 to 12 minutes. Lift foil to transfer fillet to a serving platter. Garnish with parsley and lemon wedges. Add pepper to taste. One serving is 4 ounces.

Tossed Salad with Light Dressing *(1 serving):*

Ingredients:

- *2 cups loose leaf lettuce—washed & dried (green leaf, red leaf, romaine, etc.)*
- *1/8 cup red onion, chopped*
- *½ small tomato, chopped*
- *¼ cup carrots, sliced*
- *any other veggie from list that is 30 calories or less per serving*
- *1 Tbsp. light Italian or other light dressing with 30 calories or less per Tbsp.*
- *pepper to taste*
- *Warning: croutons, crispy noodles, cheese, nuts, and dried fruit are calorie dense and will add more calories and fat above the 1600 calorie allotment.*

Directions:

Thoroughly wash all vegetables. Chop or slice ingredients, then toss together with light salad dressing and enjoy.

Dinner Day #1

Vegetable Stir Fry with Chicken or Pork *(Serves 4)*

Ingredients:

- *12 oz. (3/4 lb.) boneless, skinless chicken breast* **or** *pork tenderloin*
- *1 zucchini, sliced in half lengthwise, then cut into ¼ inch slices*
- *1 cup sliced mushrooms*
- *2 cups eggplant, cubed into 1 inch pieces*
- *½ medium red onion, sliced or chopped*
- *1 red or green bell pepper cut in half, then into thin slices*
- *1 Tbsp. olive oil*
- *1–2 garlic cloves, peeled & finely chopped*
- *8 oz. water chestnuts, drained*
- *crushed red pepper and black pepper to taste*
- *2 Tbsp. light sesame ginger or Asian style dressing*

Directions:

Thinly (about 1/8 inch) slice chicken or pork into 2 inch long sections. Wash and prepare all of the vegetables on separate cutting board from raw meat. Note: vegetables may be blanched in the microwave using a small amount of water to partially cook before stir-frying. Spray non-stick skillet or wok with non-stick cooking spray, then add 1 Tbsp. olive oil. Add garlic and onion to skillet over medium heat. Cook for 1–2 minutes, stirring frequently. Add chicken or pork and cook until no longer pink, approximately 5 minutes, stirring frequently. Add vegetables and cook until desired texture (soft or al dente), approximately 5 minutes. Water chestnuts should be added while vegetables are cooking. One minute before serving, add 2 Tbsp. light Asian dressing and mix throughout. Add pepper as desired. Serve ¼ of recipe over ½ cup of brown rice. Note: use other fresh vegetables as desired. If vegetables are not soft enough, try covering pan for a few minutes while cooking.

Lunch Day #2

Tuna Salad Sandwich *(1 serving)*

Ingredients:

- *1 can (5 oz.) solid white albacore tuna in water, drained (look for brand with 300 mg or less of sodium per can)*
- *2 Tbsp. red onion, chopped (if desired)*
- *1 stalk of celery, chopped*
- *½ –1 Tbsp. chopped cilantro*
- *1 tsp. lemon juice*
- *½ tsp. Dijon mustard*
- *4 Tbsp. (¼ cup) low-fat plain yogurt (regular or Greek)*
- *crushed pepper to taste*

Directions:

Wash celery and finely chop. Combine all ingredients together and mix well. Serve on 2 slices of whole wheat bread (about 90 calories per slice) with lettuce and sliced tomato.

Dinner Day #2

Marinated Grilled Chicken Breast *(serves 2) / Salad as Day #1*

Ingredients:

- *8 oz. boneless, skinless chicken breast*
- *2 cloves garlic, peeled*
- *1/8 cup fresh ginger, peeled and cut into chunks*
- *½ cup low-fat yogurt (regular or Greek)*
- *¼ cup cilantro*
- *½ tsp. coriander*
- *¼ cup fresh lemon juice*
- *dash of cayenne pepper, optional*
- *crushed pepper to taste*

Directions:

In a food processor, with the motor running, add garlic cloves and ginger chunks, one at a time, processing until finely chopped (chop by hand if food processor not available). Add the remaining ingredients (except for chicken) and blend. Coat the chicken breasts with this marinade. Cover and refrigerate overnight.

Brush olive oil on grill rack or use non-stick cooking spray before lighting grill to prevent sticking. Remove excess marinade, and place chicken on preheated grill rack. Cover and grill, turning 2 to 3 times, until chicken is opaque throughout and the juices run clear, about 15 minutes total or until the internal temperature is at least 170 degrees F. Divide into two portions and serve immediately.

Lunch Day #3:

Greek Salad: Arugula with Feta Cheese and Olives *(1 serving)*

Ingredients:

- *2 cups baby arugula*
- *½ cucumber, peeled, cut in half and sliced*
- *½ tomato cut in large pieces*
- *¼ cup sliced red onions*
- *5 black olives, medium-large, drained (Kalamata, optional)*
- *1 oz. feta cheese (¼ cup crumbled)*

Dressing:

- *2 tsp. olive oil*
- *1 Tbsp. balsamic vinegar*
- *drop of Dijon mustard*
- *crushed pepper to taste*

Directions:

Wash lettuce, cucumber and tomato. Chop vegetables and toss salad ingredients together (save feta cheese and olives for later). Prepare dressing with the above ingredients, mixing well. Toss salad with dressing and top with cheese and olives.

Lean Turkey Burger *(1 serving — 4 oz.)*

Ingredients:

- *4 oz. lean ground turkey (less than 10% fat)*
- *pepper, onion powder, garlic powder to taste*

Directions:

Combine the 4 oz. of lean ground turkey with spices as desired. Form into patty approximately ¾″ thick. Cook either by grilling or sautéing in a non-stick pan sprayed with non-stick cooking spray over medium heat. Broiling in the oven is an alternate method. Brown approximately 4–5 minutes on each side. Patty is done when no longer pink inside and reaches internal temperature of at least 165 degrees F. Chopped fresh onion and/or chopped green pepper (1 Tbsp. each) may be added to ground turkey before cooking to add flavor.

Serve without a bun. Enjoy with Greek salad. Condiments such as ketchup or mustard may be used if calculated into total calories and sodium for the day.

Dinner Day #3

Grilled Swordfish with Lemon, Mint, and Basil *(serves 4) / Salad as Day #1*

Ingredients:

- *1 lb. swordfish (4 steaks, 4 oz. each)*
- *2 Tbsp. olive oil*
- *3 Tbsp. fresh lemon juice*
- *3 Tbsp. chopped fresh mint leaves*
- *1 Tbsp. chopped fresh basil leaves*
- *1 garlic clove, minced*
- *freshly ground black pepper*

Directions:

Use non-stick cooking spray, then warm the grill (medium-high heat). Whisk the oil, lemon juice, mint, basil, and garlic in a medium bowl to blend. Baste the fish with lemon and olive oil mixture or put into a zip-close plastic bag with the marinade and shake until well covered. Sprinkle with pepper to taste. May leave in refrigerator until ready to grill.

Grill the steaks over medium heat until just cooked through, about 4–5 minutes per side (depending on thickness of fish). Throw away any unused marinade (do not baste while cooking). Serve hot. One serving is 4 ounces.

Breakfast Day #4

Veggie Scramble *(1 serving)*

Ingredients:

- *1 egg*
- *1 egg white*
- *1/8 cup 1% Milk*
- *¼ cup bell pepper*
- *1/8 cup onion*
- *¼ cup spinach*
- *¼ cup tomato*
- *1 tsp. olive oil*

Directions:

Separate one egg yolk (keep egg white), discard or save for another use. Combine 1 whole egg with 1 egg white (or use ¼ cup of egg substitute). Whisk together with milk. Wash bell pepper, spinach and tomato. Chop veggies. Warm 1 tsp. of olive oil in non-stick pan over medium heat. Add all vegetables and sauté for about 2–3 minutes, until, soft. Add egg mixture, stirring until eggs are completely cooked. Add pepper to taste.

Lunch Day #4

Turkey and Avocado Sandwich *(1 serving)*

Ingredients:

- *2 oz. turkey breast, low sodium (no more than 400 mg sodium per 2 oz. serving)*
- *¼ avocado, sliced*
- *1 Tbsp. light mayonnaise*
- *¼ tomato, sliced*
- *lettuce leaves as desired*
- *2 slices whole wheat bread (about 90 calories per slice)*

Directions:

Divide light mayonnaise between the two slices of bread. Layer the turkey, avocado, tomato and lettuce leaves on one side. Sprinkle with pepper to taste. Cover with other slice of bread.

Dinner Day #4

Chicken Kabob *(serves 4: 1 serving = 2 skewers) / Salad as Day #1*

Ingredients:

- *16 oz. (1 pound) boneless, skinless chicken breast*
- *1 eggplant cut into 16, 2 inch pieces*
- *16 cherry tomatoes*
- *2 garlic gloves, minced*
- *2 Tbsp. olive oil*
- *2 Tbsp. white wine vinegar*
- *freshly ground pepper to taste*
- *½ tsp. dried rosemary*
- *½ tsp. thyme*

Directions:

Cut chicken into 1½-inch squares. In a bowl, combine minced garlic, olive oil, vinegar, pepper, rosemary and thyme. Coat chicken pieces and refrigerate for 1 hour (may use zip-close plastic bag).

Note: if using wooden skewers, soak in water for 15 minutes first.

Load each of the eight 12″ skewers with the following: 1 eggplant cube, 1 chicken square, 1 tomato, 1 eggplant cube, 1 chicken square, 1 tomato half. Divide the chicken equally among the eight skewers. There may be more than 2 pieces of chicken per skewer depending on the size of cube.

Spray grill with non-stick cooking spray. Arrange the skewers on the preheated grill rack and grill over medium heat. Turn as necessary to brown evenly. Grill until the chicken is opaque throughout and the vegetables are tender, about 10–12 minutes. Remove the vegetables and the chicken from skewers onto plate using a fork.

Lunch Day #5

Turkey Chili *(serves 10: 1 serving = 1 cup) / Salad as Day #1*

Ingredients:

- *1 pound lean ground turkey*
- *1 Tbsp. olive oil*
- *1 onion, chopped*
- *1 green bell pepper, chopped*
- *1 red pepper, chopped*
- *3 cloves garlic, minced*
- *2 tsp. chili powder*
- *1 tsp. cumin*
- *½ tsp. cayenne pepper*
- *2 tsp. oregano*
- *1 (15 oz.) can red kidney beans, drained & rinsed with water to reduce sodium*
- *1 (15 oz.) can black beans, drained & rinsed*
- *1 cup frozen cut corn*
- *2 cups stewed tomatoes (no added salt)*
- *1 (15 oz.) can diced tomatoes (no added salt)*

Directions:

Warm oil in a large pot over medium-high heat. Add turkey and brown, until, crumbly. Drain excess liquid. Stir in onion, peppers, garlic, chili powder, cumin, cayenne pepper, and oregano.

Stir in both types of beans, corn, stewed and diced tomatoes. Reduce heat and simmer 30 minutes to 1 hour, uncovered, stirring occasionally. Top each 1 cup serving with 1 oz. (¼ cup) reduced-fat shredded cheddar cheese.

Dinner Day #5

Crispy Spiced Potatoes: Low-fat *(serves 4)*

Serving size: 6 wedges or ½ potato

Ingredients:

- *2 medium potatoes*
- *2 tsp. olive oil or vegetable oil*
- *½ tsp. paprika*
- *½ tsp. onion powder (not onion salt)*
- *½ tsp. garlic powder (not garlic salt)*
- *¼ tsp. black pepper*

Directions:

Wash potatoes. Slice each in half lengthwise, then in half again lengthwise. For each of the 8 pieces, slice into 3 wedges lengthwise. Total wedges should be 24. Quickly place potato wedges into a gallon-sized zip-close bag (potatoes can discolor easily). Add 2 tsp. of oil and spices to the bag. Zip close and shake the potatoes until well coated with oil and spices. Line a cookie sheet with aluminum foil and spray with non-stick cooking spray. Place wedges skin side down on the cookie sheet with the inside of the potatoes pointing up. Bake in a pre-heated oven, 425 degrees for approximately 20 minutes, until potatoes are brown and slightly crispy. Serve 6 wedges per person.

Served with 4 oz. 96% lean ground sirloin burger, grilled or cooked in non-stick skillet.

Lunch Day #6

English Muffin Pizza *(Makes 1 serving)*

Ingredients:

- *1 whole wheat English muffin*
- *¼ cup prepared spaghetti sauce (less than 400 mg sodium per ½ cup serving)*
- *2 oz. (½ cup) part-skim mozzarella cheese, shredded*
- *2 mushrooms, sliced, or other preferred low-fat veggie for pizza*

Directions:

Split English muffin in half and toast or broil to brown slightly. Spread 2 Tbsp. sauce on each half. Sprinkle 1 oz. (¼ cup) mozzarella cheese on each half and top with sliced mushrooms. Place onto foil lined baking sheet and broil for 3–5 minutes until cheese is slightly browned and warm. Watch closely so pizza does not burn.

Dinner Day #6

Chicken Fajitas *(serves 4) / Salad as Day #1*

Ingredients:

- *16 oz. boneless, skinless chicken breasts, sliced julienne*
- *3 tsp. vegetable oil divided: 2 tsp. for marinade, 1 tsp. for pan*
- *1 large onion, sliced*
- *1 red pepper, sliced julienne*
- *1 green pepper, sliced julienne*
- *2 cloves garlic, crushed*
- *¼ cup fresh lime juice*
- *1 tsp. chili powder*
- *½ tsp cumin*
- *¼ tsp. white pepper*
- *4 each—8" whole wheat tortillas*

Directions:

Mix the lime juice, 2 tsp. oil, garlic, chili powder, cumin, and pepper and place the chicken slices in this marinade. Leave overnight in the refrigerator.

Heat 1 tsp. oil in a heavy skillet; drain marinade from chicken, then cook the chicken strips over medium-high heat, stirring constantly for 5–7 minutes, or until cooked through. Add the onion and peppers; cook over medium-high heat for 4 minutes.

Divide into 4 servings. Serve with warm whole wheat tortillas. Add 1 Tbsp. salsa per serving.

Lunch Day #7

Spinach Salad *(serves 4, each serving = 1¼ cups)*

Ingredients:

- *4 oz. baby spinach (approximately 4 cups)*
- *2 hard-boiled eggs, peeled and chopped*
- *8 oz. sliced button mushrooms (about 1 cup)*
- *1 small red onion, peeled and thinly sliced*

Dressing:

- *3 Tbsp. red wine vinegar*
- *1 Tbsp. olive oil*
- *2 tsp. Dijon mustard*
- *black pepper to taste*

Directions:

Thoroughly wash and dry spinach and mushrooms. Toss together the spinach, mushrooms, and red onion in a large salad bowl.

Whisk together the vinegar, oil, mustard in a small bowl. Season with pepper, pour over the salad and toss. Separate into 4 bowls and sprinkle each salad with chopped eggs. Salad dressing can be made ahead of time and chilled.

Turkey Waldorf Pita *(serves 2)*

Ingredients:

- *6 oz. boneless turkey breast (freshly cooked, not pre-cooked)*
- *1 small apple—any variety*
- *1 stalk celery, thinly sliced*
- *2 Tbsp. dried cranberries*
- *2 Tbsp. chopped walnuts*
- *3 oz. low-fat plain yogurt (about 1/3 of a cup)*
- *pepper to taste*
- *1 whole wheat pita—cut in half*

Directions:

Roast or boil turkey breast per package directions. Do not add salt. This can be done ahead of time and served for a dinner entrée; then use leftover turkey for pita recipe. Weigh out 6 oz. of cooked turkey and dice into small cubes. Set aside in medium bowl. Wash and dice small apple, leaving skin on. Toss apple with small amount of lemon juice to keep from turning brown. Wash and thinly slice celery. Add apple and celery to diced turkey. Add cranberries and chopped walnuts to same bowl. Add pepper to taste. Stir in low-fat yogurt to coat all ingredients. Spoon turkey mixture into each half of pita. Add leaf lettuce as desired. Makes 2 servings.

Dinner Day #7

Mostaccioli with Meatballs *(makes 6 servings)*

Ingredients:

- *12 oz. mostaccioli (regular or whole wheat), cooked as directed, without salt, then drained*
- *12 oz. lean ground turkey*
- *½ cup bread crumbs*
- *¼ cup parmesan Cheese*
- *1 egg*
- *¼ tsp. pepper*
- *1 tsp. Italian seasoning*
- *24 oz. jar marinara sauce—not low sodium, but less than 400 mg sodium per ½ c.*

Directions:

Combine ground turkey, bread crumbs, parmesan cheese, and beaten egg in a medium bowl. Mix well (may need to use hands). Stir in pepper and Italian seasoning. Form 12 equal-sized meatballs, about 1 ounce each. Spray a non-stick skillet with non-stick cooking spray. Cook meatballs over medium heat, browning on all sides (about 10 minutes total). Add 1 24 oz. jar marinara sauce. Stir meatballs around in sauce. Bring sauce to boil. Cover, then turn down heat to simmer, stirring occasionally. Meanwhile, prepare 12 oz. of mostaccioli per package directions. Drain. Makes six servings of 2 meatballs with sauce and 1/6 (about 1 cup) of pasta.

49 DR SAM'S 7-DAY WORK OUT

Though this book does not gear you up to run an Ironman race, it does place you at an advantage to regain your health and live abundantly. I have formulated a workout plan that can be implemented with ease and that translates into shedding the unnecessary, unsightly, and unhealthy pounds.

I need two things from you: *first*, devote a specific time in your day for exercising, not at random hours, but a specific time, with purpose; *second*, identify what you are going to replace in your life in order to fit in your workouts (i.e., watching TV, playing video games, chatting on the phone, texting). This regimen is simple and encourages you to have a workout mentality throughout the day. There are things we all can take part in: park further from the store; walk around the office building 1–2 times at lunch; listen to music, scripture or books when walking instead of sitting and staring at a pretty person reading the news to you; walk the dog; catch up with your spouse or loved ones on a walk versus "shared" time in front of the TV; go to bed early (eliminate the unproductive and aimless time spent in the living room—snacking, watching TV, staring at the computer, drinking extra wine—and, remember, sleep deprivation is associated with weight gain); and a well-rested mind and body contributes to a more productive morning time—to eat a healthy breakfast, work out, to pray and meditate, and time to plan for your busy day as you hit the road running and not fumbling.

Did you know that the only treatment for high blood pressure in 1906 was to have the patient rest? Prior to becoming the 28th President of the United States, Woodrow Wilson had temporary blindness (stroke) from high blood pressure. He rested and walked 14 miles daily to regain his health.

We've already established that cardiovascular disease is the most common cause of death in the United States today.[112] The relative risk of having heart disease increases twofold in those who are sedentary. That means if you are not exercising, your risk of having heart disease is twice as likely compared to someone who exercises regularly.[113] Your risk for cardiovascular events will plummet as you lose weight by trading your sedentary lifestyle for simple walking!

The benefits of walking and exercising are immeasurable. The National Cancer Institute reports that physical activity is linked to at least a 50% lower risk of getting colon cancer.[114] The Journal of the American Medical Association reported that women who engaged in brisk walking for one to two hours weekly decreased their risk of breast cancer by 18% compared with inactive women.[115]

Don't you want to prevent cardiovascular disease?

Don't you want to decrease the chances of getting cancer?

Don't you want to control your diabetes and even prevent it?

Don't you want to look younger, feel younger, move faster and be more flexible?

Don't you want to increase and improve your mental alertness?

Don't you want to build stronger bones?

Don't you want to promote regular bowel movements?

Don't you want to have restful sleep, decrease colds and flu and increase your energy?

Don't you want to reduce depression, alleviate your pains, and overcome arthritis?

Then what in the world are you waiting for?

Let's walk! Let's ambulate! Let's exercise! Let's lose the weight, keep healthy and find abundant living!

Too stressed to exercise you say? I'll introduce you to my rat story in hopes of getting you excited about exercising! Rats involved in an experiment were shocked with electrodes, and continually exposed to bright lights and loud noises. At the end of one month, all these rats died. Researchers then exposed a new group of rats to the same environment, but these rats were well exercised, and then exposed to the same noxious stimuli of shocks, lights and noises. The new group of rats not only survived, but ran around healthy. [116]

Are you running around in a rat race, shocked by life's bright lights, loud noises, betrayals and disappointments? Get your gear on, and let's press on!

My plan is practical, doable, and "user friendly." It will help you with three things:

1) **S**tamina (cardiovascular).
2) **S**trength (tone).
3) **S**tretching (balance and flexibility).

If you are not accustomed to exercising, start at a slow pace of only 1 to 2 minutes. Increase the frequency, duration and intensity of your workout gradually. Do not harm yourself with strenuous exercise when walking, lifting or stretching. An aggressive approach is a set up for excessive soreness and an injury. You can simply start taking 1–2 minutes walks daily and skip the strength, balance and flexibility portions until you are more conditioned.

My top healthy ways to exercise while being gentle to the joints include walking, swimming and biking. Injuring oneself is usually due to excessive activity without first training one's body to get to a more conditioned level. Once you build up to a 10 minute walk, no matter how many weeks or months it takes you, then you may want to attempt adding the strength, balance and flexibility activities to your regimen.

Make sure you have the permission of your physician before you set out to exercise, and continue to follow up with your doctor.

Day #1

Working out is not to be done during your "spare" time or randomly; from now on, this is a set and crucial part of your day…your good health depends on it!

- Use a heart rate monitor (from a sports store); drink adequate water.
- *Stretch*: attempt to touch toes 10 times daily.
  1) Place a small pillow or rolled up towel between your knees and hold it tightly with both knees.
  2) Tighten your buttocks muscles.
  3) Stretch both hands up over your head, keeping your buttocks and core tight.
  4) Reach down and touch your toes with your hands.
  5) At first you will likely need to bend your knees to reach the toes, but this will improve over time. Caution! If you believe this or any other activity may cause injury, skip it for now.
- *Stamina*: walk, starting with 1–10 minutes at an easy pace, and increase time and speed as tolerated.
- Choose an exercise partner to keep you accountable.

**10 minutes of brisk walking daily reduces
your heart–attack risk by 50%.
20 minutes, by 60%
30 minutes, by 70%.**[117]

Walking is the easiest and most convenient means of aerobic exercise (meaning "in the presence of air," where the breathing is deeper and intensified, and the large muscle groups of the body are involved). Make sure you walk with a good pair of shoes to avoid injuring your feet and walk on level surfaces to avoid joint injury. If your joints don't allow brisk walking, then I recommend a stationary bike or elliptical machine. This will improve your *stamina* and cardiovascular health.

Too hot or too cold? Go to the mall and walk. Can't drive? Get up, turn off the TV, or if you insist, when you are watching TV, stand up and sit down at least 10 times during each commercial break. Walk in place. Jump rope in place without having a rope! Box, standing there and move your left and right hands. Can't walk? Move your feet up and down in a kicking motion. Can't move your feet? Move your arms in a circle or raise your hands up and down. Seriously, there is no excuse. You are worth the sweat.

Many of my patients ask me how high they should get their heart rate as they exercise. To calculate your peak or maximum heart rate, subtract your age from 220. For instance, if you are 50 years old, 220 – 50 = 170, your peak heart rate is 170 beats per minute. It is not necessary to achieve this heart rate for a solid workout. In fact, in my office if a patient can achieve 85% of their peak heart rate, they have reached an adequate level. The adequate level of exercise for a 50 year old person is 146 beats per minute (220 − 50 = 170; 170 x .85 = 145.5). A "safer" zone, especially for the beginner, would be 65% of the person's peak heart rate, and for the 50 year old, that would be 111 beats per minute (220 − 50 = 170; 170 x .65 = 110.5).

One way to gauge moderate activity is with the "talk test"—walking hard enough to break a sweat but not so hard you can't comfortably carry on a conversation. Exercise experts measure activity in a different way using metabolic equivalents, or METs. One MET is defined as the energy it takes to sit quietly. Mild activity (golfing with cart, canoeing leisurely, walking 2 mph) is considered to be up to 2.5 METs. Moderate activity (cycling leisurely, golfing without cart, swimming, and walking 4 mph) is considered to be up to 4.5 METS. More vigorous activity (chopping wood, cycling, downhill skiing, climbing hills, swimming, walking 5 mph, rope skipping) is considered to be from 5 METs to 12 METs.

Activities of Daily Living

ACTIVITY	METS (higher METs = exerting more energy)
Lying quietly	1.0
Sitting	1.5
Walking from house to car	2.5
Loading and unloading car	3.0
Taking out the trash	3.0
Walking the dog	3.0
Household task, moderate effort	3.5
Vacuuming	3.5
Lifting items continuously	4.0
Raking lawn	4.0
Gardening without lifting	4.4
Mowing lawn (power mover)	4.5

Approximately How Many Calories am I Burning with Exercise?

Low Activity Level	Approximate Calories Burned per Hour
Sleeping	60
Sitting	75
Standing	100
Driving	120
Office work	140
Moderate Activity Level	**Approximate Calories Burned per Hour**
Shopping	160
Golf with cart	180
Fishing	200
Golf, walking	240
Walking 3 mph	280
Walking 4 mph	330
Tennis	350
Dancing, aerobic	420
Bicycling	450
High/More Vigorous Activity	**Approximate Calories Burned per Hour**
Jogging 5 mph	540
Hiking	550
Power walking	600
Cycling studio or skipping rope	700
Cross-country skiing	750

Day #2

NOTE: The exercises listed for each day are set as goals and can be reached successfully with a slow approach and steady determination. And remember to check with your doctor before starting any exercise program.

- *Stretch*: Attempt to touch your toes without bending your knees, at least 10 times. You can touch your toes standing up or sitting on the floor. This is a good means of *stretching* and a good sign of your health and physical condition. If you can't do it, keep walking, keep drinking water, keep eating vegetables, and keep trying to touch your toes with your finger tips! You can also kneel on your left knee with your right knee in front of you, keep your back straight, lean forward, and feel the stretch in your thighs. Try this for 30 seconds, rest, and switch to kneeling on your right knee.

- *Stretch, balance, flexibility*: Standing, place your hands above your head. With your right hand touch your left toes, and then stand upright. With your left hand touch your right toes. Alternate at least 10 repetitions and 3 sets. Increase your pace as tolerated. This will help you become more limber.

- *Stamina*: Walk, starting with 1–10 minutes, light, and increase as tolerated.

- *Stretch*. More blood is flowing through your muscles after walking, and stretching is gentler on your body at this time. Get to a hallway at your home, place your left forearm and hand against the wall, left leg ahead, right leg behind you, keep your back straight, buttocks and core tight, lean forward with your upper body. Switch and do the same with your right forearm, reversing the position of your legs.

Day #3

- *Stretch*: Touch toes 10 repetitions, building slowly over time, up to 3 sets.
- *Stretch, balance, flexibility*: Stand on your right foot, and lift up the left foot. First do this with your eyes open and then try with your eyes closed. Do the opposite by standing on your left food and lifting up your right foot.
- *Strength:* Lie on your back, bend your knees, have arms by your sides with palms facing up, lift your buttocks off the floor, hold this position for 3 seconds, then return to your starting position. Repeat 10 times. This will strengthen your abdominal and back muscles.
- *Stamina*: Walk, starting 10 minutes, light, and increase as tolerated. If you don't have 10 minutes, then split it in half, walking 5 minutes in the morning and the other 5 during a break at work or during your evening hours. You don't have to go for the "all or nothing phenomenon."
- *Stretch* as above.

Day #4

- *Stretch*: Touch toes 10 repetitions, building slowly over time, up to 3 sets.
- *Strength*: Face a wall and place your hands against the wall. Tighten your thighs, buttocks and core or abdomen, push against the wall, bringing your face close to the wall, and then slowly back off. Repeat 10 times. This will strengthen your

upper extremities. You can also go to a counter, hold on to it, keep buttocks and abdomen muscles tight, and squat down as far as you can, then lift yourself up to a standing position. Repeat 10 times. This will strengthen your lower extremities.

- *Stamina*: Walk, starting with 15 minutes, if possible, light, and increase as tolerated.
- *Stretch*: Standing, place your hands above your head. With your right hand touch your left toes, and then stand upright. With your left hand touch your right toes. Alternate at least 10 repetitions and 3 sets.

Day #5

- *Stretch*: Touch toes 10 repetitions, building slowly over time, up to 3 sets.
- *Strength*: Get a sturdy chair. Keep your feet apart, parallel and pointed forward. Cross your hands and place them on your chest. Slowly ease yourself to sit on the chair, taking 5 seconds. Stay for 2 seconds. Rise slowly, taking 5 seconds and stand straight. Repeat 10 times.
- *Stamina*: Walk, 10–20 minutes, light, and increase as tolerated.
- *Stretch*.

Day #6

- *Stretch*: Alternate touching left and right toes 15 times.
- *Stamina and strength*: Raise left leg up, place back down, and then raise right leg up and down; continue to do so as if you are walking in place. May increase intensity by simulating running in place. Continue for 30 seconds. Move your arms up and down at the same time to increase your heart rate.
- *Stamina*: Walk, starting with 20 minutes, light, and increase as tolerated up to 30 minutes.

There are simple things you can do to increase your activity level: instead of sending an email to your colleague during work, get up from your chair, walk, talk, get back and count it as a part of your exercise. When 2:30 p.m. rolls around, and you're sleepy and you want a cookie or an energy drink, get up, drink some water and take a 5–10 minute walk. Give yourself the gift of a healthy life, and start walking, even if it's for 5 minutes. Your heart will thank you!

Dr. Sam's Insight

Is exercise a pain...in the butt?
No, it's a prevention...of heart disease!

Day #7

- Rest.
- Your body, heart, mind, soul, emotions, and spirit need it!

50 MY JOURNAL AND FUN FACTS

	Journal for MM/DD/Year
Exercise	Yes / No; what form; how long, calories burned
Blood pressure	
8 cups water	Yes / No
Vegetables/fruits	Yes / No
Stop smoking	Yes / No
Breakfast	I had (write down the food item, drink, and **amount of calories** for each meal):
Lunch	I had:
Dinner	I had:
Snacks	I had:
Sodas	Yes / No/How many
Weight	
Accountability	Who am I accountable to?
Total calories	Write down your total calories for the day:

What? That's in my food and drink?

Here is how much exercise a 150 pound person has to do to burn off the calories per snack…

What I just ate…	What I have to do to burn the calories!
Fries (9 oz.), 620 calories	Biking, 9 mph, 1 hour 30 min
Theater popcorn, no butter, small, 410 cal	Low-impact aerobics, 1 hour 15 min
Red velvet cupcake (1 cupcake, 5 oz.), 500 cal	Strength training, 15 reps per exercise, 2 hours
Cinnamon dolce latte, whipped cream, 410 cal	Jogging, one hour
Chocolate chip cookie, 3 oz., 440 cal	Brisk walking, 3.5 mph, 1 hour 30 min
Banana nut loaf, 1 piece, 4 oz., 490 cal	Swimming laps, light, 1 hour 15 min
Frozen yogurt, 2 cups, 370 cal	Elliptical, moderate effort, 1 hour

Yes, I'm with you…shocked!

For those who drink coffee, lattes and mochas… if you are having a Venti (20 oz) White Chocolate Mocha with 2% milk and whipped cream…it's 580 calories and 15 grams of saturated fat! Lose 130 calories and 2/3 of the bad fat by ordering nonfat milk and no whipped cream.

One breadstick at your restaurant and there goes 150 calories and 400 mg of sodium…yeah, I think you better pass…or eat only one, if it fits into your total calories per day.

Still shocked? Get your shoes on….this is how we press on!

I still don't get this portion thing...

Food	A healthy portion is a size of a...
Cooked rice, pasta or potato	Tennis ball
Meat	One deck of cards
Cheese	Pair of dice
Peanut butter	Ping pong ball
Fruits and Vegetables	Baseball

Fruits with most fiber...

Fruit	Calories (differ with size)	Fiber	Vitamin C	Carotenoids
Apple (1)	80	High	Moderate	No
Blackberries (1 cup)	60	High	High	Low
Guava (1)	45	High	High	High
Pear (1)	80	High	Low	No
Pomegranate (½)	55	High	High	No
Raspberries (1 cup)	60	High	High	Low

Richest Veggies

Vegetable	Calories	Lutein	Vitamin K
Kale (1 cup)	35	High	High
Spinach (½ cup)	20	High	High
Collard greens (½ cup)	20	High	High
Turnip greens (1 cup)	30	High	High

Foods High in Potassium

Food	Approximate Amount of Potassium
Sweet potato (baked, not fried)	700 milligrams (mg)
Beet greens, ½ cup, cooked	650 mg
Yogurt, plain and nonfat, 8 oz	580 mg
Halibut, 3 oz, cooked	500 mg
Banana, medium	425 mg
Nonfat Milk, 8 oz	375 mg
Kidney beans, ½ cup, cooked	350 mg

Testimonial #14:
It's Never Too Late

SID BEFORE

Hi, I'm Sid Goldberg, probably one of Dr. Kojoglanian's oldest patients. I'm 90 years old and going strong. I had bypass surgery back in 1986, and met Dr. Kojoglanian in 2002, when I was having a heart attack. I was on the brink of death, when he placed a stent in my closed heart artery. He also placed stents in my heart in 2003 and 2007. I have followed up with him since 2002 because he treats me as family.

I've struggled with my weight for all my adult life. Because my weight was close to 200 pounds, I was experiencing severe back pain, had slowed down considerably and was unable to walk without the aid of a walker. I'd hear Dr. Kojoglanian's voice in my mind over and over again, "It's never too late Sid!

When you lose weight, we'll get rid of this walker, and we'll stop placing all these stents in your heart!"

I finally got disgusted with what I was doing. I got disgusted with my weight and the way I looked. I'd sit and eat as if I'd never seen food, and then feel so heavy that I would just sit around even more on my couch and watch TV. My weight had steadily been increasing, but I did not want to think about it. Every time I saw or smelled food, I'd fall in the same stupid trap. I told myself not to do it, but it was as if I couldn't help myself. I obviously had paid a price with the bypasses and heart attacks, but it still didn't hit me. Once it hit me, I didn't need a pill to "help" me. It is as simple as Dr. Kojoglanian says: "Back off the food, and get off your butt." It didn't affect me until I couldn't walk anymore.

I've lost about 50 pounds in the past 3 years. I don't use my walker anymore; I'm going to give it to someone who needs it. When I visit my heart doctor, you should see the joy on his face…he is so proud of me and so happy for me! How do you get so lucky? Getting a heart doctor who saves your life and then changes your life! I may be 90, but like Dr. Kojoglanian says, "You've got more life in you now than ever before!"

So, what is stopping you? Your past? Your age? Your arthritis? Your excuses? Look at me. It's never too late!!"

— Sid Goldberg

References:

Chapter 1:

1   Roger VL et al. *Heart Disease and Stroke Statistics—2012 Update,* American Heart Association Statistical Update. Circulation. 2012;125:e2-e220.

2   Flegal KA, Carroll MD, Ogden C, Curtin L. "Prevalence and trends in obesity among US adults, 1999–2008." *Journal of the American Medical Association*, 2010; 303 (3):235–241; Roger VL et al. *Heart Disease and Stroke Statistics—2012 Update,* American Heart Association Statistical Update. Circulation. 2012;125:e2-e220.

3   *Vital Signs: State-Specific Obesity Prevalence Among Adults—United States, 2009.* U.S. Department of Health and Human Service. Centers for Disease Control and Prevention, Volume 59, August 3, 2010.

Chapter 2:

4   Heart attacks occur when either one of the two major pipes or arteries of the heart are blocked with plaque, and blood is unable to reach the heart muscle. The muscle starves for oxygen, which can lead to temporary or permanent damage to the heart walls, or even death. Symptoms of a heart attack can include but are not limited to chest pain, chest discomfort, chest tightness, chest pressure, shortness of breath, sweating, shoulder or neck or throat pain, elbow or wrist pain, shoulder blade pain, upper back pain, fainting, and "anvil" or "elephant" sitting on your chest.

5   Strokes occur when the pipes or arteries of the neck or brain are blocked with plaque, and the blood is unable to reach the brain matter. The brain lacks oxygen, leading to temporary or permanent slurred speech, blindness, loss of strength or sensation in limbs, or instability.

Chapter 3:

6   http://www.mayoclinic.com/health/water/NU00283

7   *Eat This and Live*, Don Colbert, MD, 2009, page 34; Siloam, a Strang Company

8   Martha Grogan, MD, http://www.mayoclinic.com/health/healthy-heart/ AN02175; "The Guide to Beating a Heart Attack," Ron Winslow, *Wall Street Journal*, Health and Wellness Tuesday April 17, 2012, interview with Martha Grogan, MD and Thomas Allison, Ph.D., Thompson PD, Buchner D et al.; "Exercise and Physical Activity in the Prevention and Treatment of Atherosclerotic Cardiovascular Disease." *Circulation* 2003; 107:3109–3116.

Chapter 4:

9   Roger VL et al. *Heart Disease and Stroke Statistics—2012 Update*, American Heart Association Statistical Update. Circulation. 2012;125:e2-e220.

10   http://www.cancer.org/Cancer/ProstateCancer/ detailedGuide/prostate-cancer-key-statistics

11   What is a calorie and is it different from the term "kilocalorie?" In nutrition terms, the word calorie is used instead of the more precise scientific word, "kilocalorie." Chemists use the word calorie to describe the amount of *energy* required to heat one gram of water at one degree Celsius. Nutritionists use the word calorie to describe the amount of *food* that would have to be burned to heat one kilogram of water at one degree Celsius. A food calorie is technically referred to as a kilocalorie, and many authors have merged these words to have the same meaning. The common use of a "calorie" of food energy is understood to refer to a kilocalorie. For simplicity, we will stick to "calorie" in this book. (eHow.com — What is a food Calorie?)

Chapter 5:

12   Heart failure occurs when the heart muscle is weakened and unable to pump blood efficiently to the body. This builds a backflow to the lungs, filling the lungs with excess water, causing shortness of breath.

Chapter 7:

13   Mukamal KJ, Fletcher RH, Sokol HN. "Overview of the risks and benefits of alcohol consumption." *UpToDate* 2011; 19.1:1–30.

14   Thun MJ, Peto R, Lopez AD, et al. "Alcohol consumption and mortality among middle-aged and elderly U.S. adults." *New England Journal of Medicine* 1997; 337:1705.

15   Mukamal KJ, Fletcher RH, Sokol HN. "Overview of the risks and benefits of alcohol consumption." *UpToDate* 2011; 19.1:1–30.

16   Proverbs 23: 31–32

17   www.cdc.gov/nchs/fastats/alcohol.htm; www.about-alcohol-abuse.com/Alcohol_Abuse_Statistics.html

Chapter 10:

18   http://www.mayoclinic.com/health/fiber/NU00033

Chapter 12:

19   glycemic index — a measure of how fast a carbohydrate triggers a rise in the blood sugar.

20   Phytonutrients are organic compounds found in fruits, vegetables, grains, nuts, teas and legumes that may decrease the risks for chronic diseases such as diabetes, cancer and cardiovascular disease.

21   *Dietary Therapy for Obesity*; George A Bray, MD.

22   Yang Q. "Gain Weight by 'Going Diet'? Artificial Sweeteners and the Neurobiology of Sugar Cravings." *Yale Journal of Biology and Medicine* 2010; 83:101–108;

Brown RJ, De Banate MA, Rother KI. "Artificial Sweeteners: A Systematic Review of Metabolic Effects in Youth." *International Journal of Pediatric Obesity* 2010; 5(4): 305–321;

Anton SD et al. "Effects of Stevia, Aspartame, and Sucrose on Food Intake, Satiety, and Postprandial Glucose and Insulin Levels." *Appetite* 2010; 55(1): 37–43;

Mattes RD and Popkin BM. "Nonnutritive Sweetener Consumption in Humans: Effects on Appetite and Food Intake and their Putative Mechanisms." *American Journal of Clinical Nutrition* 2009; 89:1–14;

Fowler SP et al. "Fueliing the Obesity Epidemic? Artificially Sweetened Beverage Use and Long-term Weight Gain." *Obesity* 2008;16:1894–1900;

Tordoff MG, Alleva AM: "Oral Stimulation with Aspartame Increases Hunger." *Physiological Behavior* 47, 555–559 (1990);

Black RM, Tanaka P, Leiter LA, Anderson GH: "Soft Drinks with Aspartame: Effect on Subjective Hunger, Food Selection, and Food Intake of Young Adult Males." *Physiological Behavior.* 49, 803–810 (1991);

Blundell JE, Hill AJ: "Paradoxical effects of artificial sweeteners (aspartame) on appetite." *Lancet* I: 1092–1093 (1986).

Chapter 14:

23   "How We Eat," *Rural Migration News*. Vol. 3, No. 4, October 1996, http://migration.ucdavis.edu/rmn/more.php?id=158_0_5_0;

Eat This and Live, Don Colbert, MD, 2009, page 5; Siloam, a Strang Company.

24   http://www.livestrong.com/article/321473-how-many-calories-does-the-average-american-eat/ and FAO.org. "Country Profiles: United States of America." FAO Statistical Yearbook, http://www.fao.org/statistics/yearbook/vol_1_2/pdf/United-States-of-America.pdf

25   eHow.com — How many calories should you consume in a day?

Chapter 15:

26   For a table with fiber foods see: http://www.mayoclinic.com/health/high-fiber-foods/NU00582

27   eHow.com — How to Diet to Avoid Processed Foods.

Chapter 16:

28   Martha Grogan, MD, http://www.mayoclinic.com/health/healthy-heart/AN02175;

"The Guide to Beating a Heart Attack," Ron Winslow, *Wall Street Journal*, Health and Wellness Tuesday April 17, 2012, interview with Martha Grogan, MD and Thomas Allison, Ph.D., Thompson PD, Buchner D et al. "Exercise and Physical Activity in the Prevention and Treatment of Atherosclerotic Cardiovascular Disease." *Circulation* 2003; 107:3109–3116.

Chapter 18:

29   2001–2004 NHANES study.

30   "How to Choose the Lowest Sugar Fruits," by
     Kristie Leong, MD — eHow.com

31   Anthocyanins are probably the most important group of visible plant
     pigments and are found to have one of the strongest antioxidizing powers
     of all flavonoids. Flavonoids give plants their vibrant colors and are
     plant nutrients. When consumed in the form of fruits and vegetables,
     they are potentially beneficial, triggering enzymes that reduce the
     risk of some cancers, heart disease and degenerative. Antioxidants
     reduce the destructive power of harmful molecules that cause cell
     damage. http://www.wisegeek.com/what-are-flavonoids.htm

32   Free radicals are harmful molecules that can cause cellular damage.

33   Mattes RD, Popkin BM. "Nonnutritive sweetener consumption
     in humans: effects on appetite and food intake and their putative
     mechanisms." *American Journal of Clinical Nutrition* 2009; 89:1–14.

34   Fowler SP, Williams K, Resendez RG, Hunt KJ, Hazuda HP, Stern
     MP. "Fueling the obesity epidemic? Artificially sweetened beverage
     use and long-term weight gain." *Obesity* 2008; 16:1894–1900.

35   Liem DG, de Graff C. "Sweet and sour preferences in young children and
     adults: role of repeated exposure." *Physiological Behavior* 2004; 83:421–9.

36   Daniel DeNoon. "Drink More Diet Soda, Gain More
     Weight?" WebMD Medical News, June 13, 2005, http://
     www.webmd.com/content/Article/107/108476.htm

37   Yang Q. "Gain weight by 'going diet'? Artificial sweeteners
     and the neurobiology of sugar cravings." *Yale Journal
     of Biology and Medicine*. 2010; 83:101–108.

38   http://www.mayoclinic.com/health/artificial-swee10ers/MY00073

Chapter 19:

39   Symptoms of angina (known as chest pain) can be similar to heart
     attacks and include but are not limited to chest pain, chest discomfort,
     chest tightness, chest pressure, shortness of breath, sweating, shoulder
     or neck or throat pain, elbow or wrist pain, shoulder blade pain, upper
     back pain, fainting, and "anvil" or "elephant" sitting on your chest.

Chapter 20:

40   Wang Y, Wang QJ. "The prevalence of prehypertension and hypertension
     among US adults according to the new joint national committee guidelines:
     New challenges of the old problem." *Archives of Internal Medicine* 2004;
     164:2126–2134;
     Cutler J et al. "Trends in hypertension prevalence, awareness,
     treatment, and control rates in United States adults between 1988–
     1994 and 1999-2004." *Hypertension* 2008 Nov; 52(5):818–27.

41   2010 Dietary Guidelines for Americans, page D6–4.

42   2010 Dietary Guidelines for Americans, page D6–16.

43   www.mayoclinic.com/healthy/sodium/NU00284

44   2010 Dietary Guidelines for Americans, page D6–23.

45   http://www.nhlbi.nih.gov/health/public/heart/hbp/dash/new_dash.pdf

Chapter 21:

46   Cholesterol clumps within artery walls and initiates an inflammatory process that causes an aggregation of white blood cells, collectively known as a lipid pool. This pool grows and encroaches on the artery wall causing 1) weakening of the artery wall and 2) narrowing of the artery lumen. Ultimately, the lipid pool breaks through the wall and "spills" into the lumen of the artery, where the normal blood flow occurs. This causes a "traffic jam" and either slows the blood flow or stops it. The heart muscle does not receive the blood and 1) begins to "hurt" and the patient has angina or 2) begins to "die" and the patient has a myocardial infarction, or heart attack.

47   2010 Dietary Guidelines for Americans

Chapter 22:

48   Lee IM, Cook MR, Shadick NA, Pereira E, Buring J. "Prospective cohort study of breast implants and the risk of connective-tissue diseases." *International Journal of Epidemiology* 2011; 40:230–238.

49   Backovic A, Huang HL, Del Frari B, Piza H, Huber LA, Wick G. "Identification and dynamics of proteins adhering to the surface of medical silicones in vivo and in vitro." *Journal of Proteome Research* 2007; 6(1):376–381.

Chapter 23:

50   "Vital Signs: Current Cigarette Smoking Among Adults Aged >18 Years – United States, 2009." *Morbidity and Mortality Weekly Report.* Sept 10, 2010, Vol. 59, No. 35, pages 1135–1140.

51   Chandler MA, Rennard SI. "Smoking Cessation." *Chest* 2010; 137(2):428–435.

52   Dr. Rap®, *Cut to the Heart* CD, Song # 7, "Smoked to Death," © 2007

Chapter 24:

53   Serrano CV, et al. "Association between depression and development of coronary artery disease: pathophysiologic and diagnostic implications." *Vascular Health and Risk Management*, 2011:7 159–164.

54   Litchman JH, et al. "Depression and coronary heart disease: Recommendations for screening, referral and treatment." A science advisory from the American Heart Association Prevention Committee of the Council on Cardiovascular Nursing, Council on Clinical Cardiology, Council on Epidemiology and Prevention, and Interdisciplinary Council on Quality of Care and Outcomes Research: endorsed by the American Psychiatric Association. *Circulation*, Oct 21 2008. 118(17):1768–1775.

Chapter 25:

55   Carroll D, Ebrahim S, Tilling K, Macleod T, Smith GD. "Admission for myocardial infarction and World Cup football: database survey." *British Medical Journal* 2002 Dec 21; 325 (7378): 1439–42.

56   Dimsdale JE. "Psychological Stress and Cardiovascular Disease." *Journal of the American College of Cardiology* 2008:51; 1237–1246.

Chapter 26:

57   Ridker PM, Cook NR, Lee IM, et al. "A randomized trial of low-dose aspirin in the primary prevention of cardiovascular disease in women." *New England Journal of Medicine* 2005; 352:1293.

58   Hennekens CH. "Benefits and Risks of Aspirin in Secondary and Primary Prevention of Cardiovascular Disease." *UpToDate*, 2011; 1–31.
Miser WF. "Appropriate Aspirin Use for Primary Prevention of Cardiovascular Disease." *American Family Physician* 2011; 83(12):1384–1390.
Dalen. "Aspirin for the Primary Prevention of Stroke and Myocardial Infarction: Ineffective or Wrong Dose?" *The American Journal of Medicine* 2010; 123(2): 101–102.
Wolff T, Miller T, Ko S. "Aspirin for the Primary Prevention of Cardiovascular Events: An Update of the Evidence for the US Preventive Services Task Force." *Annals of Internal Medicine* 2009; 150 (6):405–410.
Hennekens CH, Peto R, Hutchison GB, Doll R. "An overview of the British and American aspirin studies." *New England Journal of Medicine* 1988; 318:923.

Chapter 27:

59   The sole known role of carotenoids is to act as a source of vitamin A in the diet. Fruits and vegetables are the main source of carotenoids in the human diet.

Chapter 28:

60   Ecclesiastes 1:8

Chapter 34:

61   Proverbs 23:2
62   Genesis 25:19–34

Chapter 35:

63   Proverbs 18:21

Chapter 39:

64   Genesis 4:10, 6:6
65   Psalm 103:8
66   Ezekiel 33:11, Isaiah 55:8–9
67   Matthew 10:39
68   Proverbs 3:10
69   Romans 3:23, 6;23

70   Isaiah 41:10, Nahum 1:7, Hebrews 4:12–13, Revelation 1:8
71   Isaiah 53:5
72   II Corinthians 5;17–21
73   John 3:16
74   Ephesians 2:8
75   Romans 10:9
76   John 3:16, 36
77   Psalms 46:1, 118:14
78   Luke 23:42

Chapter 40:
79   Jeremiah 33:3, Isaiah 41:10
80   Psalm 121:1
81   Romans 8:37
82   Romans 8:31
83   Romans 8:28
84   II Corinthians 4:8
85   II Corinthians 12:9
86   Philippians 4:13
87   Psalm 23:4
88   Psalm 32:8
89   Isaiah 41:103
90   Isaiah 54:17
91   Psalm 40:2
92   Jeremiah 1:5
93   Psalm 13:5
94   Nahum 1:7
95   Psalm 55:22
96   Luke 15:24
97   Revelation 3:20
98   Zechariah 4:6

Chapter 41:
99   John 16:33
100   Acts 4:11–12; Isaiah 43:11, 45:22
101   Romans 2:15
102   Psalm 19:1–4

Chapter 42:
103   I Corinthians 3:16
104   Proverbs 3:2–8
105   Isaiah 58:1–14
106   Deuteronomy 8:3
107   Proverbs 9:1–6; Psalm 19:7–11

108 Isaiah 55:1–3

Chapter 44:

109 Larson MG, Atwood LD, Benjamin EJ, Cupples LA, D'Agostino RB Sr, Fox CS, Govindaraju DR, Guo CY, Heard-Costa NL, Hwang SJ, Murabito JM, Newton-Cheh C, O'Donnell CJ, Seshadri S, Vasan RS, Wang TJ, Wolf PA, Levy D: "Framingham Heart Study 100 K project: Genome-wide associations for cardiovascular disease outcomes." *BMC Medical Genetics* 2007, 8(Suppl 1):**S5**;
Wilson PW, D'Agostino RB, Levy D, et al. "Prediction of coronary heart disease using risk factor categories." *Circulation* 1998; 97:1837.

110 This risk profile is not intended to replace the medical advice of your physician, primary care doctor, or cardiologist. Please consult your healthcare provider for advice about your risks and your symptoms.

Chapter 47:

111 One cup of hot tea with 1 Tbsp unheated raw honey (ask your physician's advice if you are considering ingesting raw honey). Teas such as herbal, green, black and white teas can provide energy, enhance the immune system, improve our digestion, and provide the body with antioxidants such as polyphenols, which help reduce cellular damage and oxidative stress. Please note: drinking tea is not a substitute for drinking water. Drink caffeine-free if you are having palpitations.

Raw honey has not been heated or filtered. Commercial honey is usually heated up to 160 degree Fahrenheit; if a product is heated beyond 115 degrees, it destroys the beneficial enzymes, antioxidants, vitamins and aroma. Heating damages the nutritional and healing properties of the food. Filtering eliminates and removes the nutritional benefits of the bee pollen itself. Raw honey is safe with one exception, though rare: people can have an allergic reaction when eating raw honey, ingesting the pollen spores. Do not feed raw honey to infants under one year of age to prevent infant botulism. Ask your physician's advice if you are considering ingesting raw honey.

Chapter 49:

112 Centers for Disease Control and Prevention, "The Burden of Chronic Disease as Causes of Death, Unites States," National and State Perspectives, 2004, http://www.cdc.gove/NCCDPHP/burdenbook2004/Section01/tables.htm

113 *Mayo Clinic Cardiology Textbook.* Chapter 55 "Coronary Heart Disease Epidemiology," page 691.

114 National Cancer Institute, "Cancer Trends Progress Report—2005 Update," http//progressreport.cancer.gov

115 Anne McTiernan et al., "Recreational Physical Activity and the Risk of Breast Cancer in Postmenopausal Women," *Journal of the American Medical Association* 290, no. 10; September 10, 2003: 1331–1336.

116   Christian Leeuwenburgh et al., "Oxidized Amino Acids in the Urine of Aging Rats: Potential Marker for Assessing Oxidative Stress in Vivo," *American Journal of Physiology*: Regulatory Integrative and Comparative Physiology 276, no.1; January 1999: R128–R135. http://ajpregu.physilogy.org/cgi/content/abstract/276/1/R128

117   Martha Grogan, MD, http://www.mayoclinic.com/health/healthy-heart/ AN02175;
"The Guide to Beating a Heart Attack," Ron Winslow, *Wall Street Journal*, Health and Wellness Tuesday April 17, 2012, interview with Dr. Martha Grogan and Thomas Allison, Ph.D., Thompson PD, Buchner D et al.;
"Exercise and Physical Activity in the Prevention and Treatment of Atherosclerotic Cardiovascular Disease." *Circulation* 2003; 107:3109–3116.

Follow Dr. Sam on
RockYourPlanet.net
Facebook.com/MenderOfHearts
Facebook.com/BeaconOfHearts